# COMRADE ROCKSTAR

# COMRADE ROCKSTAR

✧

## THE SEARCH FOR DEAN REED

Reggie Nadelson

Chatto & Windus
LONDON

Published in 1991 by
Chatto & Windus Ltd
20 Vauxhall Bridge Road
London SW1V 2SA

The publishers and author gratefully acknowledge permission
from Grafton Books to reproduce 'Buffalo Bill's', from *Tulips
and Chimneys* by e. e. cummings.

A CIP catalogue record for this book is available from
the British Library

ISBN 0 7011 3472 0

Reggie Nadelson has asserted her right to be
identified as the author of this work.

Photoset in Linotron Bembo by
Rowland Phototypesetting Ltd
Bury St Edmunds, Suffolk

Printed and bound in Great Britain by
Mackays of Chatham PLC,
Chatham, Kent

I would like to thank the following for their invaluable help in providing information for this book:

Renate Blume-Reed. Ruth Anna Brown. Mike Wallace. Phil Everly. Vladimir Pozner. Johnny Rosenburg. Mona Rosenburg. Dixie Lloyd Schnebly. Russell Miller. Victor Grossman. Oleg Smirnoff. Wiebke Reed. Gerrit List. Vaclav Nectar. Manfred Dorniok. Mark Reader. Nikolai Pastoukhov. Boris Grebenshikov. Alla Pugachova. Erik and Annalise Durschmied. Lilia Liepine. Sasha Surikov. Vera Reich. Zenia Golubovitch. Anne de Boismilion.

And to the following for their help with the research for it:

Polly Apfelbaum. Celia Dougherty. Trish McKiernan.

I also want to thank these friends and colleagues for their enormous help and support:

Abner Stein. Art Troitsky. Joanna Krotz. Jo Durden-Smith. Richard David Story. Svetlana Kunitsina. Rupert Lancaster. Martin Walker. Julia Watson. Anne Graham Bell. Verity Lambert. John Saumarez Smith. Bill Boyes. Roland Joffé. Tolya Shevchenko. Yelena Zagrevskaya. Brian Siberell. Paulette Goldenhar. Maurice Goldenhar. Jonathan Powell. Alice Haemmerli. Hillel Swiller. Lesley Baxter. Peter ffrench-hodges. Elisabeth Wynhausen. Elizabeth Karnes. John Lampl. Michael Gilsenan. The Bartender at the National Hotel. Mikhail Sergeivich Gorbachev.

And, with much love, my father Sam Nadelson

For Leslie, with love.
It really is his book too.

# Contents

# New York, 1986

I was at home on a Sunday night. *The Times* lay beached, like a paper whale, on my sofa and I was only half-listening to *60 Minutes* on television. The little clock on the logo went tick, tick, tick, and the title came up on the screen: 'The Defector', the piece was called, and it was only Mike Wallace, his silky voice insinuating itself into my half-conscious brain, who dragged me to attention that Sunday night in April.

No one in America has a more hypnotic voice than Mike Wallace. He was talking about a man called Dean Reed, a rock star I'd never heard of. I looked up.

It was a very exotic picture. Dean Reed, the man in the frame, was tall, slim and handsome; he had great hair, and, although it was a contemporary picture, he wore bell-bottoms and beads. He had a narrow face, his eyes were blue, his lips were juicy and his smile was promiscuous. Straight out of Central Casting, he was the all-American boy in a Coke ad, except that, and this is what made it so intriguing, he stood in Red Square, mobbed by what appeared to be Soviet fans, plucking at his clothes, begging for autographs; gazing up at him adoringly. Behind this big American blond, the sun picked out the squashed gold onion domes of the Kremlin and the pineapple fantasies of St Basil's Cathedral. By now, I was crouched near the TV set, wondering what Mr America was doing in the heart of the Evil Empire.

The scene shifted as Wallace sketched in the life. Born on a Colorado chicken farm in 1938, at twenty, Dean Reed set out for Hollywood to try his luck. He had a nice singing voice and he looked great. He got lucky. One of his tunes went gold in Latin America and Reed headed south. In Chile, he became a superstar.

And when he saw the misery in which the people he met lived, he became a radical, but by then it was the sixties, and, like a million other American kids, Reed was ripe for conversion.

'Come with me, Deanrid,' said a talent scout from Moscow, who heard him sing at a peace conference in Helsinki. He took Dean home and made him a star in the Soviet Union, where tens of thousands of kids thronged his concerts. His albums went gold from Berlin to Bulgaria. He settled in East Berlin, where he married an East German film star, but he kept his American passport and he filed his tax forms annually with the International Revenue Service – he was not technically a defector at all. He called himself an American patriot. The Russians called him the Red Sinatra, the Johnny Cash of Communism.

On the television screen, as the music came up, Reed was singing 'Rock Around the Clock'. He did the Twist in Minsk, and then – the camera cut again – he was on stage at a Moscow stadium. Leaping into the audience, he touched people and he made them touch each other. He radiated good health. His voice was light and he thumped the guitar without finesse, but the performance was electrifying to this audience of Russian kids, prim in their white blouses and Young Pioneer scarves. He gave off body heat and, at his feet, the girls swooned, blushing, laughing, throwing red carnations, tearing off their neckerchiefs and throwing them, too, as he swivelled his hips and preached peace and love, offering them sex, politics and rock and roll all tied up together, as he had done for nearly a quarter of a century ever since he left home in 1961, his guitar on his back. He was their American; their first.

'He was the man from the land of the free and the home of the brave and Chuck Berry,' a Russian friend said to me later.

Six weeks after the broadcast, Dean Reed was dead. In April I saw *60 Minutes*; in June I read Dean Reed's obituary in the *New York Times*. He was dead, all right, his body dragged from a lake near his house in East Berlin.

'Accidental death by drowning' was the official East German report, but the follow-up stories concluded this was pretty fishy. Dean Reed was an excellent swimmer.

The item in the *Times* was halfway down the obituary page because almost no one in America knew or cared. Except for the taxi drivers. The Russian émigrés remembered.

'Ah, Deanrid, da,' they would sigh, thinking of home. 'Everyone in Soviet Union is knowing Dean Reed. Such a nice man. I am having still his *cassetski*.'

I told one taxi driver that, in America, almost no one had ever heard of Dean Reed.

'Is strange,' he said. 'Very, very strange.'

I couldn't let go of this story. I had been wanting to write a movie. This was a movie. For twenty-five years, Dean Reed roamed the world; for a quarter-century he played the radical circuit, singing 'Yiddishe Momma' to Yassir Arafat, making cowboy movies in Romania, speechifying in East Berlin. He went to acting school with Jean Seberg and Jane Fonda told him Santo Domingo was the best place for a divorce. He died mysteriously and no one knew what or who killed him. Now that he was dead, the story had an end.

After a brief flirtation with Hollywood, I went to see my friend Leslie Woodhead at Granada Television.

'I've found the man who brought rock and roll to Russia!' I said, as casually as I could. 'The Robin Hood of rock and roll!' I said, but Leslie had already commissioned the script.

Between the end of 1987 and 1990, I went looking for Dean Reed. I went to the places where he lived and worked to see the people he knew. During those three years when I travelled, to Hawaii, California and Colorado, but mostly East to Moscow and Prague and Berlin, the whole world changed. Glasnost ate up the Iron Curtain. Mikhail Gorbachev took down the Berlin Wall. By all accounts, in the Soviet Union, Dean Reed was so famous his icon was for sale in shops alongside those of Yuri Gagarin and Joseph Stalin. Dean Reed was the first rock star Mikhail Gorbachev ever saw.

# PART I

✧

## Racing Mules

# CHAPTER 1

# Checkpoint Charlie

Down a jumble of grey streets, a quarter of an hour from the centre of West Berlin, was Checkpoint Charlie and the Berlin Wall. It was the border of the world. Whenever I heard the phrase, 'The Iron Curtain', in my mind's eye I saw the Berlin Wall. Now, I saw it for real, this curtain of fortified concrete, eight feet high, twenty-nine miles long, topped with balls of barbed wire, covered on the western side with graffiti, splattered in the East with blood.

There was a raised platform from which you could view the Wall itself. From the top, I looked at the unsmiling border guards in a watchtower, peering through binoculars at the tourists, who looked back through their cameras. Between us was the dead zone of No-Man's-Land. A few months later, a twenty-two-year-old waiter jumped over the Wall because he could no longer wait, and he was shot dead. He was the last person to die there.

On the platform, a German woman was showing the Wall to a foreign friend.

'Do you think they shall take this down? They are sometimes talking so,' she said, turning to me.

'I hope so. Wouldn't it be great?!' I said.

She smiled knowingly, tucked her beautifully cut blonde hair behind her pink shell of an ear, and shouldered her Gucci bag.

'If they take it down, it shall be trouble. First Turks, next German nationals are coming. These East Germans will take our jobs. They will come in our department stores.'

That was what really got to her: if they dismantled the Wall, the East Germans would charge into the KaDeWe, denuding it of most of its 400 varieties of sausage and all of the Gucci bags. She need not have worried. Two years later, on the Sunday in November when the Wall was sliced open and East Germans raced into the West, the *New York Times* noted: 'The big department stores such as KaDeWe, were closed, despite recently passed legislation that would have allowed them to stay open.'

'You know what I am thinking?' she said.

'What?' I said.

'If the East Germans take the Wall down, we in the West will have to build another.'

The line of cars moved slowly into the border crossing. Leslie Woodhead was there, too, on that first trip East, as he was, from time to time, when I went looking for Dean Reed. Now, he looked at the men pushing little mirrors on wheels underneath the car in front of us.

'The spy's carpet sweeper,' he said.

My stomach turned over as we pulled up beside a concrete bunker and a pale border guard put his head out and stared into the car. I had never been to the East before, but I had seen all the movies.

Dean Reed's death was the subject of speculation, all of it sinister. It was widely believed that he was murdered, possibly by the East German Stasi, or the KGB. I wrote to his widow in East Berlin, but there was no reply. I called regularly; the telephone rang unanswered.

The concrete bunker was like a drive-through confessional; the young soldier, like an angry priest, snatched my passport, then snapped his box shut, leaving me to wait, pinioned in the sickly white neon light, in a No–Man's–Land without any identity.

Eventually the guard returned my passport and presented us with day visas inscribed on what felt like cheap toilet paper.

Creep, I thought silently. 'Have a nice day,' I said. The guard looked startled.

When Dean Reed went through Checkpoint Charlie, though, he always said 'Hi', to the guards, and Hans, or Heinz, or Hermann, whoever was on guard duty would go home and say, 'Dean Reed passed by today.' He was so famous that for years you could just write DEAN REED, EAST BERLIN on a postcard and it would get to him.

The empty streets that led away from the border were pitted, the walls of the dank grey buildings that lined the road were still pocked with shell marks from a war that had been over for forty years. I had imagined that in the East there would be posters with socialist slogans or banners or stylised graphics of Lenin's head, but here there were none. There were only the crappy streets with half of the street lights broken and crumbling buildings stained by the insistent rain and empty shop windows. There were no posters, no banners and no surprises, except for the most astonishing surprise of all; that I had crossed the Berlin Wall.

Before I began the research for the film and for what became this book, I swore to myself that never, never again, having once done so years ago, would I take up with a subject that could change in the middle. At the end of 1987, on this dank East Berlin street, in this, at least, I felt I was safe. Dean Reed was dead. The Wall that sat just over my shoulder was impenetrable. How could I know that in two years' time the Berlin Wall would be a pair of earrings in Bloomingdale's?

Leslie was as tenacious as a little dog with its teeth in a blanket when he wanted something and what he wanted that day were a look at Dean Reed's house, a chance to sniff around the town where he lived, and a record.

'I want a Dean Reed record,' I said at the Melodie record shop on the Leipzigerstrasse where 'Winter Wonderland' was playing. The saleswoman, who had thick ankles and thick eye-glasses, ignored me. I shouted at her.

'Dean Reed, please. Bitte?' I said, and pointed at an album. She shrugged.

'Winter Wonderland' was more her sort of thing. It was the most popular song in East Germany that year except for 'Bah Bah Black Sheep'. So far as I could tell, 'Oh Tannenbaum' was also high on the charts.

'Dean Reed, Dean Reed.' I pursued it, my voice rising. A man with a brush in his green fedora turned and shot me a disapproving look.

'Shhh,' he hissed.

The woman with thick eye-glasses turned away impatiently, nodding brusquely towards the door, and so I began to speculate that, even dead, Dean Reed was on some hit list, a non-person, a dead man whose death was a cover-up.

Outside, in the streets, the shoppers plodded by in identical stone-washed jeans, their expressions dour and disengaged. In the Alexanderplatz, a brutal piazza big enough for an army to manoeuvre in, a wind came up and drove the freezing rain. 'Be Our Guest' flickered in neon on the Stadt Hotel. The doorman there loomed up out of the gloom, wielding his umbrella like a Kalashnikov.

'Nein! Nein! Nein!'

He was furious. I was not a hotel guest and could not be admitted. There were rules. He was the doorman. This was his door.

'Go,' he shrieked and hid under the umbrella.

Across the square we found a forlorn espresso bar. Its walls were a distempered duck-egg blue and the table tops were made of scratched linoleum. But the Flying Pickets came in over the sound system and the espresso machine, which was lovingly cared for, shone, an object that was shimmery with the suggestive promise of sunny countries in which people drank good coffee and laughed.

'Halifax,' Leslie said.

'What?'

'This is Halifax, 1951. Where I grew up. The Bon Bon Coffee Bar on Commercial Street. You could listen to Frankie Mitchell and Frankie Laine and Ruby Murray on the juke box . . . you don't know what I'm talking about, do you?'

I ordered something from the menu. It was minced beef on toast, I think. Leslie shuddered.

'That looks like dog's vomit,' he said.

The Dog's Vomit Café is how I came to think of the duck-egg blue espresso bar on the Alexanderplatz.

'How could Dean Reed have lived here?' mused Leslie. 'What could he have wanted badly enough to live in this bloody place?'

Berlin must have something, something to ensnare a man like Dean Reed, I said to myself. This was just the façade; I could not see behind it. A couple of years later, however, when the façade was ripped away, it was revealed that what lay behind it was much worse, not only charmless, but polluted, impoverished, flayed, run by vile men who sat in their jacuzzis, figuring out how to starve their people.

I wanted to go home. Leslie wanted to buy a record.

In the Alexanderplatz, we got into the line outside another record store. A couple of muscular black GIs shrugged in despair as they passed. I could see that there was almost nobody inside the store, but this line of forlorn customers was made to stand out in the rain because you were not allowed in until you had a shopping basket. These were in short supply. As one customer left the shop, he handed the basket over to the next.

It didn't matter: the baskets were too small for the records. The clerks did not care if you bought anything and there was nothing much you wanted. This was my first encounter with socialism and the end of my fantasies about it. A 'Red Diaper' baby, a child of the sixties, my absolute conversion to capitalism came with a small orange plastic shopping basket in a record store on the Alexanderplatz.

Rock records were scarce. But before long rock and roll would provide the soundtrack for the revolution: the iron glove that had gripped Eastern Europe was replaced by Michael Jackson's mitten. The revolutions of the late eighties in the East looked like a rock concert: the swaying mobs with their lighted candles in Gorky Park; the crowd in Prague's Wenceslas Square, who rattled their key chains like some old punk band. In East Berlin, later that year, the kids would climb into the trees near the Wall to listen to concerts in the West, squirrelling even the most distant sounds as if they were love letters. I met a man who smuggled synthesizers and cassettes past Checkpoint Charlie, not for profit, but as a gesture of solidarity with the rock and roll underground.

'Gorby, Gorby,' shouted the kids in the trees near the Wall, as if the Soviet President were that year's rock star.

Flipping albums methodically, front to back, in bin after bin, long after I had given up, Leslie scanned each cover and found nothing. Not for the first time that day I had the eerie sense that Dean Reed never existed.

'Over here!'

Leslie was whispering.

The album was titled 'Country Songs' and Dean Reed's picture was on the cover. He wore a cowboy hat and he was smiling and he looked great. I held the album. I touched his hat. This was as good as dirty pictures. Angry, the cashier glared at me.

Schmockwitz was not on the map of places you were permitted to visit, according to the day visa printed on toilet paper. In an endless tangle of suburban streets, we got lost. Then, all at once, we bumped over the cobblestones into the village of Schmockwitz itself.

We stopped at a tavern, where I hoped there would be a beer mug with Dean's head on it for sale. I imagined that Schmockwitz, where Dean lived, was the Graceland of the East.

As I opened the door, in unison, a half-dozen hefty burghers looked up from their Sunday lunch and stared at my feet. I had no socks on. They were soaked and I'd hung them on the car radiator to dry. No one smiled. There were no Dean Reed beer mugs.

Backing off, I got in the car and Leslie drove down a narrow road between bare birch trees. Slush spattered the window. The never-ending rain fell from an oyster sky. A wrong turning led us to the edge of the lake where there was a large building that was boarded up for the winter. A sign I could just decode announced that it was a Party Rest House, and as the car wheels squealed and we backed out in a hurry, night began to close down over this slice of exurban Berlin. Paranoia turned on the projector in my head and the movie flickered into life: it was in black and white and had a creepy grain. Whoever had it in for Dean Reed, whoever killed him, was down this road and was looking for us. We would miss closing time at Checkpoint Charlie; we were way out of bounds, beyond the limits of our visa. We would spend the night in an East Berlin jail among officials who were not only communists but Germans as well, and perhaps there was a small concentration camp still open somewhere . . . Yes that would be it, a small camp. Rigid with fear, I sat, watching my socks dry on the radiator. I thought I heard the soundtrack of a German police car.

6A Schmockwitzer Damm was a low-lying, white stucco house with an orange tiled roof, a garage, a lawn and a pretty air of privilege. A large carved wooden R was perched on a post in the yard as if it were a ranch: the Double R ranch; the Dean Reed Dude Ranch of Schmockwitz. On the other side of the house from the road, was a stretch of lake the colour of metal. It was the lake where Dean Reed's body lay for four days before it was dragged to shore.

DEATH IN BERLIN FOR DEFECTOR WHO CHANGED HIS TUNE. MYSTERY OF AMERICAN POP STAR IN LAKE: IT WAS MURDER SAYS MANAGER.

DEAN REED, THE SINGER WHO WENT EAST AND THEN WANTED TO
COME IN FROM THE COLD.

The crumpled newspaper cuttings were in my purse. The Friday
Dean Reed disappeared, the journalist Russell Miller was in Berlin.
By chance, Miller had arranged to interview Reed for a magazine
that weekend and, from West Berlin, where he was staying, he
called the house at Schmockwitz. The interview was scheduled for
the next day. It was not to be, for when Miller called, Mrs Reed
told him that Dean was ill and could not see him. In the middle
of the conversation, a man came on the line – it seemed to Miller
that he had snatched the phone away from Mrs Reed. He told
Miller that Dean was in hospital and that he should go home and
would be contacted. Then he gave Miller his name and a telephone
number in Potsdam. He was Mr Weiczaukowski, he said.

Russell Miller went home and, on the following Tuesday when
he heard the news that Dean Reed was dead, he called Potsdam.
There was no 'Mr Weiczaukowski' at the number he had been
given, and so the mystery was cranked up. Eventually it spread
like a stain so that nobody who knew Dean Reed could see the
truth about his death.

'Let's go.'

It was wet and dark and I was frightened; we had seen the house.
Leslie insisted on getting out of the car to take pictures of it because
his production-designer would need these photographs, he said.
Slowly, he sauntered around the house, fiddling with his camera.
He inspected its parts and blew imaginary dust off a lens, then he
changed the lenses. He inserted each lens and each piece of the
camera into the appropriate flap in a canvas bag, which had a dozen
different flaps; it also had pockets, zips and snaps. He inserted the
camera itself in the main body of the bag, fussing with it in the
irritating way of people who are preoccupied with photography,
as if their dedication to their art is determined by the number of
flaps they have on their camera bag. I always think: why can't they
buy a postcard?

Leslie got in the car and shivered. Scared, he loved it. He had
made films in Eastern Europe before and his addiction to it was
obsessive. It tested you and then you could go home; it was a
no-exit with a revolving door.

'Cheer up,' he said, turning to take yet one more picture with
still another camera he possessed, then revving up the motor of

the car so loudly that it would wake the dead. 'This is nothing at all compared to when I was doing torture in Brazil.'

Down that country road, in the encroaching gloom, the other side of the Berlin Wall was where I seriously began looking for Dean Reed at the end of 1987. The Berlin Wall went up in August 1961. The following winter, when he was twenty-three, Dean applied for a passport and he left America, where he never lived again. In 1986, he died in this lake in East Berlin.

Four years to the day from his memorial service that June, a crane picked up Checkpoint Charlie and hoisted it away, while the foreign ministers of the United States and the Soviet Union, tapping their toes to the strains of a Marine marching band, smiled at each other. Later, the Checkpoint, which was only a prefabricated little box after all, was shipped to the Smithsonian Institution . . .

We walked down the road, a few hundred yards from the house at Schmockwitz, to a little cemetery. A few wet flowers lay on a headstone. On it, in German, was inscribed simply: Dean Reed. Born Colorado, 1938. Died, Berlin, 1986.

# CHAPTER 2

# Hawaii

When Dean Reed was seventeen, he raced a mule 110 miles for a quarter. He did it on a dare. He nearly dropped dead and so did the mule. Reed won. At the end of the race his face glowed with triumph. Racing that mule was ambitious, brave and hokey and it had the feel of one of those old folk songs where heroic men raced locomotives in their bare feet.

'I still have that quarter somewhere,' Mrs Brown said.

Ruth Anna Brown was Dean Reed's mother and she lived in a condo in Hawaii. I went to see her in Wahiawa near the North Shore of Oahu because I wanted her to tell me how her son died. We talked about the mule race. She looked for the quarter he won.

As I drove across the island from Honolulu, Hawaii seemed as far away as you could get from East Berlin and the Dog's Vomit Café. The islands were like a trail of denatured but delectable crumbs, nibbled off the coast of California and flung across the South Pacific. The sun shone, holiday-makers tanned their plump flesh, girls in bars wiggled their plastic hula skirts and everyone drank things from huge pineapples with pink parasols in them.

At the Kahala Hilton, the dolphins in the man-made lagoon sang for their supper. Loving it, we threw them more fishes. Holiday-makers, dolphins, we were all tourists locked in a palmy conspiracy of good times. In the souvenir shop, where there were toy dogs with barrels of macadamia nuts around their neck, shirts with sunsets on them and plastic pineapples with clocks in them, there were also motorised dolphins to swim in your bath.

Near Wahiawa, where Mrs Brown lived with her fond husband Ralph, the air smelled of pineapples. The fruit, whose smell made you giddy, grew on plantations that were as plush and tidy as wall-to-wall carpeting, but the mountains just beyond were jagged

15

and unprocessed and the north coast of Oahu had a breezy, ramshackle charm.

There was a storm coming when I arrived; the coconuts bobbled noisily against each other in the trees, and Mrs Brown fastened the shutters.

I liked Mrs Brown.

She was a handsome woman with fine white Scandinavian skin and hair and it gave her a powdery look, but she wasn't a fragile old lady. She was tough and funny and some of the time, she (Well! My Goodness!) camped it up some, her hands on her hips, full of self-mockery and good humour. Her back was straight and she wore a sweatshirt from the University of Hawaii, where she had just finished her doctorate in Women's Peace Studies. At seventy-four, she was immensely hospitable and naturally wary, and she had an unbending determination to see right done by her boy who was dead in East Berlin. At first we made small talk.

Mrs Brown was no fool. Courteously, she asked who I was. Dutifully, I mumbled something about the movie we were making and trundled out my leftie credentials, shuffling around cuttings from the *Guardian*, referring to a remote past on the picket lines. Ho Ho Ho Chi Minh, I mumbled. Mrs Brown got the point.

'I had that child for a special reason. I always think that Dean was born under a magic star,' she said.

Mrs Brown sat herself on the carpet between the television set and a brass-bound trunk. The trunk was full of photographs. All day long, we sat on the floor, surrounded by its contents: newspaper cuttings in three languages; records and tapes; videos and scrapbooks and copies of Dean's autobiography, written in German. The text, when I got it translated, was as self-aggrandising as any star bio I'd ever read, no more, no less, but the pictures of Dean were marvellous, made smudgy and real by the newsprint.

Everyone I met had a copy of Dean's little book and in each, in the flyleaf inside the bright blue cover, was an inscription in his big childish hand, invariably wishing the recipient peace and love and all good things for a socialist future.

Mrs Brown was rueful. She had so little of Dean left. She possessed not so much as his belt buckle – Dean's widow would not give it to her, she said. So, when a year or two later, the Colorado Historical Society organised the Dean Reed Collection, she was happy. Photographs, film scripts, diaries and a plaster casting of Dean's teeth were donated by his widow, Renate, who also offered them his dog, Emu, when the dog died.

'In no way could I justify a stuffed Emu to the Colorado Historical Society,' its director told the *Denver Post*. Mrs Brown thought it was all perfectly wonderful.

'I think Dean's looking down and saying, "Wow! I just knew I'd come back to Colorado, no matter what." '

All day long, as I sat with Mrs Brown on her living-room floor, surrounded by her souvenirs, the television was always on, and images of Dean – some from contraband videos of television specials he'd made, others from documentary films about his life – flickered across it. Pictures of Dean lay on the carpet in black-and-white and colour. A picture of Dean hung over the television set. Mrs Brown dug in her box, looking for the winning quarter from the mule race and I felt an intruder, but I couldn't take my eyes off the picture on the wall. It was a big, technicolour still, and in it, wearing a beaded Indian neckband, he looked fit, alive and vivid. It was taken not long before his death, and as I looked at it, not for the first time, I thought: Jesus, he was handsome. Finally, the verse I'd been trying to dredge up came back to me. It was e. e. cummings:

Buffalo Bill's
defunct
    who used to
    ride a watersmooth-silver
                stallion
and break onetwothreefourfive pigeonsjustlikethat
                        Jesus
he was a handsome man
            and what i want to know is
how do you like your blueeyed boy
Mister Death

Dean Reed was born on the 22nd of September, 1938, in Wheat Ridge, Colorado. It was one of a string of small towns on the fringe of Denver when Denver was still a cow town. Wheat Ridge was resolutely rural, not yet eaten by Denver's urban sprawl.

Dean went to the local schools, joined the 4 H, the Boy Scouts and the Future Farmers of America. At the local military academy he attended, he was good at sports, a fine horseman and a keen gymnast. At Wheat Ridge High, he set the record for the mile-and-a-half cross country run. In his senior year there was the mule race.

He could eat more ice cream than any kid in town – all his life he was crazy about ice cream – and afternoons after school, he worked at the local Dairy. His ears bugged him, though. They were big as jug handles. He thought they made him ugly, and he worried about getting girls. He got a guitar, figuring it would help get him some girls, the ears notwithstanding. He played the high school auditorium; he played Phipps Auditorium in Denver; he played the Harmony Guest Ranch ranch up in the mountains at Estes Park. Everyone called him 'Slim'.

It was as if Dean was in training for the sentimental cowboy movies he would one day make. Dean practised positive thinking. *The Power of Positive Thinking* by Dr Norman Vincent Peale was the biggest seller of the euphoric fifties, when the country was in its prime and it was un-American to be a failure. Kids competed at hula-hoops; kids stuffed themselves into phone booths and ate goldfish. Winning was what counted. Sometimes Dean got a little money for playing his guitar and, when he did, he gave it to the American Cancer Society.

'He always shared that way,' Mrs Brown said.

The soundtrack for Dean's teen years had the peppy beat, but none of the seditions, of early rock and roll. It had an earnest folksiness – Pete Seeger by way of the Limeliters: Folk Music for Everyone.

It sounded a typically all-American childhood, its landscape the sunny uplands Hollywood let us believe all good Americans inhabited, and it made me suspicious as hell. Fumbling in her trunk of stuff, Mrs Brown was like a woman trying to get unstuck from a chaotic dream. Outside, the tropical storm smashed open the shutters; they banged incessantly against the window frames. As she got up to fix them, Mrs Brown lurched slightly, whether from age or grief was hard to tell, then she sat down heavily in a chair, her legs falling apart a little. I wanted to ask her about the death. Who killed Dean Reed? I wanted to say. But the intrusion was too great, and, anyhow, she was well defended against it.

'You about ready for us, Ralph?' she called.

Ralph, who was wearing a Hawaiian skirt, was making lunch.

'Give me about ten minutes,' he said.

★

The video of a documentary about Dean's life flickered into play.

'Dean's dad, Cyril,' Mrs Brown said.

Wearing thick black eye-glasses, Cyril had the air of a man who had cast himself as a Lovable Rogue with the politics of Genghis Khan. Talking to a reporter on camera, he was very funny.

'Dean, he went over there to Russia and he said there was some difference between socialism and communism and I guess there was, but I could never exactly tell you what that difference was.'

I heard somewhere that when General Jimmy Walker founded the John Birch Society in 1961, Cyril joined up. BETTER DEAD THAN RED. What sweet revenge for his son to finish up a dedicated communist, if revenge was what Dean was after. Better dead than red. Poor Dean was red and dead.

'Well, Cyril was a cantankerous creature,' said Mrs Brown, who divorced him as soon as the boys were grown.

She searched for her spectacles, found them on top of her head, put them on and peered at the screen at a picture of Dean. Smiling, he was standing in front of what looked like a chicken coop.

'I kept them back in Wheat Ridge to earn extra money,' Mrs Brown said. 'I never did care much for those chickens. Come to think of it, I didn't much care for Cyril, either.'

In his way, Cyril cared for the boy, though, and the first time Dean got up to play for an audience, the old man worried himself sick. Still, although Dean sent his dad money for a ticket to come see him perform in the East, Cyril never went.

'I had no use for those countries,' he said in his corn-pone accent, putting it on good and thick for the cameras, and it was easy to see how Dean got his star quality from those two old country hams, Cyril and Ruth Anna.

Wanting the old man's love was a theme of Dean's life. He had two brothers, Vern and Dale. Dale, the younger, lived in Alaska. Vern, who was a committed Libertarian, lived in Seattle where, although he was employed at Boeing, he refused to work on military aircraft. Dean thought this was very brave and often boasted about what a good engineer Vern was. But Dean was not at all close to his brothers; most of all, he wanted his father to love him best.

'Dean's dad killed himself, did you know that?' Mrs Brown said, letting it pop out of her mouth by-the-by, as if she did not want it to count for much, but couldn't resist the effect. The landscape of Dean's mythic childhood darkened and interesting shadows danced along those sunlit uplands.

Injured in a wheat combine accident, Cyril lost a leg, and, in 1984, he killed himself because he could not afford a new one, it was rumoured. Dean told reporters his daddy died because he couldn't afford medical care and he never forgave America for failing his father. Again and again, he told the story.

'Why didn't you give him the money for a leg?' one reporter finally asked.

Dean said his dad was too proud.

Mrs Brown stopped the video, leaving her boy frozen in time. She peered at her baby, forever crew-cut. He was dead. She was in Hawaii.

As we set the table for lunch, I learned, among other things that: right up to the end of Dean's life he could walk on his hands; that he whistled when he was nervous; that he could juggle brilliantly. He adored spaghetti and Skippy Crunchy peanut butter, which Mrs Brown sent him by post to East Berlin, and turquoise was his favourite colour. ('Not red', he often cracked.) He also had medical problems. As a boy – here she grew vague – he'd had some sort of major operation and by twenty he had ulcers and trouble sleeping.

'He took a sleeping pill every night of his life,' she said. 'But only one. He never took more than one sleeping pill.'

Ralph was ready with the lunch. He was known for his fruit salad and was a dab hand with pineapple sherbet, which he produced from a white plastic gadget. It was delicious.

Outside, the rain had stopped and the sun twirled some droplets into a rainbow on the window pane. All around the apartment complex, which resembled a two-storey motel made of poured concrete, people were throwing open their windows, getting ready to go out to do the Saturday chores. There was the scraping and banging of doors and cars as the place came alive after the storm. Fit looking old people in Bermuda shorts went out of doors, sucked in the fresh washed air, hailed each other, arranged dates to play Scrabble and set off in their cars for the supermarket.

All of Hawaii was a comfy lagoon where old people, tourists, and assorted despots cavorted and basked, serviced by those who knew their tricks. Mrs Marcos had her own personalised silver napkin ring in the restaurant at the Kahala Hilton. It was an awful lot of trouble when she came to lunch, said one young waiter. Security men had to be posted everywhere and local reporters came round to see what kind of shoes Imelda was wearing.

Like the waiters, everyone who tended to the visitors was as cheery as could be, putting on muu-muus, cooking pig luaus, driving pedi-cabs, carrying suitcases, selling nuts at the macademia nut museum, working the army bases, frying McNuggets at McDonald's, dancing the hula and unfurling Mrs Marcos' napkin. They fed the dolphins and sold real estate to the Japanese, who were buying up the islands even faster than the native culture was disappearing. Every hotel had numerous courteous Japanese on the staff; Ira Yamaha, mine was called, I think.

Much of the most desirable real estate the Japanese were bidding on was around Honolulu, within spitting distance of Pearl Harbor and the Arizona Monument. The sunken battleship, entombed in the waterborne shrine, preserved World War II in a plastic box and the tourists, ferried out into the harbour, looked down fearfully and imagined the dead.

Sitting in Mrs Brown's dining room on the the other side of the world, I had the exotic idea that Hawaii was a lot like Dean Reed's East Berlin after all. Both were the result of military necessity – Hawaii might seem a paradise, but the map betrayed its purpose and it was studded with naval dockyards; and one of the islands, off limits to visitors, was owned entirely by the military and used as a firing range. In Hawaii, you lived on the surface. You had just arrived or were about to depart. In the East, Dean Reed was a kind of tourist rebel. In a sense, it was what made him a star, especially when he first arrived. He sang his heart out. He rocked and rolled. He laughed and he smiled. When he was making movies on location, he ate with the workers. In the East, Dean fed on applause and medals and desire. He was a fish out of water – a dolphin in a different lagoon – and they loved him for it.

'When he first arrived he was like something from outer space,' Mrs Brown said as if reading my mind.

He never got used to Germany, though. He was always a tourist.

'We lack certain things, Mike. Hamburgers for example,' he told Mike Wallace.

It was a joke, of course, but it stood for missing home. It was the nature of the expatriate life.

'There's a little something we like to do before meals,' Mrs Brown said.

I froze. They were going to say grace and I had already attacked the lunch. I was embarrassed. I wanted to do the culturally correct thing. But Ruth Anna Brown just smiled her smart, wry smile.

'We like to hold hands and wish each other peace and love and friendship,' she said.

In the late Hawaiian afternoon, we listened to 'My Summer Romance' on the gramophone. It was Dean's first hit tune.

'You have to understand, Dean always did what he did for a woman. First he married Patty in Hollywood. Then Wiebke and Renate in East Berlin. You could go see Wiebke, I guess. She's my friend, but she's a bitch. They were all bitches.'

She giggled.

'I guess you could say I was the original model.'

Mrs Brown showed me a photograph of the Dean Reed School, which had been dedicated recently in East Berlin.

'I have also written to that Erich Honecker to tell him to change the name of the cemetery where Dean is buried to the Dean Reed Cemetery. Dean knew Honecker. He knew everyone,' she said.

Mrs Brown was weary. I had listened to her stories and eaten her husband's pineapple sherbet and what I should have said was: thanks and take care of yourself.

'So who do you think killed him? How did your son die?' I said.

'Well, I went to see one of their policemen over in East Germany, you can just imagine. My goodness, he was a pompous man. I asked who he thought did do it and he looked at me as if I were just plain crazy. I'll never forget it. He said to me, "There are three things to consider. First, crime. Second, accident. Third, suicide."

'Then he said, "One. We do not have crime in the GDR. Two. We know Dean well and he would never have committed suicide. Three, therefore, it was an accident."

'So tell me this,' Mrs Brown continued. 'If it was an accident, why was Dean pinned under the pilings of the pier in the lake? Why were his arms stretched out so that he was pinned in a

Christ-like position? Why was he wearing two jackets in the middle of summer? Why?'

Notions poured from her like hope: that Dean knew something about Chernobyl – he was due to start filming that summer in Yalta, which was not far away; he was dissatisfied with the system – she had a letter from him as far back as 1985 saying so; he knew things about Ollie North and the Contras. He was intending to call a press conference for the Saturday he died.

The scenarios came on faster and faster. She could handle something dramatic, brave, meaningful, a death that had panache. The only unspeakable thing was an accidental death. She whispered to me of the CIA.

'There was always an agent assigned to Dean to do a "wet job", in case he got out of line,' she said.

'A wet job?'

She side-stepped the question and put on a video tape of Dean's last concert.

In a single spotlight, Dean sat on a stool on a bare stage, picked up his guitar and, a cappella, sang a song for his mother 12,000 miles away on the other side of a video machine. It was called 'Mom's Song'.

Her eyes filled up and Mrs Brown turned away. 'When I first saw that video he was already dead and I thought he was trying to tell me goodbye,' she said.

Somehow, Mrs Brown summoned up the energy to tell me one more story and as she told it, she was re-charged. In her hand was a blurry black-and-white snapshot a quarter of a century old. Dean Reed smiled up out of it. He was twenty and almost unbearably hopeful. In a white Chevrolet Impala convertible, big as a boat, he wore a skinny tie and a crew cut like his mother's front lawn. It was taken in 1958, the year he left home for Hollywood, and the story Mrs Brown told was clearly the great Reed family legend.

'Hey, mister!'

His thumb stuck out, the bum stood by the side of the road, trying to hitch a ride. Under the big blue Arizona sky, cars whooshed past the old man on the desert road. Driving his Chevy, Dean saw him from a long way off.

The radio was playing and Dean put his foot down on the

accelerator of the white convertible, a car built for a star, and Dean rode it hopefully, his guitar in the front seat beside him. He was going to Hollywood.

Unhappy about this 'singing stuff', as he called it, Dean's dad wanted him to finish his studies in meteorology at the university. Dean planned on becoming a TV weatherman after he finished. But it was summer's end after his sophomore year and, instead of heading on home to college, Dean went West.

What the heck, he said to himself. He was pretty good with the guitar. He had racked up a few successes playing Estes Park. Dean wanted a look at the big time.

Driving down the endless desert highway, he was having a ball. Anything was possible, on the road, heading West. He was going to the coast to work out on the dream machine. It was the dawning of the age of celebrity when the lives of the stars, as remote from Wheat Ridge, Colorado as Saturn, shimmered in the reflected glamour of their swimming pools.

Then Dean saw the bum. And the improbable movie of his life began.

The guy at the roadside looked forlorn and miserable. Dean, always on the lookout for a good deed, pulled over.

'Hop in,' Dean said. 'Where are you going?'

'Hi,' the bum said, scratching his face. 'Where are you going?'

'Hollywood,' said Dean.

Clocking the guitar in the front seat, the bum knew a good thing when he saw one.

'I'll tell you what. You pay for a night at a motel, maybe give me a spare pair of pants, I'll give you a name of someone in the business,' he said.

Sceptical, Dean laughed. But he was a good kid with a good heart, and he thought, what the heck.

Dusk fell over the desert. The neon came on outside the motels. Dean agreed to pay for the bum's room. He gave him a pair of pants, too, although it was his only spare pair. The bum told Dean to call up Mr Boyle Gilmore at Capitol Records in Holly-wood.

In Hollywood, the Capitol Records Building was pretty easy to find because it was built in the shape of a stack of records.

Sweet-talking the receptionist, Dean got in to see Mr Boyle Gilmore, who turned out to be the genuine article. The bum on the road was, in fact, a musician and a pal of Gilmore's from the old days.

Dean got a try-out. Next thing you knew, he was on the phone back to his mom to come on out and sign him to a seven-year contract with Capital. He was not yet twenty-one and his mother had to sign.

'Come on out to California, Mom,' he said, shouting because he was on long distance, which was still a novelty, used only for death and celebration.

It was 1958. He was twenty. He had a great smile. He could shake his hips and the girls thought he was very sexy.

Dean's dad was mad as hell when Dean quit college, but he did quit. He did a few gigs on TV, including 'Bachelor Father'. On Mrs Brown's television set, I watched a clip. In it, a girl bobbed onto the stage, her pony tail bouncing.

'How about everyone coming over to my house. I've got the new Dean Reed album and it's a real gasser,' she said.

The child on the screen had the knowing look of a TV pro, even at fifteen. She wore bobby sox, saddle shoes and an angora sweater. In rows of chairs sat an audience of teenage girls, wiggling and giggling with the calculated innocence of the fifties.

'But here he is himself in person. It's Dean Reed!'

'Twirly Twirly,' Dean Reed sang.

Bright as a button, he bounced up to the mike in that loose-jointed way that was considered slick, snapping his fingers, dancing, jumping. He wore a white sports coat and he had all the moves. He was quite polished; he knew his stuff. Behind him, a couple of plump majorettes in little white booties pranced around, tossing their batons, shaking their pointed boobies under those white angora sweaters, eyeing Dean Reed.

'Twirly Twirly,' he sang again.

Dean got himself a screen test and a contract at Warner Brothers star school. There, he studied to be a movie star and, among his friends was Phil Everly of the Everly Brothers. They remained friends for life.

'Dean's life, it was just like a movie,' Mrs Brown had said, as she reached over to shut off the TV.

I had the feeling that, once Dean left home, there were visits, but that contact with his mother was sporadic – the long-distance phone calls broken up by static and politics.

Before I left Hawaii, Ruth Anna Brown called to say that she wanted me to help her produce a television series about The Reed Family; she had a sort of American 'Upstairs, Downstairs' in mind. There wasn't much I could do in the way that she wanted me to, so I sent flowers by way of thanks for her time. She wrote to say that she had placed them on the Korean Peace Memorial in Hawaii in memory of her son, Dean Reed, the American singer who died in East Berlin. She had nothing left of his, not even his belt buckle, so she made do by putting out flowers for him and communing with his spirit at a Korean shrine. It was all there was. She had even failed to find the quarter.

# CHAPTER 3

✧

# Hollywood

Phil Everly arrived at El Torrito in Burbank in a powder-blue Cadillac convertible with tail fins; he was forty-nine.

A peppy Mexican restaurant in the pristine business district of Burbank, El Torrito was a whimsical free-standing building which stood, like a funky piece of folk art among the sleek skyscrapers that churned out movies and records and the executives who processed both.

The day was bright and hot. Inside, it was dark, cool and wonderfully gloomy and the cool gloom soothed your sun-stricken eyes. The Maitre d' had a moustache and a red vest. I whispered that we were waiting for Phil Everly and he smiled. Of course, Señor Everly.

Leslie Woodhead was there; he was in California for a meeting and, anyway, he wasn't going to pass up a chance to see Phil. Shifting his feet nervously, he watched the front door. This was Hollywood; we were waiting for a star; it was what you did in Lotus-land.

Phil's was not an easy phone number to come by, which added to the anticipation. Getting it had required a couple of dozen phone calls back to London, where friends at the BBC once made a documentary about the Everly Brothers and their reunion concert at the Albert Hall. Phil Everly, who had a sweet, southern wispy voice on the telephone, said he was seeing us just because he liked the guys from the BBC so much. He had a nice time with them. He liked those English guys. But during the whole, long, boozy lunch that followed, Phil Everly never once mentioned the reunion concert. He never mentioned his brother, Don, either.

Like Dean, Phil and his family came West in one of those now mythic old Chevrolet cars. In 1946, Ike and Margaret Everly took

27

their kids and left Tennessee for a better life, first in Chicago, then in California. Their two boys, Don and Phil, began to sing.

'Bye-Bye Love', they sang and 'Wake Up Little Susie'. In the restaurant in Burbank, as I watched out the window for Phil Everly, the songs he once sang ran through my head: 'Bye-bye, love. Bye-bye, happiness. Hello, loneliness . . . ' I knew all the lyrics.

A handsome man with a thick shock of brown hair and a baby face, he walked through the door, removing his sunglasses as he came slowly into the cool, dark room, ducking slightly to avoid the plants. He looked around in a leisurely way, not because he expected anyone to pay particular attention to him, but because he was a man who moved slowly with that easy, hot-weather grace southerners often have. With him was a middle-aged man with a bald spot. They paused for a moment, conferring, squinting, canvassing the room.

Phil took the centre of the floor naturally and, starstruck, like teenagers, Leslie and I fumbled towards him.

Then Phil saw us. He smiled, walked forward and stuck out his hand.

'Hi,' Phil Everly said, 'I'm Phil Everly.'

'Hi,' said Leslie. 'I'm Leslie Woodhead.'

The nice man with the bald spot was Phil's friend, Joe. Once Joe played bass for Phil. Once, he met Dean in Phil's company, which is why he was there, I guessed, or maybe he served as Phil's minder. Joe sold real estate somewhere around Burbank.

We sat in a booth towards the back and drank frozen margaritas out of glasses the size of goldfish bowls. Phil counselled certain dishes with the assurance and concern of an expert – this *burrito* or that *quesidilla* or whatever other fried, cheesy, spicy, tasty Mexican item that was a specialty of the house.

While he ordered, we adjusted to the fact that we were in Burbank, talking with Phil Everly, who was a legend. He was also a Republican.

'I was about as far away as you can get politically from Dean, I guess,' Phil said.

'He was a socialist and I'm a Reagan supporter.'

From the corner of my eye I could see that Leslie was looking worried. He was from the north of England, voted Labour and read the *Guardian*. I was not sure he'd ever met a Republican.

('Except Richard Nixon,' he said irritably later on. 'I have met Richard Nixon, you know.')

Phil was smoking Marlboros. 'But it didn't matter. The couple of times I went over to see Dean in East Berlin, we just played some music together and laughed a lot. We didn't really talk much about politics.'

'Was he big over there?'

'Man, he was bigger than Elvis.'

'Was he any good?'

'You can't fool crowds that size, not anywhere.'

'Big crowds?'

'Everywhere he went. And he could still walk on his hands. He was the same age as me and still doing that.'

'He was a good athlete?'

'He was a real all-rounder. He could sing, he could act. I was a lousy actor,' Phil said.

Phil and Dean met at the star school on the Warner Brothers lot, for, although Phil was already a big singing star – the Everly Brothers recorded 'Wake Up Little Susie' as far back as 1957, everyone wanted to be in the movies. The studios, awed by the success of Elvis Presley on the big screen and terrified by television, which was a dirty word in Hollywood, grabbed at new talent wherever they could find it.

Contract players like Dean learned to fence and act and wear nice clothes. They worked as bit players and walk-ons. When big shots toured the studio, they posed with them. Movie magazines showed them dressed up in tulle prom dresses or a white tux at Chasen's or the Brown Derby, like mannequins in a shop window.

In Hollywood, a handsome young truck driver became Rock Hudson, so it could happen to anyone. Universal produced movies made by Ross Hunter where the titles always seemed to appear on padded satin cushions and seemed always to star Agnes Moorhead and Deborah Rush. Married couples slept in separate beds on the screen and starlets had their dresses glued to their breasts because a starlet was not permitted to show her cleavage, although you could show the mounds on either side.

The Eisenhower Years. Did you hear the one about the Eisenhower doll? people said. You wind it up, it does nothing for eight years. But the country was prosperous, secure and confident. The

Depression and the War were over, America was aglow with affluence and stardom was awfully seductive to the twenty-year-old boy obsessed with winning. In November, 1960, Jack Kennedy was elected President because he looked like a movie star. A year earlier, Nikita Khrushchev had visited America.

Forbidden a visit to Disneyland, The Khrushchevs went to 20th Century Fox. There, they watched a rehearsal of *Can Can*, disapproved of it and met the stars and starlets. Among them was Marilyn Monroe. Having learned a few words of Russian from Natalie Wood, Monroe shook Mr Khrushchev's hand and whispered in his ear:

'We, the workers of 20th Century Fox, rejoice that you have come to visit our Studio and our Country.'

As he flew out of Los Angeles, so the apocryphal story goes, Khrushchev looked down and saw all the swimming pools.

'Now I know that Communism has failed,' he said.

Phil Everly ordered another margarita.

'To know about Dean, you had to know about Paton Price,' he said. 'Paton was the acting coach at Warners and he was a real important guy for all of us,' Phil said. 'He taught us it didn't so much matter what your politics were so long as you used your art to further what you believed in.'

'Paton was a special guy,' Phil said. 'He was a surrogate father for Dean who lived with him and his wife Tillie. You ought to go and see Tillie. She lives here in Burbank,' said Phil.

Paton Price was the acting coach at Warner Brothers, but he was, more importantly, a man of impeccable liberal credentials. Although Hollywood had been badly wounded by the anti-communist witch hunts of the early fifties, there was a sturdy left-wing community of which Mr Price was a mainstay. A pacifist, he had gone to jail during World War II. A fierce opponent of segregation and later, of the Vietnam War, he was a completely political man. Paton Price was dead. But everyone I met who had known Dean Reed had a story about Paton. In the photographs and film clips I had seen of him, he had a tense, intense face, a high forehead and a goatee. He was dying and you could see the skull beneath the skin.

At Warner Brothers, in his acting class, at his house which was a kind of salon for his students, Paton undertook to preach his beliefs, which, as Phil put it, were more about life than about acting. Because of Paton's teachings, Dean turned down the chance to star in a TV show that was then coming up; it was called 'Wanted Dead or Alive'. (There was some confusion over whether it was a show called 'Killer Diller', about a cowboy who would rather sing than fight, but most people thought it was 'Wanted Dead or Alive'.) Dean did not want to carry a gun on screen. Instead of Dean, they cast a young unknown called Steve McQueen.

On one brutal occasion, when Dean was having trouble with his lines, Paton said to him, 'Well, you're having problems, Dean, because you're sitting next to a very attractive woman and you're wondering what's under those clothes, so we can eliminate that problem.' On an empty sound stage, Paton made both Dean and the girl strip naked.

'Now you see what's she's got, she sees what you've got, now you can concentrate on putting some emotion into what you're doing,' Paton said and it embarrassed the hell out of Dean.

And I remembered Mrs Brown's bitter words:

'Most often when he came home to America, he stayed with Paton and Tillie in Burbank,' she said that day at the condo in Wahiawa.

'Paton had a lot of influence with Dean,' she said. 'Paton blamed me for the fact Dean was a virgin when he got to Hollywood. Well, just what in the world did he think I could do about that?'

'You cannot be a good artist unless you are a good human being,' Paton Price told his classes. He told them that they had to dedicate their fame, if they were lucky enough to have fame, to make this world a better place to live in. Among his students, along with Dean and Phil Everly were Jean Seberg, Don Murray, the Smothers Brothers and Dick Clark. I wondered what Dick Clark made of it all, but Dick Clark wasn't talking. Thirty years after he left Warner Brothers star school, Dick Clark, who had invented American Bandstand, was one of the richest men in America.

The smell of Phil's cigarette was drifting my way and I was dying for a smoke. Shaking out the pack, he offered me one. I confessed I had just given it up. Putting the cigarettes away, Phil chided.

'You're crazy if you go back to it,' he said.

I played the scene in my head: 'Want a cigarette?' someone

31

would say to me. 'No thanks,' I'd reply. 'Wow. You quit. How did you manage?' In reply, I would cast my eyes down and raise my voice.

'You see,' I would say, 'It was Phil Everly who got me to quit. Of the Everly Brothers.'

As a star, for me, Phil had the potent glamour of myth. Perhaps kids in Russia felt about Dean Reed the way I felt about Phil Everly. Phil was so famous that even sitting beside him in that Mexican restaurant, eating *burritos* and smelling the cigarette smoke, even chatting to the unpretentious middle-aged man he was, he was wrapped in a kind of charmed cloak that shone with nostalgia. I could see the label: the Everly Brothers. When I was a kid, a continent away in New York City and rock and roll was brand new, their names were on those first, thrilling 45s we bought, the ones with the holes big as a doughnut in the middle. You had to put a yellow plastic disk in the hole so you could stack them up on the gramophone.

Phil had a good smile and he was a great flirt. I was having a very good time. The margaritas kept coming. Phil was charming. He was smart. He was warm. He was articulate. He was witty. He had been a Marine. I knew that, at the other side of the booth, Leslie was still trying to reconcile how much he liked the singer with how he felt about Phil's politics.

Leslie loved Phil's music, too. He loved it in the way that Europeans loved America, loved it for its glory days, when it shone with imperial brass. For them, The Everlys' music forever rang with the distant sounds of America, the country of GI Joe and neon-lit motels, diners and Jack Kerouac and innocence, Marilyn Monroe and Cadillacs with big tail fins and Buddy Holly. It produced rock and roll. It produced Dean Reed.

The Russians loved Dean because when he shimmied and smiled and sang rock and roll music to them, he was the man from the American theme park. Their American.

'How did you come to play with Dean in East Berlin?'

'He just got in touch and invited me,' Phil said.

'Did you meet Renate, his wife?'

'Sure. And they really were in love, her and Dean, you know.'

'But what was it like with Dean in East Berlin?' I asked.

'We played some concerts down in Karl Marx-stadt. We had a lot of laughs. Dean was a real joker. He got me an interpreter, a lady who was one of only twelve Mormons in East Germany. There was nothing to buy, I mean how much caviar can a fellow eat? So I bought some diamonds, but they weren't much good. But Dean loved it. He couldn't go out of the house without being mobbed.'

'How did Dean make out over there?' Leslie asked.

'If Dean was doing the same business over here, he'd have been a millionaire many times over,' Phil said seriously. 'I don't hold with socialism, but, hey, Dean put his money where his mouth was.'

Lighting up, Phil exhaled the delicious smoke and sipped his drink. Across the table, Joe, the bass player who sold real estate, was listening hard.

'So who do you guys think killed Dean Reed?' he said.

Leslie recited the usual litany: the KGB killed Dean because he was wanting to come home to America; the CIA killed Dean Reed because he was wanting to come home and they didn't need another commie agitator; Dean Reed killed himself because, well, there didn't seem to be much motive for that one.

'Or maybe it really was an accident, after all,' Leslie said unconvincingly.

Phil was sceptical. He had the feeling that, towards the end of his life, Dean did want to come home.

'But he had his passport. He was a US citizen. It was easy. Why didn't he just pack up and come home?'

'What about 60 Minutes? They are pretty much on the left,' Phil said.

'I don't understand. Do you mean 60 Minutes had something to do with his death?' Leslie said, but Phil just shook his head and his reticence grew.

'Let's have another drink,' I said. But lunch was over.

'He was real big over there, though. A big star. You couldn't go into the street without the girls coming up to Dean for an autograph. It was the real thing,' Phil said again.

Outside, the sunlight was blinding. Phil had to go back to work. He was making a new album. It was his best album yet, he thought.

In the parking lot, Phil and Joe shook our hands and smiled. We all said 'keep in touch.' 'Keep in touch,' we said.

Shading our eyes from the hot California sun, we stood on the asphalt that shimmered with heat and said goodbye. Phil shook our hands again. He looked just like the boy who, with his brother, once upon a time, helped invent rock and roll, and I was a kid buying their 45s at the record store. For a minute I didn't want to go at all, as if staying on in that parking lot with Phil Everly could keep any more time from passing.

Smiling, Phil Everly put on his sunglasses, climbed into the powder-blue Cadillac with the modified tail fins and drove away, waving bye-bye.

# CHAPTER 4

# Denver

'Hi. I'm Dixie.'

Her feathery voice was frightened at first, when we met her in the lobby of the Brown Palace Hotel in Denver, but she was a handsome woman. In her early forties, Dixie Lloyd Schnebly had on a short fur jacket and polished boots under her slacks and she looked uncannily like Ann Margaret. She was Dean Reed's American manager and she figured as a main character in every news report of his death, for she told reporters that he had, without doubt, been murdered. I had been trying to reach her for weeks, but the machine in her house in Wheat Ridge only said that there was a big dog there.

Now she was here, shaking the snow off her fur shortie, for outside the city was nearly invisible in a blizzard. We had come from a tropical Los Angeles into winter. In the lobby of the Brown Palace, where waiters bustled around with huge trays, loaded with coffee and cake, the bellhops rustled up large sets of leather luggage. In the west of America, everyone was big: tall men in real cowboy hats, their wives with full-length minks on their arms, sashayed around the old hotel, greeting one another as they waited for the Stock Show to open so they could go and buy cows.

We made an odd, huddled grouping in the middle of all these big buoyant people: Dixie, her feral, rather sexy face close to Leslie's; Leslie, telling her about the movie he intended to make; Dixie's friend, Greg, a burly man with an amiable manner, who was there, it seemed, as a kind of bodyguard.

Like many Western women, Dixie was self-sufficient, but she deferred to men when there were men around.

She leaned over to Leslie.

'Gee, I'm sorry I was, like, so hard to get hold of, but you have to be careful,' she said apologetically. 'There are people after Deano. A lot of people are trying to get at me.' Dixie often called him Deano.

Many people wanted to talk to Dixie about Dean, but she was nervy. She fiddled with a pendant she wore around her neck.

'A gift from Deano,' she said rather shyly.

'It's pretty,' I said.

Like a girl with her first corsage, she smiled.

'When it first came I thought it was, like, junk, you know? And then I took it into a jewellery store and they said it was worth something.'

'It must be amber. From Russia?'

'I thought that was so neat,' she said.

Dixie's conversation was peppered with 'neats' and 'beautifuls' and she blew raspberries for emphasis. With a husky voice and a fluent way with words, she punctuated her thoughts with funny noises and she rambled, but her intuitions and insights had a loony poetic truth and, later on, she did admit that she was considered something of a poet and, diffidently, she showed me a few of her poems.

Dixie, or D.J. as many of her friends called her, was a woman in a man's world, as she put it, and it took a lot to scare her. She grew up in Wheat Ridge, where, as a girl, she first knew Dean. She still lived in her father's house, although her father was dead and she was on her own.

After high school, she married Mr Lloyd, which is how she got into the oil business in the seventies, when Denver turned into a boom town with a glass and steel skyline and a soap opera all its own. Oil made Denver rich; 'Dynasty' gave it fame.

Things didn't work out with Mr Lloyd and then, when the oil business dried up, too, Dixie took up driving. For a living she drove a long-haul rig. For weeks at a time she could be out on the road, the rig eating up hundreds of miles of Interstate, roaring across America. At truck stops she ate with the truckers; at night, she slept tucked up in the cab of her rig. No one hassled her because she knew her way around. She had her eye on the possibility of a secretarial business, and up on the north slope in Grand Junction she had a piece of property. In 1985, she met up with Dean Reed when he was home on a visit, and when he asked her to be his manager, she set aside all her other ambitions. He told her she would be his Colonel Parker.

'A lot of people want to harm Dean, you know,' she said. 'But I think I can trust you. Would you like to see where Deano grew up?' she asked, leaning towards me as if she did trust me, and when I said yes, Greg peeled away to go and sell some real estate, Dixie led Leslie and me out to her pick-up, where she told us that she kept a gun in the glove compartment. I made Leslie sit in the middle, next to her.

WELCOME TO WHEAT RIDGE, COLORADO, CARNATION CAPITAL OF THE WORLD. pop. 28,270. The green-and-white sign stood just off the exit from the freeway out of Denver.

Everywhere you looked were the mountains; everything was diminished by their presence. The Rocky Mountains dominated the city where Dean Reed was born; the mountains had formed him. As a boy, in the summer, Dean cruised the mountain passes at night, aboard his Chevrolet. He put down the top, stuck his foot flat on the accelerator, climbed the steep, curving roads and, turning off the radio, sang at the stars. Sometimes, he turned out the car's lights and steered by the light of the moon. In Denver, the Rockies were the horizon, a lowering presence, waiting to test you or trick you, as if the mountains could shrug their massive shoulders and dispose of you, a scrap of garbage on God's turf.

Dixie was a Wheat Ridge girl and she inhabited this part of the world like it was her own back porch. She could fill in the tiny things about Dean's childhood that Mrs Brown, as his mother, could not remember or never knew.

When Dixie and Dean were kids, Wheat Ridge, like the other small towns at the foot of the mountains, was a rural village where people went visiting on horseback. For a day out in town, ladies put on their hats.

Sometimes, Dean courted his girlfriends on horseback; sometimes, he galloped over the empty fields to where Dixie waited for him back of her house. She was just a kid, still in pigtails, but she was, of course, in love with Dean, the handsome older boy and he was nice to her in a brotherly way. 'Little Dixie', he called her and they rode horseback together.

'Everyone had a horse around here, even me,' she said. 'And I was raised poor as dirt. Deano thought he was poor. But I was the poor one,' she said, and it was as if they had engaged in a 'poor' competition. The anger rose and died away in her. I tried not to look at the glove compartment. Leslie listened to Dixie attentively.

What really rankled with Dixie, though, was how, when Deano went to Hollywood, she could not buy his records because her mother was very strict and didn't want her to have spending money. Her best friend, Karen, could buy Dean's records and that hurt worst of all. Dixie's mother did not approve of Dixie or of her men, but her dad was proud of her and they had some neat times when he was growing up. He loved goofy gifts and she always bought him a toy at Christmas, but her father was dead now and all she had was the little house in Wheat Ridge.

'What about Dean's dad?'

'He was something else,' she said. 'He never got over Dean being a communist. Cyril taught at the local high school and was a big womaniser. Ruth Anna Brown was one of his students. When Ruth Anna divorced Cyril, Deano was shattered. In those days, people didn't get divorced, you know,' she said.

The instant Freudian in me went to work: so Cyril was a womaniser with a wooden leg, who killed himself, and all his life Dean tried to get his daddy's attention.

'We're coming to his house,' she said quietly.

Degraded by the growth of Denver, Wheat Ridge had no centre left, only a shabby shopping mall and the Blue Swan Motel, where a vacancy sign hung from a post. There was another out at the Humpty Dumpty Motel and, on the roof of Verne's Cocktails, a pink neon martini with an olive in it flickered, or maybe it was a Manhattan with a cherry. Across the street was a plain white church.

'I don't think there was much churchgoing in Wheat Ridge,' Dixie said. 'Dean's people were not churchgoers,' she added, although she herself was raised a Catholic.

'That's the Small Animal Farm, off Wadsworth Avenue, and that's the house Dean grew up in.' It was a two-storey bungalow with a front porch and a tidy front yard.

'Once, they put the house on a flat bed and moved it over here, about a block away from where it used to be, because this was a nicer area. That was pretty common in those days, if you could get a better location,' she said.

'That's where Dean's mom kept her chickens.'

A low, long shed, it was made of chicken-coloured cinder blocks and it could have held maybe four or five thousand birds.

'I'm telling you just so's you'll know where to find it in the future,' said Dixie, looking at the shrine.

For a while we sat in the truck outside Dean's house.

'Was Dean very political back in high school?' Leslie asked.

'Dean was not particularly political in high school, but he was a gung-ho kid. He did track, hence the race against the mule. He was a gymnast, a swimmer. He did it like he did everything. He was a track alcoholic, a music alcoholic, whatever he did, he did with maximum commitment. Later, he was a political alcoholic, but not back then.'

'But what was he like?'

Dixie turned on her smart switch and said, 'He was very naive in some ways. He was terribly shy in relationship to girls. When he went to Hollywood, he was still a virgin. I mean, everybody did It back then,' she said. 'My homecoming queen in high school was pregnant. Everybody was pregnant.

'When I met him later, there were two Deans, the public man and the private one, and he was definitely a political alcoholic.' She repeated it, because she saw Leslie thought she'd hit on something worth knowing.

Leslie shifted the conversation towards Dean's death. Dixie grew wary. It grew dark. I thought about the gun and as we drove away into the night, Leslie edged towards me and away from Dixie, pretending to reach over for a pair of gloves he had left on the dashboard. From somewhere police sirens wailed. Alongside the entrance to the freeway was a tangled mess of steel that had once been a car. The pick-up skidded and Dixie drove badly, as if talking about Dean had drained her and she could no longer concentrate. She announced that she was taking us back to her place, then she missed the exit that she must have taken every day.

Her face glowed in the reflection from the headlights of on-coming cars.

'There are so many things I could tell you,' she whispered, veering out of lane. 'I know I can trust you. I think I trust you. Can I?'

I nodded in what I hoped was a trustworthy fashion and Dixie smoked a cigarette and told us she had given money to the Sandinistas, for Dean told her it was a righteous thing to do, but she let slip that she felt Fidel Castro was the devil incarnate. Her politics emerged from the weird libertarian swamp where liberalism flipped backwards to meet the crazy right. Colorado had its own peculiar mix of do-gooder and neo-Nazi; this was the heartlands: there were a hundred million handguns in America. One of them was in Dixie's glove compartment.

Confused, she believed what Dean believed in: a sentimental socialism that was part peace and love, part free medicine, but she was a girl raised on the anti-communist catholicism of the middle fifties in the middle of America, and as a result, she was now scared of everything: the CIA; the KGB; CBS.

Eventually, she found the exit she was looking for, drove off the freeway and pulled up in front of a small grey house. She did not ask us in, but jumped out of the truck and ran towards the door. In the window sat a big sad dog with a huge pink tongue, staring out into the night.

Within seconds Dixie emerged, never explaining the detour, only stopping to wave at the dog.

'His name is Bear,' she said, and I realised it was the dog on the answering machine who was supposed to scare off intruders.

'I can take care of myself,' said Dixie. 'You know what I mean?'

Outside the Brown Palace, Dixie parked the pick-up. The snow began to fall harder on the city with its beautiful soap-opera skyline. The streets were flayed and salted; the city had no depth and the mountains no colour, as if they were made of cardboard.

The horrible scrape of the snow ploughs ran through the night, like fingernails dragging a black board. The steel and glass skyscrapers were empty. The oil was gone. Denver was dying.

Dixie was calm and thoughtful now and she said she would think about letting us have her files on Dean. She withheld information not because she was a tease, but because she was scared to death.

'We'd love to make this movie right,' said Leslie. 'But we need your help.' And Dixie was, of course, tickled, as people always were when you promised them a movie. She was interested in the possibility, of course, one that would tell the truth about Dean

Reed's life and which would involve her in what had been the great episode of her own.

'I had not seen Dean since 1963, when he came home to a Wheat Ridge High reunion. The kids were excited because he had been to Hollywood by then.'

In 1985, Dixie met Dean at a film festival in the Tivoli Center in downtown Denver. 'Hi, Dean. Do you remember me? I'm Dixie,' she said.

He didn't know who she was, but it didn't matter. He smiled at her. She could see that he might be a big star over in Russia, but he was the same slim cowboy she remembered.

'Little Dixie, of course I remember. You come on into the show with us,' he said and without another word, took her in with him.

'It was beautiful,' she said.

In between, for more than twenty years, she kept a scrapbook on him, waiting for him.

'Wouldn't you? I mean, you know, how many of your class-mates get to be so famous?'

'Dick Cheese, Mr Cheese.'

The public address system at Stapleton Airport in Denver ran through a never-ending loop of names: 'Dick Cheese. Mr Cheese. Brett Falcon. Mr Falcon. Margaret Bird. Ms Bird. Wayne Sick. Mr Sick' and so on, until it looped back and began all over again with 'Dick Cheese'.

It was snowing again in Denver, the morning after we saw Dixie, and the planes were delayed. Up and down the corridors of the airport, travellers wandered, looking for something to do, to buy, to eat. The airport was huge; so were the people, the natives and visitors both, and they glowed with unearthly health, like creatures in a Ray Bradbury novel.

The men were big and so were the women and the children seemed to have grown at an abnormal speed. These large people were stuffed into down coats and vests; on their feet they wore huge plastic ski boots in pink and baby blue, in which they marched around, stiff legged, unable to bend their ankles. As they cruised the shops, as they scanned the luggage carousels for their bags, they resembled vacationing families of Yeti with pastel feet.

Among the passengers were young couples, barely out of their teens, their own babies slung casually into backpacks. Returning home, setting off on a journey, they coped with ease. Their ancestors would have come West in covered wagons and now, they too, were going to do business with nature, in the mountains. Every one at the airport was big, handsome and healthy and they were all travelling, because moving on was the American thing to do. This was a planet inhabited entirely by Dean Reeds.

Waiting, I got out the police file Mrs Brown had given me, along with the autopsy report. These were the banal summaries of officialdom – the police, the forensic experts in Berlin – their brutal expressionless accounts of what had happened to a human being. This was 'The Final Report Concerning the Death Under Suspicious Circumstances of United States Citizen Dean Cyril Reed'. Taking into account the autopsy and the criminal investigation, so-called, it was concluded that there was 'no evidence of traumatic violence', 'no evidentiary basis for suicide', that 'the suspicion of crime has not been confirmed'. So the Police of the German Democratic Republic concluded, 'It can be presumed that Dean Reed died by accidental drowning.'

In the grim medical log which was the autopsy, the only anomaly was a reference to 'so-called Canuto's trial cuts . . . in a typical place as can often be seen in cases of suicide'. The cuts were very superficial, it was noted. But it was inconclusive.

Mrs Brown was certain Dean's death was not a suicide; he had everything to live for: he was at the height of his career; he loved his wife; he was preparing his biggest movie role ever.

Dixie Schnebly believed that Dean had been murdered.

'Dick Cheese. Mr Cheese,' the loop started again and I wondered if anyone ever reported in, because the names seemed to play over and over for as long as you were in the airport, as if for travellers who were lost because America was so big out here, and so lonesome.

Leslie was going to Ethiopia to make a film and I was heading home to New York and then to Russia. After Dean Reed's last visit to Colorado in 1963, it was more than twenty years until he came home again. I was glad when my plane was called.

# CHAPTER 5

✧

# London: the 9.40 to Moscow

I never made it to South America. By the time I went looking for Dean Reed in late 1987, the obsession was with the East. It was the hottest story of the second half of the century. In Russia, the monolith was breaking up, like ice floes in spring, I thought, but it was the wrong metaphor. It was as if, beyond the Berlin Wall, for decades Darth Vadar had beckoned, evil, unknown. Suddenly, you could look. Lift the visor and see inside.

Any movie we made about Dean would inevitably be about Russia. About Germany. About the end of the Cold War. About the revolution which liked its music good and loud. I was convinced that every Western journalist who went to Moscow did the rock stories first because it was reassuring to see Russian kids with pink hair and rings in their ears, waving their fists; it made them look exactly like us, and, after all, you didn't kill your own kind. So here I was in pursuit of the man who brought rock and roll to Russia, and South America felt like a side-show. Who cared about Nicaragua when, in Moscow, there were 5,000 rock bands and in East Berlin, even in 1987, the kids crouched near the Wall, eavesdropping on a concert on the Western side.

'Police pigs,' they shouted. 'Tear down the Wall,' they shouted in the same breath. For their pains, the policemen gave them a kick in the teeth.

On my way East, though, I plugged into people who had known Dean in South America. Energised by news of his death, a whole network sprang into life, electric with information or memories. I must have eaten a hundred meals with Dean's rememberers, chasing their rich scraps, the tiny articles of faith, the improbable fantasies they all had stored in their memory disks. Chilean expatriates remembered his beauty as they mourned their beautiful

43

country; an Argentine woman in a Los Angeles restaurant thought of Dean as perfectly *raffiné*; Marcello, a New York waiter who once worked in a Buenos Aires television studio and saw Dean perform. Marcello had contacts in Miami who knew Dean and he gave me their addresses.

Fired up by contact with the star, they had a kind of fatal attraction for one another, and every now and again, as news of our film was passed along, the phone would ring and a new one checked in with a covert agenda, a mysterious whisper and the crackle of excitement that drove them whenever they thought about him.

'I knew Dean Reed.'

A throaty voice inserted itself into my telephone.

It belonged to the Countess Nyta de Val. She claimed to have known Dean in South America and she wanted to talk. She lived in Florida, but she was on her way to London – to see her publishers, to set up her cabaret act – it wasn't clear, but I was headed for London too. There were still no direct flights from New York to Moscow. The week before I got the 9.40 out of Heathrow to Sheremetyevo, I met the Countess in a Chinese restaurant in Soho that had a picture of Mick Jagger in the window.

The Countess ate spare ribs and said she made Dean Reed a star. She was a cabaret star herself, she said, a well-known *chanteuse*, and it was her contacts in Hollywood that brought him south. In 1962, a year after 'Our Summer Romance' went to the top of the Chilean charts, Dean Reed beat out Elvis Presley in the South American Hit Parade poll, 29,330 to 20,805.

An imposing woman of a certain age, the Countess, who was Czech, wore a leather skirt as voluminous as a sofa. Her head was tied up in a silk scarf and a hat sat flat on top of it like a pancake on an egg cosy. She wore several pairs of eyelashes and, as she handed me a photograph, she lowered them with the demure *moue* of a sixteen-year-old coquette.

In the picture, she stood with Dean on an Argentine beach, their arms wound around one another. She wore a bikini and had the figure for it. He had a great body, young and lean.

'We were lovers,' she said.

'Women wanted him, but the men were not jealous. He played the nightclubs, he played the stadium. All his singles went to number one. He wore a light blue, how do you call this Italian fabric? Gaberdine! A gaberdine suit the colour of the sky, very tight and he was beautiful,' said the Countess, and ate another spare rib.

Dean went south on a hunch, the way he raced the mule, the way he gave the bum his extra pair of pants. Movement was everything and, like a conjurer's hand, it blurred the illusion. Life was a stunt, a gamble, a race to get to the party, wherever the party was. Fed up with Hollywood – later he would say it was a prostitution camp – he simply left. Maybe he'd heard 'My Summer Romance' was a big hit in Chile. Maybe it was the Countess. Maybe Dean was just plain restless, tired of being cast as a prop at Chasen's.

In February, 1962, when he was still a starlet at Warner's star school in Los Angeles and had a few hits on the provincial charts, he applied for a passport, stating he intended to depart from the US for South America at New York on March 9, 1962. His passport was issued at the beginning of March, and, like all American passports in those days, it was marked: 'Not valid for travel in Albania, Cuba and those portions of China, Korea and Vietnam under Communist control'. On his application, Dean listed his hair as brown, although everyone called him blond and his eyes as green, although they always looked blue as the sky-blue gaberdine suit. His height, it was stated, was six foot one.

Almost as soon as he got the passport, he left; he didn't tell his agent or his room-mate; he just picked up his bags and left the house. A few years later, he sent a postcard saying, Merry Christmas.

An unknown kid with a backpack and guitar slung over his shoulder, he arrived that spring in Santiago, expecting a modest welcome, perhaps from the local deejays who were playing his tunes on the radio.

Viva Dean! We want Dean!! Viva Dean!!!

The blue-eyed god had come down from the north, and when he opened the shutters to his hotel room that faced the Presidential Plaza in Santiago, he saw half a million upturned faces.

We want Dean!

Even when he closed the shutters, he could still hear the roar.

There was a deejay at a Santiago radio station; his name was Ricardo Garcia and although he dutifully plugged 'My Summer Romance' because the kids liked it, he did not think much of

Dean's singing. On the other hand . . . on the other hand, when Garcia saw him in the flesh, he knew Dean was hot. The looks were something else, Garcia thought. Dean was very, very sexy, what with the big hair and the big white teeth. His looks were his most important talent and he could warm up an audience the minute he got on the stage.

'He was a naive gringo come to "do" Latin America,' Garcia said. Like a character from a movie musical, Dean was called The Magnificent Gringo.

'Brainwashed,' the Countess muttered, grasping at a spring roll.

'The communists brainwashed my beautiful Dean. Later, later, he went on a trip to Russia and fell ill, he was hospitalised and they brainwashed him and shipped him back. *Gott in Himmel!*'

She picked her teeth and turned bitter. Her own hatred for the communists was all-consuming. Her father, a Czech government official before the War, was murdered by the commies, she announced, reminiscing dreamily about the good times, when she was a child and sat on Mussolini's lap.

'When my mother died, all Dean could say was, "Good, that's one countess less,"' although he adored her.

'Brainwashed,' she whispered.

In South America, Dean saw the writing on the wall and it said: YANKEE GO HOME. He was shocked. Like most Americans, in finding out he was not universally loved, he was hurt. It was his first exposure to the sour fruits American imperialism had borne in South America.

'I saw poor people crawling on their bellies with their last little bit of something for the church,' Dean would say.

He began to read. He wrote to Paton Price and Paton wrote him back, and Dean remembered the things he had been taught and he set out to dedicate his fame. He wanted to save the world.

Heady times in South America: revolution was in the air. Already a sex symbol, when Dean acquired a political agenda, he was unstoppable. Within weeks of his arrival in Chile, he took out advertisements in the newspapers, urging Chileans who opposed atomic testing to write to President Kennedy. When he set out for a tour of northern Chile and Peru, the American Embassy told him his actions might be contrary to the best interests of the United States. Dean claimed there were attempts to stifle his freedom of speech, noting he was an admirer of Mahatma Gandhi, Bertrand Russell and Linus Pauling, was opposed to warfare and military service, and had been a conscientious objector since the age of eighteen. He announced that his friends at home were planning to sue Secretary of State Dean Rusk because of the unconstitutional attempts in Lima to suppress his, Dean's, freedom of speech. In Hollywood, Dean's friends duly sent a telegram to the State Department, expressing outrage at Dean's treatment, and it was signed by several of Paton Price's students, as well as David Dellinger, who later became famous as a member of the Chicago Eight.

Dean did not cancel his tour, of course. Every time he was opposed, whenever he realised that the State Department had taken an interest in him, it charged him up: this wasn't just the movies, this had the smack of real adventure. It was always high noon in Dean's South America.

'He was an idealist,' said the Countess. 'You could fool Dean easily. But he could get to 5,000 workers and tell them how to vote. He was a sincere man. Not like that fat little Allende, who used to wash his hands every time he met the miners.' The Countess spat when she mentioned Salvador Allende's name.

South America was Dean's coming of age. Professionally, it made him a star. He appeared on television in Lima; with a troupe of 'Twisters', he performed at the Astral Theatre. Roaming the continent, he gathered a following of fans.

Ban the bomb! Dean shouted whenever he could, but, then so did a lot of us. The times were ripe in Latin America, what with the young Fidel in Cuba and Che only just dead, his handsome death mask imprinted on everyone's brain. In Chile were the poet radicals like Pablo Neruda, and the radical folkies like Victor Jara, who had a dashing moustache, and they accepted Dean, even though he was a gringo. At last, Dean found a community.

It was more than a little ironic, because Jara's folk-song movement was intended to fight the tide of American culture that poured down like shit on Chile, as Jara saw it. Chile was a dumping ground for singers who couldn't cut it up north and there was a profitable trade in it, because so long as the pop stars had fair hair and tight pants, the girls went mad for the singing gringos.

Dean separated himself from the pack; he cast himself as a political man and he had a real genius for it. He could sell the rhetoric because it was as simple as a pop song, because he was a true believer. The willing student for Paton's political raps, he was ripe as fruit in South America, for he could picket embassies and sing for the workers, he could go up the Amazon with his Indian comrades. At concerts, because he was so handsome and so surprising – this American, who was, politically, a good guy – people bought the slogans he stitched in-between the songs. For Dean, life had meaning; he saw himself as an emissary, as an ambassador of peace and he said so, to anyone who would listen. Now he was no longer just a dumb blond out of some Hollywood starlet stable; he was a man to reckon with. The South American experience became a theme he played out the whole of his life.

Dean married Patty, a pretty beauty queen with bouffant hair whom he'd met at his agent's office in Hollywood and by 1964, they were living in Buenos Aires, where Dean had a television show and a handsome suburban villa. It was a charmed life. Then, right-wing gangs shot up the house and someone smeared a hammer and sickle in red paint on his garage door. Dean and Patty got guns. For Dean, it was a turn-on; it was like sex. He became increasingly more radical.

'Brainwashed,' the Countess said again, straightening her hat.

Like everyone else, she remembered Paton Price.

'Paton screwed Dean up. They used to send each other telegrams about how great the Pill was, about how many women they both screwed.'

Paton Price haunted this story; I backed into his ghost everywhere, and always, the stories turned on politics and Dean's sexuality, his inadequacy in Paton's view, and Paton's ridicule. Mrs Brown said Paton blamed her because Dean was a virgin when he got to Hollywood; the Countess said they wrote each other dirty letters. Odd, of course, because all his life, Dean said Paton was his greatest friend, his mentor, teacher, father.

Odd how everything I heard about Paton Price sounded like a slogan, as if he had printed his protégées straight through with them, like a stick of Brighton rock. Although Mrs Brown and Phil Everly expressed only admiration for him, I began to take a dislike to Paton Price for he appeared to me peevish and manipulative, an ideologue with a rigid moral rectitude.

'He screwed Dean up.'

The Countess's contempt was complete, and her story rambled.

She had fairy tales about bank accounts and Porsches Dean received in exchange for errands he did for the East German Politburo. Like so many others, her ideas were half-cooked, and chasing Dean Reed was like chasing smoke. She was convinced the communists killed him.

'He knew too much. Over there in the East is like the Mafia. Once you were in, you could never get out,' she said.

As she saw it, Dean was a 'Manchurian Candidate', run, turned, used, a traitor but a victim, too. But, having eaten all the ribs, and turning to the fortune cookies, the Countess started on a tale about an out-of-body experience in which she met her dead father, who told her where the Czech government treasure was buried.

In 1963, around the time Dean Reed was already crooning his heart out in Santiago in the pale-blue gaberdine suit, a Russian kid called Artemy Troitsky heard 'Surfin' USA'. It was the first rock and roll record he ever heard, and because he could not find 'surfin' in his English dictionary, he figured it was some kind of dirty word. He was eight years old.

I first met Artemy Troitsky in a Thai Restaurant in South Kensington the same week in early 1988 when I ate Chinese food with the Countess de Val.

Troitsky was a Soviet rock critic with half an inch of stubble on his handsome jaw. He was travelling in Britain to help promote *Back in the USSR*, his book about Soviet rock.

Troitsky had a cold. He snuffled into his lemon grass soup and blew his nose. It was his first trip to the West. He was my first real Russian. He said his Western name was Art.

Wearing black jeans and sweater, an olive green T-shirt and jacket, and a new pair of sneakers, Troitsky had walked that morning from Bloomsbury to Chelsea. His feet hurt.

In the beginning the two of us made the sort of chitchat that seemed appropriate in those first heady days of Glasnost. Art's favourite writers were Gogol and Cervantes, although when he was younger he read Kurt Vonnegut and J. D. Salinger. *Catcher in the Rye* was Art's favourite book. In Prague, where he grew up – his father worked there as a journalist – he wore a yellow hat with a peaked brim because he could not get a red hunter's cap like Holden Caulfield's.

'I only believe in rock and roll and John Lennon,' he said.

In London, Art spent most of his time going to gigs, sometimes three in one night. Johnny Rotten was fantastic, said Art. At the Limelight he heard Pop Will Eat Itself. 'They were very good.' Art's green eyes shone. 'I had a great time. I almost ate myself.'

I asked if he had been shopping, but he didn't like shopping much, he said. 'I do have a long list from my wife, Svetlana. She wants a sun lamp and a riding costume from . . . ' he consulted a scrap of paper. 'Moss Bross. Svetlana is not allowed out of the Soviet Union at the same time as me. She is hostage,' Art said.

There was an uneasy silence while we ate some squid salad and drank more beer.

'You know, we have had in Moscow an American singer named Dean Martin,' Art said.

Art had very nice manners and this was his first trip to the West, so I supposed he was trying to make an American connection for my sake.

'Dean Martin,' I said. 'Really?'

'Dean Reed, I mean,' he said. 'I mean Dean Reed.'

'Dean Reed? You knew him? You saw him? Where? Tell me!'

So far, the pieces I had accumulated for the puzzle were out of Dean's life in America – his childhood, his Hollywood days. Here, by chance, because it was a friend who had brought Art to lunch, was a real Russian who knew Dean Reed.

'Tell me everything!'

But Troitsky just blew his nose again. 'Come to Moscow,' he said. 'I can introduce you to his interpreter, Oleg. Oleg Smirnoff. KGB surely, but also very charming. Also there is best friend of Dean's girlfriend. She was a Page-Three Girl, his girlfriend. She killed herself when Dean Reed died. Big breasts. Very big.' Art tugged unsuccessfully at the front of his black pullover.

My head was spinning: Dean had a girlfriend in Moscow and an interpreter from the KGB! Art Troitsky blew his nose one last time and said he would like to meet a real businessman, because he had never met one.

'Come to Moscow,' he repeated.

I said I was coming.

# PART II
✦

## THE MAN WHO STOLE ROCK AND ROLL

# CHAPTER 6

# Moscow

'Come with me, Deanrid.'

Out for a stroll and a smoke in a Helsinki park, Nikolai Pastoukhov got lucky. Pastoukhov was the head of the Komsomol – the Soviet Youth Organisation – and a delegate to the World Peace Conference in Helsinki. It was 1965. And Pastoukhov – he sometimes thought of himself in the third person – was bored out of his skull. The conference was dull. The women at it looked like dogs. The Chinese were contentious and intractable. The speeches were incessant. Pastoukhov escaped. Strolling in the park, having a smoke, he ogled the pretty girls in their mini skirts. Right up to their asses, he thought, and tried not to lick his lips.

Pastoukhov's attention was diverted, though, by the sound of music. A little group had gathered and at its centre was a handsome young man with a fine head of hair, playing the guitar, his hat on the ground. He was working his passage back to Argentina, he said. But he was not an Argentine. He was an American. His name, he said, was Dean Reed.

Stamping out the dying butt, Pastoukhov looked the American over. God, he thought, the American had the little group in the park eating out of his hand.

As head of the Komsomol, Pastoukhov was always on the lookout for an acceptable entertainer to pacify his Young Communists and prevent their wholesale defection to the decadent music of the West. (Damn Bitles! Pastoukhov thought, as he often did, for Beatlemania had swept the Soviet Union.) Here was this handsome American with a real cowboy hat, plucking his guitar, singing peace songs. Pastoukhov had a little talk with the young man who, to his wonderment, espoused peace and love and the socialist cause. This was the jackpot! Pastoukhov said to himself again, drooling over the Finnish girls (so short! Right up to their asses!)

'Come with me, Deanrid,' he said.

At the hall where the peace conference was in progress, Pastoukhov pushed Dean onto the rostrum and turned to the delegates. The room was packed.

'Here is new blood come to us in peace movement from America,' Pastoukhov said and, as Dean Reed began to play, he stood in the wings and watched, holding his breath.

That night, when Dean first played the World Peace Congress in Helsinki, Bertrand Russell failed to show. Pablo Neruda, the Nobel Prize-winning poet from Chile turned up, but not Russell. The Master of Ceremonies, a doddering old Finn, was hysterical. Bertrand Russell's secretary, who was there, took up the Chinese line, which was that you cannot talk World Peace until there was World Revolution.

'Bullshit,' the Soviets cried.

'Bullshit,' thought Pastoukhov, bored to death with this idiotic babble and desiring only a cigarette.

'Stop him! Stop him!' some people yelled at Russell's man.

'Let him speak,' others shouted.

Dean looked out over the hall. He was twenty-seven. He had played big in South America – the nightclubs, the union halls, the soccer arena – but this, this was something else! He had never had an audience like this before.

At Helsinki, the audience was cold as a meat locker, cold as the Cold War itself. Maybe Dean looked out into the sea of stony faces and thought: I can make a difference; I can make the difference between war and peace; I can make people touch each other. Even at twenty-seven, Dean was never short of a good opinion of himself.

He picked up his guitar and sang 'Marianna'. He sang cowboy songs and he sang something that to Pastoukhov, at least, sounded a lot like rock and roll. Pastoukhov held his breath.

From the podium Dean greeted the delegates – the chubby Chinese in Mao jackets, the dewlapped Soviets, their chests webbed with war medals, and he made them sing. He told them to hold hands. He told them they had to hold hands, even if the girl sitting next to them looked like a dog.

When that wasn't enough to liven things up, Dean leaped off

the stage, climbing over their legs, striding down the aisles. He *made* them hold hands! The delegates started laughing. The delegates started laughing at the crazy American. Dean roamed the hall some more, then he bounded back onto the stage, picked up his guitar and sang 'We Shall Overcome'. Before long, the delegates were singing too. A missionary among the unconverted, Dean sang American spirituals and cowboy songs and rock ditties. In the wings, Nikolai Pastoukhov grinned his shit-eating grin; he knew a good thing when he saw it. 'Come with me, Deanrid,' he said. And by nightfall, Dean Reed was on the train to Moscow.

With Pastoukhov, he travelled in a private compartment which belonged to the Deputy Premier of the Soviet Union. Deputy Tikhonov was a celebrated poet and he greeted Dean as a fellow artist. Through the June night to Leningrad, Tikhonov read his poems aloud and Dean played his guitar – you could just imagine him singing 'The Midnight Special'. Pete Seeger had toured the Soviet Union to great acclaim a few years earlier and his American folk music was much esteemed.

Inside the opulent little carriage, with its red plush seats, its antimacassars, its gleaming samovar, toasts were proposed. Outside in the white night, the shadowless fields sped by. At Leningrad the train pulled into the Finland Station. Pastoukhov took Dean to the Astoria Hotel for lunch. There was a jazz band in the restaurant and he asked Dean to sing. It was a kind of audition and Dean sang his heart out, and the audience fell in love with the young American. Bingo! thought Pastoukhov.

And so Dean's final conversion began on the stage at Helsinki, although he was, in fact, an official delegate from Argentina and Pastoukhov's tale of the pick-up in the park was a bit of old man's embroidery.

Finishing his tale, Nikolai Pastoukhov leaned back in his chair and pulled on his cigarette. The old man was past seventy now, but vigorous and canny. Cigarette ash tumbled down the florid, flowered tie that covered half of his dark purple shirt, the colour of grape juice. He was the editor of *Pravda Selskaya Shizn*, which translated roughly as *Pravda Country Life*. It was the nation's main agricultural newspaper.

I had followed Dean to Moscow and then to *Pravda Country*

*Life*, where, in the lobby, people sat with their feet in puddles. Over the sound system, Dave Brubeck played 'Take Five'. On a tiny television, a commissionaire with mittens watched blurry images of Mikhail Gorbachev talking to people in the street.

Upstairs in Pastoukhov's office, there was neither a typewriter nor a note pad, only a bank of plastic telephones with blank faces and a row of Christmas cards on a shelf bereft of books. 'Happy New Year,' Nikolai Pastoukhov said, for it was the beginning of 1988.

Pastoukhov dropped the butt from his cigarette into an ashtray and lit up again, his mouth pulling in smoke between huge dewlapped jowls, like a friendly hound enjoying a smoke. Like all Russians, he had real narrative talent. Still wrapped up in the tales of his discovery of Dean Reed in a Helsinki park in 1965, he gave those old jowls a good shake.

'Deanrid!' He said it as a single word, the way Russians often did, as though it might have been a slogan or a product, the way you might say Kleenex! or Communism!

'Deanrid!'

Within a year of the Helsinki conference, Dean was back in the USSR. Pastoukhov wangled him a recording contract with Melodiya – the state recording company had never before issued a rock and roll record – and a tour. In Moscow, he played the Variety Theatre. In reporting performances at the Moscow Theatre, *Pravda* noted that Dean Reed 'left his country as a sign of protest against the unjust war in Vietnam'. Posters all over Moscow announcing the performances showed that he was blond and played the guitar and hinted at an 'exotic' biography. It was such big news that even the *New York Times* got wind of it, which was pretty rare in those days for a Western newspaper. On page forty-seven on 28 November, 1966, the *Times* wrote: US SINGER CHEERED IN MOSCOW THEATRE.

Dean was twenty-eight and he had that big head of hair like Jack Kennedy as he stepped into the centre of the stage at Moscow's Variety Theatre. He sang like crazy for the audience: folk songs, ballads, Latin American songs he learned in Chile, show tunes – 'Maria' was a big favourite in Russia – some of his own antiwar songs. He wore fancy, silky clothes and had a very slim waist. He moved his hips like a star; he could belt out the Twist in a style the Russians adored; he could croon Beethoven's 'Ode to Joy' like an Italian gigolo.

No one in Moscow had ever seen anything quite like him. Not just handsome . . . American!

For an encore, Dean sang 'Ghost Riders in the Sky' and it became his signature tune in Russia.

At the end of the concert, the audience cheered, clapped and whistled and stamped their feet for twenty-five minutes.

Soviet kids were crazy for western music. Late at night, a whole nation of teenagers crouched under the covers in the dark and fiddled the knobs of ancient radios, raising the Voice of America, where they heard the siren call of rock and roll.

For the most part, Russian kids had to settle for folk songs celebrating tractor production or mustachioed pop stars with plastic smiles. Bureaucrats tried to replace the Twist with new dances for socialist youth. The *Moskvichka*, the *Terrikon* and the *Herringbon* were not a success.

As chief of the Young Communists, Pastoukhov knew there was a void to be filled and Dean Reed was a miracle. Here was a real American in cowboy boots, who sang something a lot like rock and roll and who was ideologically correct. He was put into the care of the Ministry of Culture. His official minder was Georgy Arbatov, the director of the Institute for Canada and the United States, and an influential player in Soviet-American policy, some said.

When Dean arrived, the propaganda machine cranked up. Dean was a star in America but America brutally rejected him for his politics, the stories said. No one in Russia cared. The lust for Western culture was huge but undiscriminating, and nobody cared if Dean Reed was run by the Komsomol or the Communists or the Soviet cosmonauts, or a monkey, as someone said. What mattered was that Dean Reed was a real American singing rock and roll in English. Even compared with Pete Seeger he was a marvel, for Seeger, after all – skinny, Harvard bred – was an earnest folkie who was interested in local folklore. But this, this Deanrid . . . Oh Boy! What a catch! Like a panda for a zoo.

Dean's arrival in the Soviet Union had all the verve, the heroics, the aspirations of his conquest of South America all over again. Although he continued to live with Patty in Argentina, then moved on to Madrid and to Rome, he went back again and again, tempted by the adoration the Russians gave him, seduced by the feeling that he mattered so much.

On his first tour of the Soviet Union, Dean played twenty-eight cities and he sang 'Yiddishe Momma' to a little old lady with a round face. Again and again, he went to Russia to record, for concerts, as a peace delegate. He made rock videos, after a fashion: Dean riding his motorbike; Dean clowning in parks, on river boats, singing 'Yesterday' and 'Heartbreak Hotel'. Kids who saw him in the early days carried the memories around like snapshots in their schoolbooks.

On 'Go For It, Boys', a televised competition in which young men vied in several categories for the title of 'Most Macho Male', Dean appeared as the celebrity host. Everyone I ever met in the Soviet Union remembered Dean. He was as big as Frank Sinatra.

And he was impressed with what he saw in the Soviet Union. He spoke with the comrades on long plane trips across the country – pictures show his face wreathed in smiles under the big fur hat. It turned him around. He studied Marxism-Leninism. A little boy gave Dean his Pioneer's Badge. At the Kremlin Wall, he posed beside John Reed's grave.

The better Dean got to know the Soviet Union, the more he liked it and, as he became the first authentic superstar, he grew increasingly impassioned with its politics. In 1971, he sent an open letter to Alexander Solzhenitsyn, which was printed in the magazine *Ogonyok*. It went:

> Dear Colleague in Art Solzhenitsyn . . .
> Mr Solzhenitsyn, the society of my country, not yours, is sick. The principles on which your union relies are healthy, pure and just, at a time when the principles on which our union are built are cruel, selfish and unjust.

Nikolai Pastoukhov was restless. I asked about the rest of Dean's career, but because he had played no part in it, he was not interested and he waved the question away with an impatient gesture.

'Yes, yes, he travelled a lot. He left South America and went to live in Italy, then to Berlin. He settled in Berlin because he met a woman.'

I asked about the death.

'Officially, he drowned. But was very good swimmer. How it

happened? I don't know. Maybe provocation. American press call him "Kremlin agent", "notorious communist". He annoyed Americans.'

Glee spread across Pastoukhov's face and engulfed his features. He winked. Then he fixed his face in a sombre expression. 'This sad news of death I received and was shocked, he was very young, very handsome. He was the first from the West. He talked about peace and friendship; we were very much impressed. He visited Siberia, he said his visit recollected his native Colorado in United States. He liked to make out autographs, to be mixed with girls. But I think he has no time for this sexual business. He is good boy . . . Look.' Rummaging in his 'perhaps bag' – you never knew when there might be a sudden special on bananas or socks in Moscow – he pulled out a photograph album. Pastoukhov pushed an old magazine cover with a picture of Dean under my nose. 'He has written here: "To my lovely papa from the son, Deanrid."'

'Always he calls me papa, because I give to him birth here in Soviet Union,' added Pastoukhov.

Pastoukhov leaned back in his chair and the old eyes filled up, but it was hard to tell whether it was from affection, self-pity or cigarette smoke. He grew evasive.

Chasing Dean Reed was a chase after fantasy, through tangled webs spun by those who adored him, and there were plenty of them: lover, mother, daughter, father, son.

'He called me his second mama,' older women said. 'I was second papa,' said the men, and when I met an American journalist who once interviewed Dean Reed, she said, 'I never slept with him, of course. We were just friends.' But I hadn't asked.

They were enchanted because he was so alive, because, if he was always on the make, it was usually in pursuit of love – theirs, the fans', the world's – it didn't matter. As a result, all these papas and mamas and lovers wanted nothing to do with the dark side of Dean Reed, but only to keep his memory intact. It made me think of the figures in little plastic domes filled with snowflakes that you bought as holiday souvenirs and could take out now and again to remember where you had been.

*

Pastoukhov's assistant arrived to show me out. A man in a suit and sneakers, he spoke exquisite French and looked exactly like Klaus Maria Brandauer. I said so, meaning it as a compliment, but he looked crestfallen. 'What about Charles Bronson? Everyone says I look just like Charles Bronson,' he said.

As I was pulling on my coat, Pastoukhov eyed my mother's old mink appreciatively. 'I remember very fondly America. Americans come here. We go to America. Little farms. We travel up and down Mississippi River.'

'What year was that?'

'1978? 1979?' he said.

'So. You are liking this Glasnost?' he added.

'Oh, yes. Isn't it wonderful?' I said. 'Isn't it amazing. Wouldn't Dean Reed have loved it . . . it's . . . '

He shrugged doggily.

'1978, that was real *détente*,' he said again.

For a moment Pastoukhov looked thoughtful. He opened his mouth and shut it: his journalist's heart no longer stirred and, anyway, he was starting a ski holiday in the morning, with his girlfriend. We shook hands. We exchanged addresses.

'So maybe I am visiting United States, I stay in your house, OK,' Pastoukhov said.

Then he bellowed with laughter so that his hound-dog jowls shook and ash from his cigarette toppled on his tie one more time.

# CHAPTER 7

# Gorky Park

In the subway train, the Muscovites stood and sat, behind books and newspapers, secret and unsmiling, as blank as the faces on Nikolai Pastoukhov's telephones. One beanbag of a woman, who seemed to have been stitched permanently into her overcoat, clutched a string bag triumphantly. It held a rush of yellow oranges. Fruit was more precious than gold in a Moscow winter and there must have been a special on somewhere. All over town that day I saw oranges spilling from suitcases or stuffed into net bags.

The Moscow subway was everything that had been promised. The walls were marble and granite; there were chandeliers and stained-glass windows; there were stations like Ivana Trump's hotels and stations as streamlined as Rockefeller Center, where the Art Deco bronzes glittered just for the pleasure of the strap-hangers at rush hour. In the subways, the imperial desires of Mother Russia had been handed over by Stalin to the working classes and I would not have been surprised to find walls made of solid silver. For five copecks, you could ride for ever.

Warm, efficient, safe, the subway was the only institution in Moscow – perhaps the only institution in the country – which worked, but it failed to give up the secrets of its underground success to the rest of the city. Here, amid the subterranean splendours, was the only place that Art Troitsky felt that he was on firm ground.

At the Gorky Park Station, Art was waiting, chic in the casual black clothing he purchased in Tallinn's street markets and, with him, was his wife Svetlana. Six feet tall, in perfect Italian boots, Svetlana Kunetsina was twenty-eight. But you could still see the join where a large, gawky teenager had evolved into this butterfly.

She was more Scandinavian than Russian. She had beautiful manners; she was a passionate feminist, itself a rebellion in a country so brutal towards its women, and she was systemically incapable of being on the take, which amounted to a kind of dysfunction in Moscow. It made her different from everyone else. To some it made her seem haughty. Westerners loved her. Every Westerner who met Svetlana fell for her, perhaps because she was so un-Russian. Or maybe it was just for her legs.

A light snow fell. The black, iron gates to Gorky Park shone with gold filigree. Inside the park was a silvery, moon-shaped ice rink on which skaters raced, twirled, stumbled. From the loudspeaker system came the insistent strains of 'Nel Blu del Pinto di Blu'.

'*Volare*', Domenico Meduno warbled. The skaters circled. The music changed to the 'Skater's Waltz' and the show-offs spun onto the rink. Millions of distant little stars twinkled coldly and, as we trudged off into the park, following Art unquestioningly, the ground was frozen solid. Skaters sped in and out from among the stands of black trees.

In a clearing, near the embankment of the Moskva River, was a building painted the same blue as the café in East Berlin, and I wondered if there was an oversupply of duck-egg blue paint in the Eastern Bloc. An old man without any teeth was its gatekeeper. Waving a filthy handkerchief at us, he blew his nose on it and stuffed it up his coat sleeve. He did a little Charlie Chaplin dance and snatched our coats, locking them away in a sealed cupboard. It was useless to try to hang on to your coat in Moscow – perhaps it was bad manners, or bad luck. Perhaps the doorman was afraid the pockets concealed something dangerous.

I was hungry. Mondays, Moscow's restaurants closed for cleaning and I'd had nothing to eat since early morning when, with the take-it-or-leave-it look that came with the breakfast, a sullen waiter in the hotel dining room tossed a couple of limp hot-dogs on my plate. Art had promised dinner, and somewhere, from the bowels of the building, came the smell of cooking.

As we followed Art down a long corridor, music rattled from behind closed doors. In the hidden maze of ramshackle rehearsal rooms, Moscow's rock bands practised their liberation. In the basement was a cooperative restaurant, which was then the polite word for private enterprise. It was very dark.

The building belonged to Stas Namin. A rock star, he was also the grandson of Anastas Mikoyan, the former premier of the Soviet Union, and politics ran in Stas's blood; so did commerce.

He was the quintessential promoter – wily, political. As a young cadet at the Military Academy, he formed his first band and, curiously, no one seemed to mind. Stas used his family connections so cunningly that, long before Glasnost, he was recording for Melodiya in Russian, which, in the seventies, was astonishing. Stas even had a line on foreign equipment; Cat Stevens once gave him a synthesizer, presumably before Cat took up the veil and became a devout Muslim.

Now, Stas was Mr Rock and Roll and he presided over this building in Gorky Park where there was an outdoor theatre at the back and this restaurant in the basement.

Pictures by local artists were just visible in the faint glow from the candles in the Chianti bottles; in one of them, Stas was portrayed as a fat, naked woman. Loudspeakers were stacked up like cubist sculptures. The music was by Stas's own band, the Gorky Park. Stas's sister did the cooking. The room smelled of burned lamb.

We all shook hands, made rock and roll small-talk and sat down at a table in the corner. I felt like crying. On it was more good food than I'd seen in all of Moscow: tomatoes, cucumbers, stuffed grape leaves, fish salad, hot meat pies. Stas Namin wanted advice about a name for this new venture – what would sell it to foreign visitors? he asked. But, inevitably, it became the Hard Rock Café.

We began to eat and Art Troitsky drifted away as Russian men always did. In the smoky distance, he crouched and talked with other men. They smoked Marlboros. Young, hip, thin, dressed in the international brotherhood of black clothing, they looked, nonetheless, like all other Russian men. They could have been dissidents or KGB agents, or miners, their circle was closed. They whispered among themselves and smoked the cigarettes as if they wanted to eat them.

After a while, Art reappeared. With him was a young man in glasses. 'This is great! The guy I wanted you to meet happens to be here, tonight. Surprise. We have had good luck. This,' Art said, 'is Oleg Smirnoff.'

'What do you mean, "happens to be here"? I thought that's why we came,' I said.

Looking at me gravely, Svetlana shook her head.

'But I thought we had come here specially to meet Oleg, Dean's interpreter, the KGB agent with charm, the . . . ' I said. Svetlana looked at me again.

Oleg Smirnoff was a Soviet nerd. He had round spectacles and a row of ballpoint pens in the breast pocket of his plaid button-down shirt. He wore a blue pullover. He spoke nearly perfect English. Aggressive, reticent, promiscuous and secretive all at the same time, Oleg was like a young Hollywood agent on the make.

'So. Dean Reed,' he said after sitting down next to me. 'Dean was a great guy. He was as American as an apple pie.'

'How did you meet Dean Reed?' I said.

'Dean Reed is first singer for my generation. First time, I am sixteen, in front row at concert. Dean Reed jumps down and together we sing "The Saints Go Marching In". It was great.'

'Great,' I said.

Oleg was not listening. 'Ten years ago – 1978? – I was a student translator. I got a call to work for Dean, but I said, No thanks. Who is this guy who's telling us how to run our lives? Dean did that. But I was wrong. He was an emotional Democrat. What I didn't see until later was that he was an idealist in a wilderness. He taught kids here to believe in the possibility of idealism when it was impossible.'

Unwrapping his various secrets, Oleg spread them fulsomely, talking about Dean Read without stopping, except to order another Pepsi.

'The words were important, that's why he needed an interpreter. I would sit on a stool on stage, just next to Dean. Talking to the audience was as important as the songs. We each had our own spotlight,' Oleg said.

'Every song was a page from Dean's book of life. He wasn't complicated or well-read, but he believed. He was an innocent. He had a minder in the East German Politburo who was responsible for him there; here Mr Arbatov was Dean's Godfather. Dean wrote about socialism. He made one big mistake, though, and he regretted it. He criticised Solzhenitsyn and then wanted to apologise, but he would have to acknowledge he had been used. He knew it, though. Anyhow, you couldn't apologise.'

Oleg was in the mood. Wiping his glasses, he talked incessantly, his elbows on the table. He leaned towards me. He had an audience. For ten years, Oleg and Dean were together – in Siberia, where Dean sang 'Tutti Frutti' for a handful of loggers; in Kiev; in Minsk, Mongolia, Tashkent and Moscow. 'I believe in music,' Dean sang and everyone adored him, eyeing his slim waist.

Girls followed him everywhere. Girls tried to rip his clothes off. The stage-door Ninas pursued him relentlessly. Dean could have any woman he wanted in the Soviet Union, said Oleg, who could barely stop himself salivating.

'He was a very shy guy,' Oleg said. He was pleased with the little rhyme he'd made and he repeated it. 'A shy guy,' he said.

Oleg got plenty of action, too. He siphoned off the girls who didn't get through to Dean, he said, and he smirked when he said it.

'Did Dean speak Russian?' I said.

'Not much. A few words only,' said Oleg.

'Dean wanted to be keeper of the flame . . . but everybody wanted to own a little piece of Dean,' Oleg said mysteriously.

'Could anyone have a piece of him?' I said. 'How much did it cost?'

Oleg was silent. He sucked his drink from the bottom of the glass and averted his eyes. For half an hour, I'd been drawn in: we were in a club in a basement which, if it smelled of burned lamb, nonetheless had the black walls, the loud music, the lank-haired kids, the booze of all clubs. But this was Moscow, still a secret, underground city, still a society where a million half-facts made up a forgotten history as hidden as the little wooden dollies you bought in the souvenir shops. Oleg had a part to play. He was a man from the Soviet theme park and secrets were his trade. For a decade, this man had been closer to Dean Reed than anyone else in the Soviet Union. It made me understand that Dean Reed was, however cuddly, a function of officialdom.

Suddenly, his face seizing up in anger, Oleg removed his glasses and put his twisted features close to mine.

'How do I know who you really are?' Oleg said.

'I've told you, I'm writing a movie,' I began patiently.

'Oh yeah? Yeah? How do I know? How do I know you're going to preserve the memory of Dean properly?' Oleg said.

Christ! I thought, he's going to leave. He had videotapes of Dean's concerts and I wanted to see them. I looked around for

Art, but Art had gone with Stas and the boys into the maze of little rooms at the back of the Hard Rock Café.

I was also a little frightened. I tried to suck up to Oleg. 'So, did you play an instrument as well?'

'It wasn't my job.'

'No, of course not. I mean, why should you? So when did you last see Dean?'

'I can't remember,' he said. 'I stayed in his house the last Christmas – Dean took Renate to London, and I stayed in the house in East Berlin to look after the dog and have a holiday. Germans!' He spat it out. 'In Germany you went for a walk, people said hello to the dog but never said hello to you. I don't know how Dean stood it.

'If you took down the Berlin Wall, half of the people would fight for the system, the other half would rush to the other side. Here, everyone would fight for the Fatherland,' Oleg said, opening up again. But the enthusiasm was gone and he turned back into a prissy party-hack.

'Who do you think killed Dean?' I said, exhausted finally, not much caring if Oleg defected from the conversation or not.

He drew himself up and fingered the row of pens in his pocket. 'He was killed by the forces of evil,' he said.

'Which forces?' I said.

'You decide,' he said.

It was after one and the subway was shut up. There were no taxis in Gorky Park. The only way back to town was in Oleg's car, and, looking straight ahead, he drove silently until he pulled his tinny car up to the front door of the National Hotel, where the hard currency hustlers stamped their feet in the snow. As I got out he shook my hand in farewell. His hand was clammy and it made me shudder.

The next morning, I was going down in the elevator to meet Art and Svetlana when a couple of Romanians – they looked like father and son – got in on the second floor. They wore Sergio Valente jeans and they spoke English quite well. They smiled wonderfully.

'First floor?' I said.

'Ground floor, please,' they said.

'Where are you from?' I said.

'Romania,' they grinned. 'Maybe you have heard of it. Bucharest?'

I had heard of it, all right. Ceausescu and his wife had turned the country into a Stalinist nightmare – this was long before the crowds rooted them out and shot them. What could I say about Romania? It was home to the men in the elevator. Dean Reed made movies in Romania and he claimed to know the Ceausescus. These men in their fancy jeans were probably officials, but they smiled nicely and I was a sucker. Romania, Romania . . . I had it.

'Yes, of course, I've heard of it. Very good food,' I beamed back. 'Pastrami!'

They beamed harder.

'You speak very good English,' I said, and they beamed some more.

'Where are you from?' said the younger Romanian.

'New York City,' I said.

Oz! You could see it written on their faces: that they knew I had come from a magical planet. Oz or Shangri La or Eden or Bloomingdale's, it didn't matter. Satisfied, the Romanians nodded at one another and I knew I had become a postcard from the trip to Moscow – a real New Yorker in an elevator in the National Hotel. For a minute, I was their American. I was their Dean Reed.

As I got out of the elevator, I saw Oleg. In a good, grey suit he was coming through the revolving door. The front hall porter, who looked like Leonid Brezhnev in a cardigan – all the porters, in fact, looked like Brezhnev – did not challenge him.

I got out of the lift. Oleg got in. I did want his videotapes.

'Hi, Oleg,' I said. 'How's business?'

He grunted.

'What are you doing here?'

'I am working,' he said.

'Can I have those videotapes of Dean Reed's concerts? Can I have a look?'

'Maybe.'

Suddenly I didn't care and was weary of his games. 'Working? Yeah? What as?' I said.

'I am working on cementing international relations,' said Oleg and the elevator doors shut.

# CHAPTER 8

# The Bar at the National

At the National Hotel in Moscow, I got a room with a view of a drainpipe. At the front desk, a woman, who wore two cardigans and spoke soft, old fashioned English, did not smile. I was not entitled to a Class A room.

'But you see, this is my first trip to your country and I want a room with a view of RED SQUARE! And I want . . .'

All around me in the lobby of Moscow's best hotel, tourists shuffled across an expanse of turd-coloured linoleum, looking for something to buy. There was nothing in the souvenir shop except wooden dollies, vodka and bad fur hats. At the front door, as always, Leonid Brezhnev's brother barred the way to Soviet citizens, admitting only foreigners, who showed the slab of cardboard that served for a passport to the National.

'Here you may want,' said the woman in the two cardigans, 'but here you may not necessarily get.'

'They have a plan for you,' a friend said.

It was a lifetime of not getting, in a country where no one got. This big, rich country that stretched across eleven time zones was reduced for most people to a tiny plan, to twenty square metres in a shoddy apartment block, to a school where everyone wore the same clothing and a job where everyone did the same chores. 'We pretend to work, they pretend to pay us,' the proverb went. For twenty years, while Brezhnev reigned, nothing happened and no one cared.

What they did get was Dean Reed, with his shining complexion, the good hair, the blue eyes, the fancy shirts and the will to make them sing a little. He delivered escape.

I got a room with a view in the end. Outside my window was Red Square, big as the landing pad in *Close Encounters*. Suspended by day in frozen pink sunlight, at night it was backlit by clouds that drifted in from a power station. The red neon star – 5,000 watts of it – on top of the Kremlin's Borovitsky tower, blazed among the real winter stars.

Across Red Square, St Basil's looked rich and whimsical, a Spielbergian starship just touching down after a trip to the Arabian Nights, a pile of red and green striped pineapples, of squashed onion domes and spires and gold, all filigree and inlay. Such a pretty thing.

Make me something unique, Ivan the Terrible said to his architects and they made him St Basil's and he asked, could they make him another. Yes, they said, and thought about a new arrangement of striped pineapples and golden onions. Yes, we can, they said, and Ivan had their eyes put out.

I liked Moscow best at night. I liked it in the snow, its natural element, its grandeur underscored by the sweep of empty squares, vast plazas as burnished and forsaken as the uninhabited ballroom of a tsar's palace. Night hid the cracks, and the hoods gave the city a cosmopolitan feel.

Fur hats? Roubles? Sex?

The hard-currency hustlers and the pimps were concealed in the shadows of the Bolshoi Theatre, which was pink as bubble gum, its columned portico rising up like a Russian version of Tara.

I sat in my window and watched as the tourist ants made their way past the Tomb of the Unknown Soldier towards Lenin's tomb itself. There, Lenin lay in his marble box in the square near the wall where the generals were buried. Here, I sat at the National Hotel where, from the balcony of Suite 101, Lenin lectured the masses. All of it seemed oddly familiar. The American Revolution was a remote woodcut of tiny eighteenth-century figures in wigs in a formal landscape: the Russian Revolution was movies. So completely inscribed on my cerebral celluloid was it, that I knew every sequence by heart – the close-ups, the crowd scenes, the tracking shots – all of it recorded the day before yesterday, so precisely that in documentaries, as often as not, Sergei Eisenstein's fictional footage showed up, intact, as historical evidence.

What did Dean make of it all when he arrived in Moscow in 1965? His conversion on the stage at Helsinki notwithstanding, the radical politics he picked up in South America apart, there was nothing in his blood to account for his passion with this place.

Dean had not, after all, spent his youth watching Eisenstein movies at the Museum of Modern Art or marching for civil rights in Selma, Alabama. Dean was at the Wheat Ridge Dairy, eating ice cream, and attending meetings of the Future Farmers of America.

Still, looking out at the brilliant stage set, I could picture him in the middle: the Star. Comrade Dean Reed. Between the Magnificent Gringo in the pale-blue suit in Santiago and the Soviet superstar, lay only that first encounter in the Helsinki Park.

There was a knock on the door.

It was Martin Walker. He was wearing very tight jeans and a fur hat a foot high. It had been awarded to him for extraordinary feats of macho fishing by some Siberian tribe. Martin was the *Guardian's* correspondent in Moscow and he had exploited Glasnost brilliantly, rediscovering the Soviet Union for his readers as a place where people had sex and permanent waves, listened to rock and roll, ate Chinese food and did not have Tampax. There were no sanitary napkins anywhere in the country. Art Troitsky was Martin's best friend, which was not surprising. We went to the bar.

The bar at the National drew the gossips and the high rollers and it had a chancy edge-of-the-world feel. At night it throbbed with possibility. I sat with Martin and we gossiped. My Romanians were there at a table with a couple of fat, East German businessmen in green loden coats and grey leather shoes. There was a textile man from Atlanta, and a 'professor' from Bloomington, Indiana, with a wispy chin beard. Professor of what? I asked, and he turned away, no longer garrulous, returned to a secret world.

Behind the bar, a pair of young waiters with the sullen, smooth, empty faces Russians sometimes have, played an interminable game of chess. I watched them through the prism of a glass case, which held two chocolate buns and a pyramid of Pepsi Cola cans. Beside them was an ancient *babushka*, her head encased in a cotton scarf, her body draped in a dress or coat – it was hard to tell which – and she watched the chess game, her broom in her hand, frozen in time behind the chocolate buns.

The noise of the deal-making grew – deals in roubles, sables, sex, potatoes, who knew what? Everyone and everything was for sale at the bar of the National.

At a table in the corner were a pair of hookers, one in red satin, the other in a yellow angora sweater with glitter on the shoulders, which were padded out like a quarterback's. Ignoring the Germans

in grey leather shoes who hovered over them, waiting for customers with hard currency, the women ate chocolate-covered
cherries from a large box on the table, reaching into the frilly
papers with a steady rhythm and popping the candies whole into
their big, red mouths.

Martin, who was taking it all in – you could tell that the bar at the
National would be a column in the *Guardian* by the following week –
scribbled a list of people for me to see. His contacts were astonishing.
Then we went out to eat Chinese food at the Mei Hua.

At night, a minor form of tourism in early Glasnost was making
the rounds of the cooperative restaurants. We ate Indian food at
the Delhi where Mr Rajneesh Kumar Verma had the spices and
the rice flown in and where a Russian band played eerie imitations
of Stevie Wonder and Dire Straits and a fat bride shook her bosoms
to the impeccably mimicked lyrics of 'Money for Nothing, Chicks
for Free'. With Art and Svetlana, we went to the Skazka, a club
for tourists and *apparatchiks*, where there was a floor show and a
gypsy fiddler who played everything. He played 'Hava Nageelah',
he played the 'Mull of Kintyre'. A male exotic dancer, his pectorals
oiled to a shine, began his routine. He jumped around, then posed
on a bed of nails.

'A representative of the Soviet Socialist Sado-Masochistic Republic,' Art said sarcastically, but the audience was wild for it. A
magician coaxed golden coins from behind Art's ears, then stole
his watch, while Svetlana and I shared a pear the size of a melon.
As the juice ran down our chins, I understood that, for a price,
you could get almost anything in the Soviet Union.

The Skazka would have been a perfect venue for one of Dean's
impromptu concerts. He would have held Svetlana's hand, looked
into her eyes and sung 'Yiddishe Momma' to her, then treated the
tourists to one of his comic songs. 'Old Cowboys Never Die
(They Just Smell That Way)' he would have sung. Whatever his
politics, he was once a man who was completely alive. I was
suddenly so sorry that Dean Reed was dead.

Like Dean, in my first week in Moscow, I was full of tourism. I
went to the Ukraina Hotel, a Stalinist wedding-cake of a building
that towered over the river. In the lobby, where tourists stomped
their feet in brown puddles of slush, Dean once encountered the
black Ukrainian girl singer who appeared later on his television

71

specials. While the astonished tourists watched, he grabbed her hand and together they gave an impromptu rendition of 'La Bamba'. I went to GUM, where, astride the rococo fountains, Dean played his guitar among the beautiful glass-covered galleries. There was nothing to buy at Moscow's biggest department store but plastic gilt models of the *Battleship Potemkin*. At the Museum of Musical Instruments, I saw Dean's guitar. It had a little, yellow, smiley face pasted to it and it was signed.

'Dean was very popular, he had a beautiful voice,' said Anatoly D. Paniushkin, the director of the museum on Fadeyev Street. 'He gave a concert for us here in the museum. It was so sad he could not go to America, where they rejected him.'

In Red Square, I waited in the snow in the line for Lenin's tomb. Some of the comrades, their ears bare – for only tourists and wimps turned down the ear-flaps on their square fur hats – ate ice cream. Alongside gruff Bulgarians and impenetrable Albanians, were a group of cheery Cubans, who spoke lilting Spanish. As the line was halted in its progress at regular intervals by the arrival of official delegations, the Cubans chattered happily, although they must have been very cold. Their shoes appeared to be made from cardboard and they would, no doubt, have rather been at a baseball game.

Inside the granite mausoleum in the very centre of Red Square, Lenin lay in a plastic box, stuffed. A little, shrivelled man with a bald head and the familiar pubic beard, he wore an utterly bourgeois black suit. It was a face completely without humanity or humour. Backlit, he resembled a plastic dolly. His skin had a curiously orange cast and his hands were twisted, like an arthritic's. I met a brain surgeon later who said that Lenin had a peculiar malformation of the cerebellum – for years, slices of his brain were kept in jars in scientific labs and studied – and that it resulted in the deformation of his hands. It also killed him, although for years, his enemies gleefully circulated the rumours that Lenin had died of syphilis.

In the airless tomb, the crowds shuffled past, prodded on by men in uniforms. The whole, stifling history of the Soviet Union seemed to be entombed in here, the way the War was boxed up in the Arizona Monument in Honolulu.

Once, inside Lenin's tomb, a tourist observing the mummified man in the plastic box, drew back, startled by what he saw.

'My God, Lenin's lost an ear,' he shouted.

Lenin's ear had fallen off. The tomb had to be shut up for days while officials searched for Lenin's ear.

'Have you ever been to Lenin's tomb?' I asked Art that evening at dinner at his flat.

He barely raised his eyebrow. 'Have you ever been to the Statue of Liberty?' he said.

'Rada set out her stall to get Dean Reed,' said Alla and blew her nose. She accepted a beer and a cigarette and sat down, cross-legged, on the floor of the Troitskys' flat on the Horoshovskoje Chausee near the Begovaya subway station.

'Alla's best friend, Rada, was a friend of Dean's,' Svetlana explained, translating for Alla, who spoke a sexy, cooing Russian. 'A close friend,' she said, gravely. Across the room, Art pulled at the front of his pullover to remind me we were talking of the *page-three girl* with big breasts. 'Very big.' Art mouthed it.

'She set out her stall to get him,' said Alla.

Alla wore a little Lenin badge, tight jeans and a home-made pinafore. Red lips, big dark eyes and frizzy hair, she was a gypsy girl from Moldavia – half Hungarian, half Romanian. Her husband was a film-maker. He was away in Sweden. She wept for her dead friend, enjoying herself enormously. Then she lit up a Marlboro.

'She is very emotional about this,' Svetlana whispered.

Alla rearranged herself, blew some smoke into the air, sipped her beer and launched voraciously into her friend's unhappy story, stopping only to wipe away the tears that brimmed up in her big eyes and ran down her pink cheeks. All it needed was the violinist from the Skazka.

'Rada loved Dean from age thirteen,' she said. 'Rada was a big girl (Art pulled his sweater again) whose ambition was to become famous or to meet famous people, and when she saw Dean on television, she loved him to death, even from afar, even when she was only thirteen years old.' Alla drew breath.

Years and years passed. Rada collected all of Dean's records, went to his concerts, watched him on television, bought pictures of him, daydreamed about his slim waist and the way he moved, like all the other girls she knew. Unlike the others, Rada had a plan.

When Rada grew up, she went to work as a model for the painter, Victor Kropotkin. When she was sixteen, she heard that Dean Reed was back in Moscow.

She borrowed a nude portrait of herself from Kropotkin's studio. She got a taxi and tied the big canvas onto the roof. She went with the taxi to the airport to greet Dean. Huge crowds were waiting to meet Dean and, with them, was Rada with her taxi and the picture of herself, naked, on the roof.

After the incident with the picture, Rada and Dean were inseparable. Or so she thought, because Rada was a very unstable sort of girl and everyone knew Dean had lots of women. Rada thought Dean would leave his wife and marry her, even though, some years, they only saw each other once or twice, when Dean was in Moscow and had the time. She covered her ears when people told rumours about Dean. Rumours that he had an illegitimate child in Moscow, for instance. The truth was even worse. The truth was he loved his wife.

If Dean saw other girls, what he told Rada was that he could give himself entirely to two, three women a day, maybe more. That's how it was for him. He could give that much. Rada was sure Dean loved her best, sure he would marry her.

Then Dean died. There was hardly anything in the official press, but the news was known in Moscow. Rada took many pills. She drank a lot. She ended up in a mental hospital, where she had been before.

'The hospital was on the outskirts of Moscow, but Rada managed to escape.' Here, Alla paused for effect and added: 'Rada had her pockets full of pills! Next day,' she whispered, 'Rada's body was found, sprawled on a rubbish heap, on the edge of town. All that she left behind were her diaries.'

Weeping steadily now, Alla was smoking, drinking the vodkas that Svetlana handed her for comfort. She implored us to help her: Rada's mother wanted to sell her daughter's diaries, Alla said. Could I not help?

Art said: 'Alla says Rada kept very good diaries. Her mother wants to get them published, not for the money, but because her daughter was the friend of a big star, which was almost like being a star.'

'Rada was in love with Dean,' said Alla.

'But he treated her so badly,' I said.

'He was a big star. He was a man. He had the right,' said Alla.

Quietly now, Alla sat, crying. Dean Reed as a womaniser began to emerge from the puzzle and I wondered how many other girls he had left behind him, bruised, in Moscow, convinced that he had the right because he was a star. I wondered how much the diaries would, in the end, cost me.

After Alla told her sad tale and had another good cry, she went home and we sat down to dinner. There was chicken and pickled garlic, cucumbers and cheese, chocolate cake and red wine.

'Stalin's favourite vintage,' Art said examining the label.

At the end of the meal, Svetlana ate cherry jam with her tea. It was the only time in Russia I ever had what could pass for a race memory: my father liked to eat cherry jam with tea. He said it was a Russian custom.

Svetlana was preoccupied. We were full of the pleasures of Glasnost, but she did not believe in the interesting melodrama of revolution. Hers was a vision born in queues and waiting rooms.

'Did you ever believe in Communism?' I asked.

'Not for one single day in my entire life,' she said. 'Not when I was a little girl and drew wigs on Lenin in my school books.'

In the Soviet Union things would deteriorate, Svetlana believed. The lines would get longer. The meat would get scarcer. Everyone would get meaner. Maybe it was O.K. for the men, who sat around Moscow's restaurants with their Western pals, arguing, drinking, laughing. Maybe glorious Glasnost was O.K. for them, but she saw no reason to stick around to spend four hours in line for one chicken.

'I think I will send Svetlana to the West,' Art said.

'What? Like a parcel?' Svetlana banged her fists on the table; the plates jumped. 'You don't understand.' This was addressed to Art. He looked bemused.

'I waited in line for a chicken four hours,' she said.

'Why do we need a chicken?' Art said.

'I don't care about a chicken. But you would care if our friends had nothing to eat. I don't want to wait for a chicken. I want to be doing my work,' she said.

Svetlana turned to me. 'Can I say this in Russian and Art will translate?'

'Yes, of course.'

Eyes blazing, fists clenched, Svetlana let out a torrent of Russian.

'Well, first thing I say is that Svetlana is absolutely wrong. Then I translate what she says,' said Art.

Even among men like Art – liberal, liberated, cosmopolitan – women were a subspecies. Perhaps Gorbachev was the exception. I'd read that Raisa married him because he was the only unvulgar Russian man she had ever met.

I thought of Dean Reed, who said he could love many women in one day. I thought of Alla the gypsy, and her luckless friend Rada.

There was a New York City subway map on the wall of the Troitskys' flat and, in the living room where we ate, a large Sony Trinitron monitor. It didn't work as a television set, of course, because the broadcast standards were different in Moscow. But it was the only set Art found stylistically interesting, so he used it as a monitor for his video player.

Sipping his Avocat liqueur – the kind that looked like snot – he reminisced about his conceptual punk band. It was called Vladimir Illych.

'We wore Komsomol outfits and we had several big hits such as "Lenin is Alive" and "Lenin, Come Back" . . . after *Lassie Come Home*. There was also "Brezhnev is Knocking at Your Door".'

'Of course, the band existed only in our heads,' he added.

'When Dean Reed first arrived, he did numbers like "Blue Suede Shoes". This meant something for us,' Art said. 'There was nothing in Soviet culture that reminds me of my dreams. Rock was a concentration of all good things.'

The times were ripe for Dean Reed. The kids longed for rock and roll and there was none. The roots of their desire and the rebellion it represented went deep. This was Art's territory; he had invented it, and he talked fluently.

'No living Western performer of rock and roll ever came to USSR. Dean Reed was young. He was playing guitar. He was American. We believed.'

In the fifties, Russia's passion for America came from the movies and the records which the Red Army captured in Berlin after the War, and so it was that Johnny Weismuller, the first and the best Tarzan, and Sonia Henje, captured the hearts of post-war Moscow. For among the films the army brought home was *Sun Valley*

*Serenade*, a kitsch caper which featured Sonia doing sit-spins on an ice-rink in an ermine cap. But it was because the picture had a soundtrack by Glenn Miller – Miller débuted 'Chatanooga Choo Choo' in it – that the *Stilyagi* adored it.

The *Stilyagi* – the Style Hunters – ruled Moscow's street corners, and they cared only for clothes and for dancing. In platform shoes, zoot suits and fat ties painted with Hawaiian palms, they wore their hair in Ducks' Asses, slicked back with loads of grease. Officials who caught them, shoved them up against the wall and cut their hair off, but the *Stilyagi* persevered and they held cocktail hours and listened to jazz. Louis Armstrong and Duke Ellington were heroes, but above all, there was Glenn Miller. 'Chatanooga Choo Choo' was their anthem.

The *Stilyagi* were Art's nostalgia heroes. To his mother, who was at Moscow University at the time, they had no charm at all. She despised them because they had no spiritual values. They were empty. And stupid and interested only in clothes. They wanted only to dance the *Bugiwugi*. It was just what the intellectual old folkies of the American fifties felt when they looked at low-rent blue-collar rockers like Elvis with his greasy hair and swaying pelvis. How the old folkies despised rock and roll! Light years later, when the Berlin Wall came down, a man, looking through the brand new hole in it said, 'I am looking in West Berlin and I like to dance!'

'I hear rumours that the KGB house-band's favourite tune these days is "In the Mood",' said Art.

The fifties carried with them the first youth subculture and for Art, it had the charm of kitsch. The taste for kitsch went deep with Art. In Russia, kitsch was a rebellion. If you couldn't get anything good – and there wasn't anything good to get – you settled for what was lousy and made it into a style. Kitsch was a put-on, a parody, a form of survival. 'Up yours', it said to conventional taste and the furniture of officialdom. Moscow had its own breed of cosmopolite and, the poets notwithstanding, its humour was tough, urban and seditious. The more freedom Moscow was allowed, the more it was inclined to put Gorbachev's face on toilet paper.

Shifting to the floor, pouring himself another drink Art continued his trip down nostalgia row to his period of choice which was, of course, the American fifties: the musicals; the cars; he could see the world as if it were enshrined in a baby-blue Harley Earl Caddy with tailfins, a lot like Phil Everly's. Many Muscovites remembered those cars from the brochures they took home from the American exhibition in 1959.

At the exhibition, where Nixon and Khrushchev faced off in an American model kitchen among the Frigidaires and the Mix-o-Matics, Coca Cola was served in plastic glasses by girls who smiled.

Lining up to sample the drink, many said it tasted like shoe polish, then, still sneering, lined up for another glass. And the plastic glasses! And the smiling girls! Who ever heard of such a wonderful thing? And there were the cars. Lovely cars, in many pretty colours, with musical names. Cars that went with rock and roll music. Carrying away the brochures with the pictures of those cars, people studied them in secret, for years, as if they were art.

The taste for rock and roll grew, of course, with these glimpses of the magical West. Paul Anka and Pat Boone were hot in Moscow, so was 'Love Potion Number Nine'. Electric guitars came in through Czechoslovakia and a group called the Revengers played standards by Little Richard. It was all unofficial, of course. Kids strung wires across a table and called it a guitar; they made themselves into bands through sheer willpower, ripping off telephones whenever they could, so that, in one period, not a single public telephone in Moscow worked. The production of records required similar ingenuity and *Records on Ribs* were invented. You stole X-ray plates, rounded out the edges with a pair of scissors, cut a hole in the middle and recorded on top of them. In the underground, rock flourished on top of pictures of your Uncle Sergei's lungs.

But by the early sixties, when Soviet youth was full of enthusiasm over Yuri Gagarin, the Cuban Revolution and the 22nd Party Congress, 'Decadence and disaffection were out of style,' Art said. 'For the Russians, these were the gung-ho years of the hero astronaut, and Soviet culture could even withstand the Twist.'

The bureaucrats said 'Of course, it is all nonsense, this tweest, the music is for idiots, but let them fool around, it is nothing terrible.'

And then, Brezhnev. In 1964, the years of stagnation ground into play. Only the distant sounds of the Beatles singing through the crackle of static on illicit radios sounded like life to Art's generation. For them, the rest sounded like a raging silence.

Beatlemania swept Russia. Beatles bands were formed. A Beatles album was an almost undreamed-of treasure and for half a rouble you could rent a Beatles poster for a day just to dream on. Fans wore jackets without lapels called *Bitlovka*.

'Elvis was nice,' Art mused, 'but Elvis was an exotic. The Beatles had melodies. The Beatles were wonderful. The Beatles came knocking at our hearts.'

Still, the Beatles were not official and never played Russia, unless you counted the by-now legendary stopover at the Moscow airport en route home from Japan.

When Dean Reed arrived, he leaped into a void, an empty space as big as all of Russia. He seemed, literally, to have snatched rock and roll away from the West and brought it East in his bag.

'The Robin Hood of rock, eh?' said Art.

Dean Reed was brilliant propaganda. If you turned down the speechifying, what you got looked like rock and roll. Anyhow, the Soviet kids had the habit of tuning out what they did not need. Watching Soviet propaganda films about the horrors of the West, they turned off the sound and read the edges of the picture to see what was really happening in the streets, in the shop windows. They turned down the sound and read the shoes. They read Dean's boots when he arrived in Russia.

'He wore cowboy boots and he came from the land of the free and the home of the brave and Chuck Berry,' Art said. 'He meant everything.'

He polished off his Avocat. It was late. I asked what records he wanted from New York.

'Cab Calloway,' he said. 'And early Louis Prima.'

# CHAPTER 9

# Pozner's House

On the desk in Vladimir Pozner's flat was a glass model of the Empire State Building. The walls were lined with books in half a dozen languages; an American quilt hung on the wall.

'Go and see Vladimir Pozner. He's a smart man and he knows everyone. I'm sure he knew Dean Reed,' Martin Walker said.

So I had come, across Moscow in the snow, to a building where a few brooms were parked in the corner of the courtyard. Melting snow had turned to slush and dripped on a couple of rusted bicycles. I rang the bell. Vladimir Pozner opened the door.

'Hi,' he said in English. 'Come on in.'

The face was utterly familiar. Pozner had appeared so often on television in America that he was the most famous Communist in the country, with the exception of Mikhail Gorbachev. *Our* commie, polished, witty, urbane, a man who knew his way around a sound bite.

When Pozner began turning up on the box a decade ago, in the middle of the Cold War, people were perplexed and intrigued by the anomalous Russian who spoke colloquial English, rarely used the conventional dreary rhetoric of the Soviet hack, and was very slick.

Was Pozner a Kremlin mouthpiece? Something more sinister? A mole? He looked like one of us, but he was one of them, a member of the Communist Party who rarely deviated from the official line.

In the 1980s he set up the Spacebridge, a sort of intercontinental chat show which allowed the citizens of Seattle and Leningrad to talk to each other by satellite about democracy or Bon Jovi or whatever interested them. Pozner was fifty-four and he had the perfect face for the messenger between cultures: the good cheek-bones, which the cameras loved, gave the face a Slavic cast; the fast-breaking all-American smile warmed it up; the receding hairline made it accessible. Like all of the great TV performers, Pozner was both aloof – as befitted a media royal – yet so knowable that people in the street thought he was their cousin.

Affably, he offered Scotch and slippers that winter day in Moscow, and as he began to speak I was spooked. I don't just mean that he had an American accent, I mean that in the tiniest detail – intonation, inflection, verbal mannerisms – he talked like . . . me.

'I thought Dean Reed was a terrible phoney,' he said, but before I had time to absorb this startling news, he added, 'You'll have to forgive me because I did not like Dean Reed at all. I'm a folk music man. The music teacher at my school in New York was Pete Seeger.'

'What school was that?' I said.

'City and Country,' he said.

'Really,' I said. 'Where did you grow up?'

'24 East 10th Street, in Greenwich Village,' he said, 'I don't know if you . . . '

I knew.

We had grown up on the same block. We had gone to the same school. Although we were fifteen years apart in age, the particulars of our childhoods were identical. We reminisced – about Bluie, the librarian and Ottilie, the cook and Al in Shop – City and Country was a school so progressive you could major in Shop; about Sam the newspaper man and Wanamakers Department Store, where Pozner bought his first bike, and hootenanies with Pete Seeger . . . I had come 5,000 miles to the heart of the formerly Evil Empire to find myself with a man who had . . . Bluie for Library!

'Do you still have an American passport?'

'I never did,' he said.

Vladimir Pozner's cultural coding was quintessentially cosmopolitan. Survival was bred in the bone. His father's family were Spanish Jews who migrated to Poznan in Poland, and then to St Petersburg. In order to enter a university, which was forbidden to Jews, they converted to Russian Orthodoxy. In 1922, Pozner's grandfather

left Petersburg in the wake of the Revolution; in 1940, his father
fled Paris as the Nazis marched in.

The family settled in Greenwich Village. Vladimir was six. He
grew up during the War when America and Russia were allies and
his two heroes were Joseph Stalin and Joe Di Maggio. In 1948,
with Churchill's Iron Curtain speech at Fulton, Missouri, the Red
Scare began in America and the Pozners fled again, first to Berlin
and then to the redemption that was Moscow. All his life, Pozner's
father nurtured dreams about the romantic Revolution of his youth
and he instilled them in his son. The family history looked like the
history of the twentieth century.

Pozner adapted to life in Moscow. He passed his exams. He
became a journalist. He joined the Communist Party.

'It is easier to believe if you are ideologically motivated. I've
always been very political,' he said.

In 1979, Pozner first appeared on American television, and he
was cool. Cool for a cool medium. In a perverse way, ordinary
Americans admired him because he was loyal. He was also very
good-looking.

But loyal to what? Was he even a journalist? Who pulled his
strings? Many liberal American journalists considered him a Soviet
snake-oil salesman. The mistake was to consider him out of con-
text. Just because he looked like a Western journalist didn't make
him one. It didn't make him a dissident, either. He was a man
doing his job. He was a survivor.

'With Gorbachev, it's a whole new ball game,' Pozner said.

In aid of the new *détente*, Pozner also appointed himself Com-
missioner of Soviet baseball. In 1986, Pozner went back to New
York for the first time in thirty-eight years. In the taxi from the
airport he saw the skyline.

'In the distance, I saw New York. And my heart stopped . . . '

In the streets, he stared at people and he knew them all, knew
how they felt, who they were; he was one of them.

'I wanted to cry out, Hey, you, all of you, look, it's me, I'm
back . . . I love you.'

When I met Pozner again, it was in New York. I couldn't shake
the sense that he was an American.

'Of course I am. I got my idealism here. Tom Paine was my
hero. When I read *Catcher in the Rye*, I thought: Holden Caulfield
is about me.'

As we walked down Fifth Avenue on a brilliant winter day, the buildings glittering like cash, he looked around him with the possessive ease of a man who had come home. 'This is my town!' he said, as if he wanted to eat the city.

Putting away the school newspapers, purple with the ink from the ancient mimeograph machine that I knew too well, Pozner drank his Scotch.

'Well, Dean Reed. I thought he was a phoney. I thought his music was junk. I thought he was plastic Hollywood beefcake. The first time I saw him, to tell you the truth, my hair rose up at the sight of that hustler. He wasn't stupid. But he wasn't sophisticated politically either. Who else have you seen?'

I said I had seen Nikolai Pastoukhov.

'No shit. How is the old hack?' said Pozner.

'He's now editing *Pravda Country Life*.'

'How the mighty have fallen,' he said, pleased.

'He says he discovered Dean Reed when he was walking in a park in Helsinki.'

'Pastoukhov, incidentally, never took a walk in his life. I'll tell you something. Dean Reed lived here for a short while. He couldn't be a star anywhere else. Nothing really worked for him. He went from Hollywood to South America, to Italy – I think he made spaghetti westerns with Yul Brynner – finally even to the Soviet Union. He came here to milk a very naive cow. More Scotch?'

I nodded. Pozner poured.

'I couldn't stand him,' he said bitterly. 'You think of Paul Robeson, or Vysotsky, or Pete Seeger, for that matter, who stood up for their beliefs . . . Dean Reed just took it where he got it. He was very good-looking, it's true, so he was a big star with women, and he also fulfilled the image of people who knew America from films we grew up on. Dean was certainly used by the regime.'

'Who do you think killed him?'

'Frankly, I don't think he was important enough for anyone to bump off,' said Pozner. 'Unless he knew something important by chance. But the US Embassy wasn't interested. A lot of people said there was a woman involved. *Cherchez la femme*,' Pozner said, and I wondered whom he meant. My letters to Dean's widow, Renate, were still unanswered.

'Didn't he sort of bring rock and roll to the Soviet Union?' I said.

'He had no talent, that's why no one heard of him in America. And he didn't bring rock and roll to the Soviet Union. The Beatles brought rock and roll. When Pastoukhov and his sort discovered Dean Reed, they thought they were giving the kids something.' He shrugged contemptuously. 'They thought they bought the Beatles and they didn't even buy Pat Boone.'

It was Friday evening as I walked away from Pozner's house and into the Arbat, and I could hear a million voices chattering, gossiping. Moscow was a huge café where everyone knew everyone and everyone chattered all the time. Everyone had a story to tell. Gossip was like cash in Moscow; it was often the only commodity worth having; information was still so carefully controlled by the state even in 1988 that, although the telephones were free, in this city of eight million, there were no telephone books at all.

I thought I had begun to know Dean Reed; listening to the gossip, I thought I had barely cracked the surface. I thought of Pastoukhov, who said Dean Reed was a fine young man who didn't have time for 'sexual stuff'; of Alla who said he had two or three women a day. Oleg said he taught the Russian kids democracy but he criticised Solzhenitsyn, telling him that he was wrong, that the Soviet Union was not a sick society, that it was America that was sick. In Oleg he had an official minder; in Georgy Arbatov an influential godfather. Millions of kids believed in him. And Vladimir Pozner thought he was a fake, a creature of the establishment. But, then, what was Pozner? One Moscow wit described Pozner as an 'official call girl'.

It took me months to realise what Pozner's rhetoric reminded me of: it reminded me of Dean Reed. It was the rhetoric of the American left. I had grown up with it. I knew it by heart. My mother, the commie, I thought. My mother who, during the Depression went on bread marches wearing the Persian lamb coat her father had given her, just as I marched against the Vietnam War in designer jeans. In Moscow, I missed my mother.

'They thought they bought the Beatles and they didn't even get Pat Boone,' Pozner said.

But Dean played rock and roll and tens of thousands of kids in the Soviet Union would have died to meet him. Girls tore his clothes off. Later on, he was given the Lenin Prize for Art and Literature.

'I am the only American with a Lenin Prize,' he bragged.

In the Kalinin Prospekt a little crowd had formed. At its heart was an old crone with a crate beside her. The crowd pushed forward.

'Pineapple,' she said. 'Pineapples.'

The crowd looked sceptical.

The old woman tore open the crate and extracted from it tiny white boxes. The crowd moved in. Showing her gums in a triumphant smile, the woman tore the cardboard away and held up her proof: a slice of frozen yellow fruit. It was not unlike a slice from the pineapples that grew on the plantations near Mrs Brown's condo in Hawaii, except the Moscow pineapple had no smell at all.

Inside the record store nearby, I looked for Dean Reed's records in vain. I wondered if they were out of print or out of stock. I found a Pat Boone album, though, and on it was a picture of Pat in white buck shoes. I bought it for Art. He was in heaven.

# CHAPTER 10

✦

# East Berlin

'You are the best-looking man in the world.'

Wiebke practised the line to herself, her tongue getting in the way of the English words. She looked across the room at the man in the white turtleneck sweater and tried again, because she was determined.

Wiebke first met Dean at a reception at the film festival in Leipzig in 1971. Everyone was there. It was an annual event on the leftie circuit, where deals were, no doubt, cut on films about radical embroidery in Slaka. In any case, the room bulged and throbbed with people drinking, talking, making deals. There were a couple of elderly Americans, two members of the 'Hollywood Ten' who, persecuted by McCarthy had lived in embittered exile in Europe ever since. Old men now, they talked too much and cracked cynical jokes.

Wiebke craned her neck, but she couldn't see her husband, who was also a film maker. All she could see was the man in the white turtleneck with the blue eyes. Every other woman in the room was staring at him, too.

A clever, curious girl, she was thirty, worked part-time as a model and had trained as a teacher. She adored music and art: she was especially into Simon and Garfunkel, the Beatles, the Mamas and the Papas and Leonard Cohen. Their records were not always easy to come by in East Berlin, but there were ways, and Wiebke was hip. She tossed her hair back – it was cut pudding-basin style, like Paul McCartney's, only longer – and looked at the man at the other side of the room.

'What an astonishing-looking man,' said one of Wiebke's girl-friends, who was standing next to her. Wiebke ran out of the room.

She found a friend who was a photographer and she whispered in his ear.

'O.K.,' he said.

He let Wiebke carry his light meter back into the reception, where she saw Dean again. She knew he was Dean Reed. Everyone knew. He was already big in the Soviet Union and word filtered through. He was the centre of attention. He was dazzling. From the second he set foot in East Germany, he was a star.

Dean had serious things on his mind. He was talking earnestly about his plans for a gesture of solidarity with the North Vietnamese. A group of Americans gathered, trying to decide what to do about Vietnam. Give blood? What were the alternatives? The two blacklisted old geezers cracked up because Dean wanted to send white doves to Vietnam.

'Why don't you send the blood of the doves, Dean,' said one of the geezers.

'How about we drink the blood of a couple of white doves, Dean?' the other cracked.

Dean didn't mind. He went on talking, while all the women in the room stared at him. Dean had seen news footage where some pretty North Vietnamese girls pushed bicycles loaded with provisions and ammunition up the Ho Chi Minh trail. He wanted the delegates to load up bikes and push them into the market square at Leipzig as a gesture of solidarity. The American lefties thought this was a hoot.

'That's a good one, Dean,' said one of them. 'That's wonderful.'

Dean didn't care. He went right on talking.

Wiebke tossed down a few vodkas; she hardly ever drank, but she was nervous. She had made her way over to Dean.

'You are the best-looking man in the world,' she said. She blushed horribly. Dean laughed and said something back to her in English, but she didn't understand. She used up all her English with the one sentence: 'You are the best-looking man in the world.' She got it off a Little Richard album.

'Victor.'

Victor Grossman lived in East Berlin. He was an American who had defected and he worked as an interpreter.

'Yeah, Dean,' Victor said, sizing up the situation.

'Let's get away from all this,' Dean said to Wiebke. 'Come up to my hotel room.'

Victor translated.

'I'm not going to do something as sleazy as that. I don't want to compromise my husband, who's quite well-known here,' Wiebke said.

Victor translated this, too.

'Let's go to my place,' Wiebke said.

At the apartment where Wiebke was staying, she drank some whisky. She was really nervous because her relationship with her husband was a brother-and-sister thing, as she said to herself. Here she was with the best-looking man in the world and she felt like a virgin. Within an hour she and Dean were in bed. Then he flew away to Moscow.

She was curled up in a chair one day and the phone rang. A girlfriend picked it up. 'It's your Dean. From Moscow, I think,' she said.

'Hello? Who are you?' said Wiebke, trying to locate some English. She wanted to say 'Where are you?' but it came out wrong.

'Who are you?' she said.

'Dean Reed,' the voice answered.

'I know it's Dean Reed. Who are you?'

'Dean Reed! This is Dean Reed.'

It was a terrible mess.

Wiebke hired Fräulein Schultz to teach her some English. She worked hard at it. The Fräulein was seventy-five and proud that she was still a fräulein. They worked on English with 'Cecilia', a Simon and Garfunkel track.

'I want to discuss getting sex-talk right,' said Wiebke to Fräulein Schultz. The Fräulein was appalled. 'Making love in the afternoon' was the line in the song that gave her the most trouble.

Wiebke persevered, and when Dean returned to East Berlin to begin work on a film a few months later, her English had improved. The relationship blossomed. Dean was some catch. He had his own minder, who was a member of the Politburo. He experienced the privilege that artists enjoyed – nice housing, good medical care. He always wore that white turtleneck. Rock and roll in East Berlin had its ups and downs and, as often as not, it took its cues from the USSR. Once again, Dean was a godsend. The East German Communist Youth Organisation presented him with its gold medal.

In 1972, Dean made his first German film. In *The Good For Nothing*, an adaptation of a nineteenth-century novel, Dean was deliciously miscast. His German was lousy. It didn't matter. In a long pageboy and a shirt with a ruffled bosom, he looked great. He was American. Politically, he was a dream. He said all the right things, and the political limelight did for Dean what the cameras did for other stars: it loved him a lot and it turned him on.

What a catch! Then Wiebke got pregnant.

'It's the kid or me,' Dean told Wiebke. Although he didn't put it quite so harshly, it came to the same thing. She didn't want a kid, not without a husband, so she had the abortion. It was easy enough to do in East Berlin, even then.

They began seeing each other and he took her to Moscow with him. In those days he could draw 60,000 for a concert. Women followed him openly in the street. Wiebke was astonished. After a performance one night, a girl tried to rip his cowboy shirt from his back when he came offstage. A bit of cloth came off in the girl's hand and she stood there, looking at it and weeping. Another slipped him a note. 'I'll meet you at midnight,' it read.

Before a performance, he whistled from anxiety. When Dean began whistling, Wiebke knew he was worried. He had enormous energy. He lived off big rushes of adrenalin, and then, at the end of a day's work, or after a concert, as it drained away, he was exhausted. He fell into a chair one night at the Ukraina Hotel, staring at the green chenille bedspread with little cotton balls on it. He couldn't stand or speak. He shut down, like a light switch.

In Moscow, out of the blue, Dean asked Wiebke to marry him.

'Would you like to be my wife?' Dean said. She was startled.

'I would like two days to think the situation over,' she said.

He was not pleased at all, although it was a phrase she learned from him. 'I would like two days to think it over,' Dean would say whenever he had a difficult political issue to deal with.

'Unless you're my wife I can never take you places,' Dean told her.

She knew it wouldn't last. She thought to herself: this is not for good, but it's going to be a hell of a lot of fun while it lasts. So she said O. K.

They got married and Dean did take her places. He took her to Venice. He took her to Cuba. He took her to America where, like

Leonard Cohen, she stayed at the Hotel Chelsea, and on a plane to L.A., she saw Kojak in the flesh.

Wiebke finished her story, staring at the remains of the kebab on her plate.

'Have some wine?' I said.

I wanted to get Wiebke to tell me what Dean was like in the sack.

'No, I may not. I am driving,' she said.

We were eating lunch at the Stadt Hotel in East Berlin. Leslie Woodhead, who had finished some filming in Ethiopia, had come along to see how the project was shaping up. He could not resist a trip across the Wall and I was glad. Wiebke turned on when there was a man in the room.

I met Leslie in West Berlin, and we took the subway to the Friedrichstrasse Station to find Wiebke. Friedrichstrasse Station in East Berlin was three stops from the Zoo Station in the West, and it was a much odder way to come across the Wall than through Checkpoint Charlie. It was banal and had no melodrama. You got into a subway car; the train juddered across No-Man's-Land; the passengers read their paperbacks or their finger nails and got out. You barely saw the Wall. But at the turnstile in the station there were border guards with guns, the requisite exchange of hard currency for worthless East German marks and the visas inscribed on toilet paper.

It was raining. Outside the subway, alone and in small groups, people scanned the crowd anxiously, waiting for relatives from the West. The hard-currency hustlers turned up the collars of their leather jackets against the weather and scanned the crowd for the suckers.

Wiebke was in her late forties, but looked a decade younger. Small-boned, pretty and tough, she looked a little like Dixie. She had a blond ponytail and wore good leather boots and a cheerful expression. She was gregarious by any standards; for an East German, she was practically noisy. Her English was very fine – fluent, full of nuance and detail. She learned it as a result of her marriage to Dean, and she worked as an interpreter.

We got into the tinny orange car of which she was dutifully proud and she pointed out the opera house that had been restored to its pre-war grandeur. I asked about the Wall and she produced a standard, and quite spirited, defence. I had heard it all before: the calm conviction that the system, if not perfect, was better than most. As we drove, she talked of the haemorrhage of talent, which made life impossible in the East before the Wall was built; of how the East had suffered in the War. She wasn't at all aggressive about it; she simply believed.

At the Stadt Hotel, where, a few months earlier, a sullen doorman had turned us away, Wiebke had things in hand. A table was booked. The waiter smiled. It was clear that Wiebke was very well-connected. The meal over, we stayed on, talking and drinking coffee.

As always with stories about Dean, the tales were as much about the teller. Dates went missing; anecdotes were obscured, but it didn't matter. What really mattered was the sense of this huge life that Dean led. The more I learned, the more I thought Dean's life was like some gorgeous fruitcake, stuffed with unlikely details that made your mouth drop, too big for the cake plate.

For instance, Wiebke said that Dean divorced Patty, his first wife, in Santo Domingo because Jane Fonda told him that Santo Domingo was the best place for a divorce – Jane was a friend of Dean's – and when he got there, he ran into trouble with Yul Brynner.

Jane Fonda? Santo Domingo? Yul Brynner? I tried to piece together the muddle of dates and events, and all the time Wiebke kept moving forward.

In Moscow, after the peace conference at Helsinki, Dean arranged to interview Valentina Tereshkova for Argentine television. The first Soviet woman in space, she would not kiss Dean and was embarrassed. Back in Buenos Aires, where he was then living, Dean was questioned by the police and, when the military took over the country – the sequence of South American coups is always hard to keep up with – he was expelled. In 1966, still married to Patty, he went to live in Madrid, made a couple of pictures, and moved on to Rome.

For the next half dozen years, Dean commuted between South America and Europe and the Soviet Union. Deported from Argentina, threatened by the Right, he tried to get in again by travelling to Uruguay. He was arrested. To the world who knew him, he had the glamour of a political cowboy, moving faster and faster, and he wrote it down in his autobiography that was printed on the crappy paper. So did the FBI and the State Department. It took two years for Dean's file to arrive on my desk, courtesy of the Freedom of Information Act. But when it did, the account of his exploits in South America, was, so far as I could tell, absolutely accurate.

After an illegal entry, a policeman in Uruguay who had previously arranged his deportation, recognised him. 'Hello, Dean, I always suspected we would meet again,' said the policeman.

By 1967, Dean was living in Rome where he made Spaghetti Westerns (This wasn't a life, it was a mini-series!) He made eight altogether: in 1967, there was *Buckaroo*; in 1968, *20 Steps to Death*, *The Three Flowers* and *Adios Sabata*. In 1969 came *Death Knocks Twice*, *Pirates of Green Island* and my favourite, *Machine Gun Baby Face*.

Sometimes, late at night, you could still catch *Adios Sabata* on television. In it, Dean worked with Yul Brynner. Dean was taller than Yul, but Yul was the star. Dean played their scenes standing in a hole on the beach that had been specially dug for him. Dean told the story for the laughs, but it clearly got up his nose that he was less important than Yul.

When Dean went to Santo Domingo to get the divorce from Patty, he laughingly told the press about how he was taller than Yul. Next thing he knew, he saw a story in the paper that Yul had arrived in Santo Domingo.

And in 1970, when Dean applied for a new passport – his old one had expired – his height was listed not as six foot one, as it was on his original document, but as six foot four, but then, by 1970, perhaps Dean felt he had grown taller.

Like America, Dean courted trouble in foreign places and he said it was for honour's sake. Part true believer, part bad boy, he played politics because it was subversive and sexy and it got him in the news and was loads of fun. He was a star at the big party and, in the sixties, there was always a party somewhere.

In Rome, he joined anti-war speakers at the Piazza Navona. In Rome, he put on a suit and, flashing his American passport, talked his way into the US Embassy. From the steps, he turned to the waiting crowd of antiwar protestors who stood outside the gates and he raised his fist.

'Ho Ho Ho Chi Minh,' he shouted.

In South America, he washed an American flag at the entrance to the US Consulate. It was 1972, the year that Richard Nixon was driven to the Miami Convention by his own paranoia. Washing the flag became Dean's emblem. He proclaimed that he was cleansing it of the blood of North Vietnam. Making it clean, clean for Dean.

Dean had come of age in the late fifties; he never smoked dope or jammed with a band in a basement, Wiebke said. His naiveté, his belief, the enthusiasm were carried around, undiminished, the way he carried his guitar on his back. His exploits were well-chronicled by the international left-wing press and he was known to millions. Long after the rest of America shaved off its beard, grew cynical and took out a mortgage, Dean was stirring things up and getting arrested. He loved going to jail. Except for the gay guys.

In South American jails, there were plenty of gay guys. Homosexuality was a crime in Argentina. And they wanted him. 'Give us Dean! Give us Dean!' they cried merrily, and banged their tin mugs on the bars of their cells. As Dean told it, these men had faces so painted up, you would not believe, he said. 'I was never so frightened in all my life,' Dean said. 'You be good, Dean, or we will give you to them,' the guards said on one occasion. Instead, the guards gave them Dean's washing – the gays did laundry for a price – and it never came back. 'They tore it up into little strips for souvenirs,' Dean said, whenever he told the story.

The South American stories, which reminded him of some of his most heroic days, were threaded through his life like the lurex in his stage costumes. He loved telling them the way he loved telling about Yul Brynner and the hole in the beach, or the Russian general who gave Dean his watch.

Across the table I could see Leslie thinking: How in the hell are we ever going to make a movie about this promiscuous life, about all this STUFF?

'Of course, he was a Virgo,' said Wiebke thoughtfully.
    'I see.'
'Like me,' she said. 'Both Virgos. Stubborn, obsessive, perfectionists. He didn't have hobbies. He didn't read much, except politics. He didn't go to the theatre or the opera, or have interest in sports. He was interested in propelling his career. He craved attention. Once we were in a boat with Victor Grossman. Dean

disappeared. We got crazy. We looked over the edge of the boat, and suddenly, he bobbed to the surface. "Look, I've drowned," he said and, rising from the water like Jesus Christ, he burst out laughing.'

Wiebke shuddered, finished her story and signalled the waiter for a bill.

I opened my bag to get some money to pay it. Wiebke stopped me.

'Please,' she said.

'It's O.K.,' I said.

'No, I will pay and if you like, you can pay me back later,' she whispered, glancing over her shoulder at the waiter. Then I understood: she wanted the dollars.

Wiebke stuck her elbows on the table and put her chin in her hands. 'Sex and politics. That's all Dean was interested in. Sex and politics.'

'Sex?' I said. 'Really?'

She didn't need much encouragement. 'When he was twenty-one, Paton Price – you know of Paton Price?' she asked.

We nodded.

'Paton asks him to do a love scene with Jean Seberg in acting class,' said Wiebke. 'Dean and I went to see Jean Seberg, did you know?' she added maddeningly, just as she was about to get to the good stuff.

'What about the love scene?' I said.

'Dean didn't know what to do. Paton Price took Dean aside and said "You're a virgin, aren't you?" Then he took him to a whorehouse and got him the best prostitute. She was black.'

'I see,' I said.

'Afterwards, the girl said to Dean, "You're a natural." '

Paton again.

Paton who was angry with Mrs Brown because she sent Dean to Hollywood a virgin; Paton who wrote letters to him in South America about the women he screwed, who made him strip naked in class and sent him to a whore. Paton Price. The Manipulator. Dean always said: 'I am no puppet.' But wasn't Paton his God-father? His puppet master? The best friend of Dean's life: Paton Price.

'Was he?' I said.

'Sorry?'

'A natural.'

Wiebke changed the subject. The next afternoon, at her house in East Berlin, Wiebke showed us her nudie shots of Dean doing push-ups on the carpet.

Wiebke's house was in the Berlin suburbs. It had a garden and a swimming pool – a sumptuous house for a single woman and her little girl, even if the pool had dead leaves in it. It was five minutes' drive from Dean's house at Schmockwitz.

We ate *coq au vin* in the kitchen. Over the table, a shelf held a dozen brightly coloured packets of tea that Wiebke hoarded. I asked if food was hard to come by. Only the mushrooms, she said. And oranges. You could only get oranges at Christmas.

Natasha ate with us. Wiebke's daughter by Dean was twelve. A slight, fair, pretty girl, she had her mother's face imprinted on her, like a pale photograph. She smiled shyly and hardly spoke. She refused to speak English, Wiebke said, because she was angry at Dean for leaving her. And for dying. She was mad at him for dying.

A cuckoo clock chirped from the living-room wall. Wiebke got out the box of pictures as Mrs Brown had done in Hawaii. In a hundred images, Dean was scattered across the floor.

There were photographs of Dean turning somersaults in the air, of Dean rolling around with the dog, of Dean doing push-ups on the rug without any pants on. There were pictures of Wiebke bare-breasted, which she showed without any embarrassment, even though Leslie was there, or maybe because he was.

Natasha crept quietly into the room and curled up in the corner of the sofa.

I tried to get another look at the picture of Dean doing push-ups bare-assed, but Wiebke had moved on and was staring at her wedding pictures. Dean wore a cowboy shirt with an eagle on the front. Wiebke wore a muu-muu from Hawaii and platform shoes. Everyone had such such a good time, they forgot to speak English, even Victor Grossman. Feeling left out, Dean grew petulant and remote. Wiebke wondered what she was doing there.

'It was the first time since we met we didn't make love, our wedding night,' Wiebke said.

After Dean and Wiebke were married, they built the house at Schmockwitz. She gave up her career. He chose women who were

self-possessed and competent, but as soon as they were his, he
wanted them to stay at home. ('A whore, but only for him,' Leslie
said.)

Dean could be erratic, even volatile, Wiebke said. His moods
could change on a dime. 'Once he became so furious he smashed
at the furniture with his fists. Once we turned up at some cinema
where tickets should have been left for him and they weren't. He
could not handle it. He wanted to go home and despair,' she said.
'I said, Dean, let's go out and have a good evening, but he said
"You don't know what it's like when I'm checked in this way. It
makes me feel dreadful. I can't cope with it." '

They tangled about clothes.

'He wore those cowboy clothes. He had a red jacket. "He looks
just like a trained monkey," my first husband would say.'

They fought about his music.

'Once, when Dean was practising I said, I've heard that song
thirty times, I'm going into the garden. Dean became hysterical.
He said "Patty used to love to hear it a hundred times." I said,
Good for Patty. I'm not Patty.'

'But I think he knew his limits,' Wiebke said. 'He would put on
Frank Sinatra and he would say, "I wish I could do that." ' In
Wiebke's box were bundles of letters tied together with ribbons.
'To be opened in the event of my death,' one was marked.

The letter, written before a trip to the Middle East, described
the necessity of this visit to the Third World. It was what a man
had to do, said Dean. You could not ask others to put themselves
on the line if you did not do the same thing, he wrote to Wiebke.

'As soon as things were going bad in his personal life, he got on
a plane for some revolution. He would go somewhere really stupid
and dangerous. He played a kind of Russian roulette,' said Wiebke.

In the early seventies they travelled together. To Colorado. To
Hawaii and to New York, where she was sick as a dog in a
restaurant in Greenwich Village. She thought it would be interesting to stay a while in America but Dean said 'No, I cannot, I have
no career here. I am a political man.'

She adored Cuba, although Dean was disappointed because Fidel
was out of town. Dean had played for Ortega in Nicaragua and
for Yassir Arafat at his headquarters, and he no doubt anticipated
sharing a cigar and a rap with Fidel. Nonetheless, he was impressed
by Cuba; it was the only place in Latin America where there

weren't great disparities between the rich and the poor, although Wiebke was surprised that everything was run by white people. More and more often, I was astonished by the naiveté of people in the East. It was as great as mine.

'The music in Cuba was wonderful,' said Wiebke. 'Dean made his best record with some Cubans. They have natural rhythm, you know,' she said.

In a letter Wiebke showed us, Dean talked of the reconciliation with his father that had occurred when he went home to America in 1978. They had been fishing together.

'I really feel I have his love and respect now, and that he now loves me more than Vern or Dale, but he never told it to me,' Dean wrote.

'Getting his father's attention was the most important thing in Dean's life. He thought his father was very brave to commit suicide. Dean saw the movie of *Whose Life Is It Anyway*? He said a man has a right to end his life. Renate said, "No, he has no right," but Dean thought he had a right to do that.'

I turned the page over.

'Please be out of the house by the time I get back, otherwise this is going to be a problem for me.'

It was a startling slide. Just piss off, the letter said. And they split. And Dean told Wiebke he was bringing a red-haired stewardess home to Schmockwitz and would Wiebke please beat it. It was 1978, and Natasha was still a baby.

'Was Renate already in the picture?' I asked.

'He knew Renate. He knew her from the time he came to East Germany.

'There were many women. He used to come here and say, "Can't you teach these girlfriends of mine to cook?" He had a different girl every weekend to cook, but he liked my goulash,' she added gleefully.

Just piss off, he told Wiebke and didn't bother to help her find a place to live. Or so she said, and, as she rambled, Wiebke was convincing.

'He could have helped, you know. He had powerful friends on the Central Committee. But he did nothing. He didn't bother with Natasha. When he married Renate and adopted her son, Sasha, he bought him videos of Mickey Mouse and Donald Duck. For

Natasha he bought junk. Couldn't he buy Natasha a Donald Duck, too?'

Wiebke didn't waste any time finding the house with the pool five minutes' drive from Schmockwitz. A whole house, with a pool, all to herself. It made you wonder a little: who did Wiebke know?

'Renate could never have a child by Dean. After we had Natasha, he had a vasectomy!' she said. Her tone was not quite vindictive.

'You would like some coffee?'

We had coffee and coconut cake. Natasha had baked it for the occasion.

'Would you like to play something for us, darling?' Wiebke asked her little girl. Natasha went to the piano and began. Then she got up abruptly and ran out of the room and Wiebke's mood changed.

'Shall I play for you the song Dean and I made together?' Wiebke asked, suddenly coy.

They had gone to Prague together to record it. Dean recorded most of his albums in Prague. Wiebke turned on the record player. The song was called 'Together', and it had a spoken interlude.

'Tell me you love me,' Dean whispered.

'I love you,' Wiebke said.

'Tell me you need me.'

'I need you,' Wiebke said.

'Tell me you respect me,' Dean cooed.

I turned my head away, wanting to eat the carpet to stop myself giggling. I did not look at Leslie.

'I respect you,' said Wiebke's voice.

In spite of her feisty style, it was all deeply felt; she had gone all the way to Prague to whisper that she respected Dean on the mushiest of all the tracks he ever put down on wax.

'He didn't even make a special effort to get our song special plays on the radio,' she said irritably.

# CHAPTER 11

✧

# The Karl Marx-allee

In his flat near the Karl Marx-allee in East Berlin, Victor Grossman kept his Pete Seeger albums in a yellow plastic shopping bag from Tower Records. The flat was on the eighth floor of a post-war housing block. Like scabs, the tiny beige tiles were peeling off the façade.

We had trouble getting to Renate. Renate was the key, but I couldn't get through. Instead, I went to see Victor Grossman, who knew her. He agreed to contact Renate. In his flat we talked and waited for the telephone to ring.

Good-natured, shrewd, vain, Victor first worked for Dean at the documentary film festival at Leipzig. They had a few laughs.

'I was rung and asked to help interpret for an American rock and roll singer. It wasn't my sort of thing, but I agreed,' said Victor, who was a folk music man himself.

He was astonished.

'He was a real rock and roll singer, who looked rock and roll and came from Colorado, but spoke in what we call a progressive or left-wing way, and I wasn't used to this from a rock and roll singer,' Victor said.

I knew what Victor was thinking straight off: in his heart he thought a rocker from Colorado ought not to have been a radical who spoke of peace and freedom. As far as Victor Grossman was probably concerned, anybody born in America west of the Hudson River, east of San Francisco, was certainly stupid and probably a fascist – I was willing to put money on it. Sometimes, I knew how he felt.

'Dean was a star from the moment he arrived. Girls here fall for anything Western. "The Golden West", they called it,' said Victor.

'One girl bragged her Italian lover gave her one hundred lire. She thought that one hundred was a lot of money.'

In Victor's flat, which he shared with his wife – the kids were grown up with children of their own – back issues of *Mother Jones* and *Rolling Stone* were piled knee-high. Galleys of *Veil*, Bob Woodward's book about the CIA, were sprawled out on a large work table that held a computer. Dictionaries in Russian, German and English were stacked beside it.

'Have some cheesecake,' said Victor. Backing out of the tiny kitchen, he elbowed aside the curtain strung on a metal rod that did for a kitchen door. In his hands he clutched a large metal cake tin. Shoving aside a pile of manuscripts, he put the cake tenderly on the coffee table.

'Go on. My wife made it,' he said hopefully, like a man who was intending to have a large slice himself, but not before his guests have been served.

I ate a lot of cake on the Dean Reed story, especially in East Berlin and Prague. Cake-eating, as a ritual, seemed to feature as significantly in the German Democratic Republic as smoking Marlboros did in the Soviet Union, or Kents in Romania. As soon as you arrived – at Wiebke's, at Victor's – the coffeepot was filled, a cake produced. Victor pushed a large knife into the tin and, getting some leverage on it, gently prised out huge slabs of cheesecake.

'Good, huh?'

In the seventies, when Dean was a superstar making movies, Victor was part of his road show and could thicken up the story with anecdotal tit-bits: the ragged gypsy girl Dean befriended on location in Romania; his camaraderie with the stunt men (you got paid by the stunt in Eastern Europe, and Dean saw to it that everyone got an equal piece of the action); the horror of the directors when he insisted on doing his own stunts. In one case, even after he broke his wrist, Dean persisted in climbing a castle wall for a sequence in a film. He demanded that his stunts were filmed in a single shot, so you could tell it was Dean himself performing. He often spoke of himself in the third person.

Idolised by fans, his politics acceptable to the Party, Dean became a minor but potent player in the East. He claimed to know Erich Honecker and Gustav Husak. He made speeches and was honoured by the Czechs with the Julius Fučik Medallion. He played concerts in Sofia and the Bulgarians presented him with the Dimitrov Medallion. When, on a visit to America in 1978, he was arrested and sent to jail, the East German propaganda machine clanked into action and the legend of Dean Reed grew.

In a Buffalo, Minnesota jail, Dean began a hunger strike and he wrote a letter about his suffering to the people of East Berlin. In it, he crowed about the solidarity among the prisoners, but mentioned wistfully how he dreamed of eating goose, especially now it was almost Christmas. His letters were larded with the international rhetoric he was so good at.

In East Berlin, the media devoted its single-minded attention to his arrest. It was a story as big as that of Angela Davis a few years earlier, when the black activist was tried for murder in California. (The Davis story was a favourite and in 1973, Angela Davis and Dean Reed were the only two American delegates at a peace conference in East Berlin which, for years, remained a landmark on the leftie's Eastern circuit.)

Obsessively, the media reported the details of Dean's detention: on November 6, *Neues Deutschland*, the official East German newspaper, gave front-page coverage to Dean's telegram of greetings to 'the people of the GDR and Erich Honecker'.

From his jail cell, Dean wrote to Erich Honecker. Joan Baez sent a telegram to President Jimmy Carter to protest Dean's incarceration. So did Pete Seeger and Shostakovich. An international incident was in the making. On 11 November 1978 the *New York Times* got into the act:

> Four Soviet composers appealed to President Carter today to obtain the release of Dean Reed, 'a singer and actor' on trial in Buffalo, Minnesota on charges of trespassing during a protest demonstration at a powerline construction site.

Trespassing? Trespassing? It was so minor an infraction even a German couldn't get exercised over it. It was more than a little embarrassing when it turned out that the judge offered Dean his choice: a $500 fine or three days in jail. Dean made a speech and went to jail.

Every morning in jail, he rose early and, from his cell, he sang for the other prisoners. 'Oh what a beautiful morning, Oh what a beautiful day,' Dean sang. It was one of his favourite songs and he often sang it when he was in jail.

'Give it a break, Dean,' the other prisoners shouted. 'Give it a break!'

Like Dean, Victor was an American in Berlin. Unlike Dean, Victor was perfectly cast for his life. He did not admit to missing much living in the People's Democratic Republic. Except maybe an avocado. And a Jewish salami. It was impossible to get a Jewish salami in East Berlin, he said.

He was sixty-something, a plump American who wore a plaid shirt and sandals. He fretted a little that day we first met. He had not yet booked his summer holiday. If you missed the final booking date, your holiday was kaput, even if there were still vacancies. Victor intended to visit Soviet Georgia with his wife.

I think Victor was a little fed up with talking about Dean Read. Concealed behind that amiable, bland face and the round spectacles, was a not inconsiderable ego. He was an American in East Berlin, like Dean. Like Dean, he ought to have been a star.

'He's an exotic here, isn't he?' asked Mike Wallace when he interviewed Grossman about Dean Reed for *60 Minutes*.

'Perhaps, a little bit. Because, of course, there are not so many of us Americans around here, you know. I'm an exotic here, too, basically.'

'But, he's blond and, er, somehow . . . ' Wallace said.

'Yes. So many people here are blond, you know,' said Victor.

'That's true. That's true,' said Wallace.

'I'm more exotic than he is, in that sense,' said Victor, who was losing his hair.

Dean was a cowboy with flashing blue eyes who wore white turtleneck sweaters and tight bell-bottom pants. Victor Grossman was just another Jewish leftie in sandals, who looked like my uncles.

While we waited for the telephone to ring, Victor pulled one leg over the other, polished his spectacles and told his story. He grew up in New York and went to Harvard. During the Korean War, he was drafted. The Army asked if he belonged to certain left-wing organisations.

'Did you?'

'As many as I possibly could,' he said.

'The Communist Party?'

'Yes, of course.'

Refusing the draft was illegal. Being a leftist was illegal. Victor kept his mouth shut, joined up, went to West Germany and served nearly his whole year without incident, although, as a Jew he felt uneasy: there were still plenty of fascists around.

Then the letter came. The Judge Advocate, noting that Victor Grossman had concealed his illegal affiliations, ordered him to report to the nearest Military Court. Victor panicked.

In his head, Victor must have played out scenes of his Court Martial. Senator Joe McCarthy's voice plagued his sleepless nights: 'Are you now, or have you ever been . . . ?' G-men in Homburg hats chased his dreams. Images of prison haunted him: hardened criminals and Victor among them, a kid who grew up in New York, whose parents sold books, a commie, a pinko traitor, as bad as a guy who hit on little girls!

Making his way to the Danube River, which was still divided, Victor jumped in. Stuffed his papers in his pocket and jumped, just like that, swam across, and came up on the Russian side, clutching those papers, looking to defect.

He couldn't find a Russian.

For twenty-four nightmare hours Victor wandered around the sector, clutching his papers, looking for a Russian. By the time he found one it was pretty hard to explain where he had been all that time.

Still, they took him in, debriefed him, and resettled him. He went to university and moved on to East Berlin, where he married Mrs Grossman, had a couple of sons and got down to the business of being a journalist and translator. He had a GDR passport with the word 'American' stamped across it.

As a Jew he found West Germany scarier than the East. In East Berlin he never made a secret of his Jewishness. He believed the GDR made a conscious effort to reject fascist ideology. He believed the German Democratic Republic made an effort to evolve a just socialist society. Victor didn't have to buy the package; he had grown up with it. He wrote books about folk music and took his holidays in the Soviet Union, and, after thirty years, Victor Grossman still believed. He knew that it was not paradise on earth, but his basic convictions were intact. In the East there were great gains in education and in medical care. Neo-Nazis and big business ran West Germany; A. G. Farben was a name that often popped out of Victor Grossman's mouth. Were there Gulags? Perhaps, he said, perhaps they were not unlike the prison farms of Arkansas. Victor heard a wide range of opinion expressed in East Berlin. Maybe you didn't hear the non-leftist view in political meetings, but you heard it at the supermarket. You heard discussions of West German TV; people watched the American soaps obsessively. There were shortages, yes, but there was music, theatre, art, opera. There were world-class sports.

'I don't actually care much for sports,' Victor added.

Victor was a man in a time warp. In spirit he was true to his origins. You could put him in a museum with a label: Young American Communist Man, *c.* 1952. He was a Henry Wallace Progressive. He grew up when the Soviets were America's brave war-time allies. His role models must have been those urban coastal Jews in America, the union organisers in San Francisco, the New York dreamers and booksellers, like his parents, the believers who hoped for a better way of life for their kids and for the dispossessed, who thought, whatever its drawbacks, and all systems had draw-backs, that the socialist ideal, realised, would feed body and soul. 'All them cornfields and ballet in the evenings,' said Peter Sellers as the union man in *I'm All Right, Jack*. That was what the American dreamers thought, when they thought of the Soviet Union and even of its satellites: All them cornfields and ballet in the evenings.

In East Berlin, Victor was one of a tiny group of Western expatriates. Victor Grossman did not think he would ever see America again; he still owed the United States Army some time, but, as the years went by, if Victor missed America, it became more and more remote.

'Will you ever go back, do you think?' I asked.

'I think this year we shall have our holiday in Soviet Georgia,' he said.

In Victor's apartment, the telephone rang. Speaking briefly into it, he covered the mouthpiece.

'It's Renate. She says she will see you, but not before Sunday, if that is convenient for you.'

One more delay. We had a thousand questions. Victor had to get to the travel agency.

In the elevator, he was silent, concentrating on his holiday, I think. We shook hands and agreed to meet on Sunday – he would translate for Renate. Leslie and I were going back to West Berlin for the night, and then to Prague.

'Is there anything you'd like from West Berlin?' I asked.

Victor hesitated.

'Please let us,' I said.

'Well, I would like an avocado. It is thirty years since I last saw one,' he said.

The metallic sound of the goose-stepping guard at the Memorial to the Victims of Fascism rang out with chilling irony as Leslie and I drove away from Victor's into East Berlin, looking for something to do.

At the Kino, *Die Mission* was playing. I wished it were *Tootsie*. It had been a big hit in East Berlin, and I could have used a laugh. Robert De Niro speaking German did not seem an appetising way to spend the evening. I had seen him schlep his weapons in the string shopping bag up that mountain in English already, and once was enough. As he manfully shouldered his own good-hearted message around the globe, Dean would have identified with De Niro, *Die Mission* and the net bag.

I suggested a visit to the opera, for which East Berlin was famous. Leslie looked horrified. Opera was something fat ladies did if they couldn't get a job with a rock and roll band.

'Let's have a drink instead,' he said.

A few blocks from Checkpoint Charlie was the Grand Hotel, an island of comforting Western decadence in the heart of the righteous socialist state.

Inside the lobby, the illusion began to fall apart. It was as if hoteliers from another planet had reconstructed a hotel from a blueprint made after a single visit to earth. The elaborately carved period furniture was imitation veneer on top of chipboard; the courteous young managers in striped pants had the beady eyes of security guards; there was a swimming pool in the hotel, but it was too small for real swimming, and the tropical solarium looked out on a sodden, chilly city.

In the café, a grave little all-girl orchestra played skilfully, but without any feeling, for the clientele, who were more interested in the enormous bowls of ice cream than in the pretty renditions of Brahms.

A young woman in stone-washed jeans – the uniform of the well-to-do youth of the East – sat opposite her mother, who wore a hat and ate whipped cream off her spoon with her pinky raised in the air. Smiling, she nodded at her daughter, as if lost in the illusion that this was the Berlin of her gay youth and nothing at all had happened.

When the old lady in the hat got up to gaze at the cakes in a glass case, the younger woman leaned over. She spoke good English. 'It is nice for her. Next time, I save enough to take her to the swimming bath, too.'

I scrounged a few loose dollars from the bottom of my bag and gave them to the young waiter for a tip. Confused, worried, he clenched his teeth. Then he smiled. He had it. 'Have a nice day,' he said, in exchange for a couple of loose, crumpled dollar bills. 'Have a nice day.'

The Grand Hotel accepted Diners Club, American Express, Visa, Eurocard, Eurocheques, Avis cards, Hertz cards, dollars, pounds sterling, deutschmarks, Swiss francs, French francs and Yen. 'Money makes the world go round,' went the song in *Cabaret*. Money, money, money. Joel Grey leered out of the gloom as the cabaret *Meister*, singing about money and jingling the coins.

The Grand Hotel did not accept East German money.

Nothing in the East shocked me more than the way these countries degraded their own currency. It eroded the whole structure of society; it made people willing to sell themselves for a few bucks, and I hated it. When in the fall of 1989, East Germans began jamming the trains that would take them west through Hungary, they tossed their banknotes on the station platform with contempt and spat on them.

At the Grand was an Intershop, an official hard-currency store. With their noses literally pressed against the glass, the East Germans out for the evening looked in at the displays of leather coats from West Berlin, at French perfume and Italian silks. Inside, still more families cruised the goods, but without hard currency, there was nothing else they could do. Why didn't they smash the windows in rage? Why? What did Dean make of it, with his medals from every dictator in the East – the Bulgarians, the Romanians, the Czechs? Did he have a secret agenda? Was he working for democracy from within, the worm in the apple? Perhaps he remained a tourist in Berlin, in Moscow, seeing only what officials intended him to see, unaware of the corruption.

'How could he be?' said Leslie, who had barely said a word all day long.

Leslie drove, he took notes, he ate cake, but he kept a thin-lipped silence, which was unlike him, for he was always ready for a laugh. I knew he was beginning to take against Dean Reed for, more than anything, he could not stand the naiveté.

'I don't get his politics, you know,' Leslie said.

Dean Reed's politics were naive, and straight as a die: US democracy was only a choice between Pepsi and Coke; imperialism ruled the West; the East featured benign state socialism and free medical care. Dean had a rationalisation for everything, even the invasion of Afghanistan (the Afghans denied women their rights). He had the line down pat and was much given to shtick about the arms race and the human race. Mike Wallace told him he sounded like an editorial in *Pravda*.

Unlike Victor Grossman, however, Dean had parents who were neither Jews nor lefties, only the memory of Paton Price and his platitudes. It didn't quite fit. Dean seemed to have been hatched out of the head of a half-formed idea he picked up between Wheat Ridge and East Berlin. But what I tried to explain to Leslie was that he truly believed. Believed in the way only Americans could believe, because they alone could afford to.

In the time I spent in the East, I only met two true believers. One was Victor Grossman; the other was Vladimir Pozner. In a sense, both of them were, even in exile, New York Jews.

Leslie was desperate to get out. At the border, we discovered we still had East German money. You were forbidden to take it west. The bank at Checkpoint Charlie had closed. Both Leslie and I were too obedient, too paranoid, to stuff it in our pockets and lie, which is what anyone else would have done. We drove back into East Berlin.

Leslie, who had been to Eastern Europe a dozen times before, had been changed by East Berlin. Staring at the money in his hand, he gave up whatever tiny shreds of belief in socialism he might once have espoused.

'It's crap,' he said. 'Crap. All of it crap. The politics are crap. The money is crap. The furniture, the clothes, the schools. Crap.

It's a conspiracy of mediocrity. From the Berlin Wall to Vladivostok, they've cheated everyone and everything is crap.'

'Stop the car,' I said.

'What for?'

'Just stop, O.K.?'

Looking anxious, he pulled over to the kerb. It was dark. A man in a hat walked along the street, staring at us. The man disappeared, and all I could see was the rococo outline of the opera house against a purplish sky. In the distance, beyond the Berlin Wall, lay West Berlin, the neon dream city. It made the sky glow the way Las Vegas does when you come on it, all of a sudden, out of the desert.

I got out of the car.

'Where are you going?' said Leslie.

'I'll be right back.'

Looking around once more at the empty, dark, wet Berlin street, I took all of the shitty, crumpled, greasy money and shoved it in a bin on top of all the other rubbish. Then we fled for the West. I could hear Leslie breathe out.

'I had a minute of panic. I thought I might be trapped the other side of the Wall,' he said.

# CHAPTER 12

# Prague

Vaclav Nectar was an improbable rock star. A tiny, cherubic man who was trained as an opera singer, he had the direct, dimpled gaze of a five-year-old. *Un vieux garçon*, the French would have called him. He was a man with the face of an elderly baby. His friends called him Vashek. In Prague, he was Dean Reed's best friend.

In the driveway of Vashek's little villa in the perfectly bourgeois suburbs of Prague, on a day so lovely it was ironic all by itself, a mirrored ball from a dance hall that had shut down lay, discarded, near the trash bin.

'I can't think of anywhere to throw it away,' said Vashek.

On the other side of the drive was an ancient tree. 'My wife's father planted it when she was born,' he said.

Mrs Nectar, an ex-ballerina with safety pins dangling from her apron, had a cold. She smiled wearily, produced a plate of creamy cakes and left us to watch a video of Vashek's group, the Bacilli.

In doll-face make-up, he warbled and postured. All of the Bacilli wore masks and their biggest hit was called 'The Clown'.

Leaving the video on in the sitting room with its carefully matched three-piece suite, there followed a little tour of Dean Reed memorabilia, carefully hoarded, placed in positions of honour around the house: windchimes from Colorado; a big tin samovar from the Soviet Union; a chromium clock from somewhere social-ist and a little brass lamp from India.

'Dean had a tremendous capacity to warm up the public,' Vashek said. 'He could win them immediately, then state his political convictions. People would take it from him. He spoke in English. He was the master of communicating. I learned from him: the public must be yours the moment you've sung your third song.

He did the international hits: Everly Brothers. "Ode to Joy". "My Yiddishe Momma", which was tremendously popular here,' he said, and added, 'Come, please.'

In the basement of Vashek's house was a secret rock and roll museum. On a row of shelves, back issues of the *New Musical Express* were stacked tidily alongside newspaper cuttings and record albums. There was an old gramophone. And the walls were completely papered with posters of Mick Jagger and John Lennon, of Elvis and of Dean Reed, Vashek's hero. Except, in a sense, it was Cliff Richard who made Vashek a star.

In 1968, Vashek tuned into a radio broadcast from the Albert Hall in London and he heard Cliff Richard sing 'Congratulations'.

'I was much taken with it,' he said in his formal way. Three days later, adding his own Czech lyrics, Vashek recorded a cover version of Cliff Richard's 'Congratulations'. It became the anthem for the Prague Spring and its lyrics went something like this:

> The poplars are blooming. The mud is gone. Music should play because the trees are green. I think spring is coming. I met a nice girl in a nylon blouse and invited her out for a Martini Dry.

Vashek, who was star-struck, longed to meet his hero. He had once seen Cliff Richard backstage at a concert, but he was too shy to say hello.

The music died when the Soviet tanks rolled into Prague in 1968. The sound of the tanks and the sound of the music – the sound, above all, of the Beatles – formed a generation east of the Berlin Wall, exactly as the sound of the music and the sound of the blades of the helicopters beating time to it in Vietnam, formed ours. Except that in Prague, after the battle, the music died, literally.

It was a city addicted to music: Paul Anka had played Prague once, so had Manfred Mann. So pervasive was rock and roll in the sixties, that when the writing team of Sucy and Slitr – their hits included 'Mr Rock and Mr Roll' and 'Vain Cousin' – opened the Semafor Theatre in Prague, within five years a million visitors came, which was equal to the entire population of the city.

In the sixties there was a surge of Western culture – Beatles bands flourished. In his book about rock and roll in the East, Timothy Ryback describes a delicious moment when, in 1965,

Alan Ginsberg was made student king. He announced that rock and roll 'had shaken loose the oppressive shackles of Stalinism.'

What a howl it was when they made Ginsberg king and carried him around town. He was thrown out of the country for subversion, perversion and wearing flowers in his hair. The Soviet invasion destroyed the gaiety, but it took time before the music absolutely died, before Dubček's good natured system faded away and the country was strangled by dread.

In 1969, The Beach Boys came to Prague. In Czech, the Beach Boys were known as *The Boys from the Seashore*. It was all as sweet and loony as Shakespeare's Seacoast of Bohemia.

'Help me Rhonda, help help me, Rhonda . . . ' the Lucerna Hall rocked all night. And the lead singer of *The Boys from the Seashore*, Mike Love, said how happy he was to be in Prague. That night, he said, he wanted to dedicate a song to Alexander Dubček who was in the audience. It was called 'Breaking Away'.

When the tanks rolled in, it was also the end of the music of chatter in the street that, during Alexander Dubček's Prague Spring, had risen to a delirious hum. The banners and flags that crowded the city's sight-lines, extolling socialism and Lenin and Brezhnev, flapped to a tuneless breeze. In Wenceslas Square, for twenty years afterwards, it was as if the soundtrack was shut off.

It was the most beautiful city in Europe, where melancholy floated like dust through the stucco-coloured air and there was a slow, drifting accretion of inertia. In every window in the shabby arcades around the square, in every car, taxi, and shop were pictures of Lenin. Slogans pasted on exquisite baroque buildings testified to the joys of socialism. Groups of children, with sullen faces were herded, silently, through the Klement Gottwald Museum of Socialism. As the hard-liners tightened their grip, all of the rock clubs shut up and Prague's top band, the Plastic People of the Universe, went to jail. But the shop windows were solid with sausages. Into this heartbreakingly lovely town, stunned into weary acquiescence by Husak's neo-Stalinist repressions and a load of salami, walked Dean Reed and it was like Christmas.

Could Dean sing? Did he have talent? Did it matter? He could carry a tune and he had a nice sentimental style. I always thought if he had stayed in Hollywood and plugged away at his trade, he could have had a decent career, in the early sixties, at least. He could have been Fabian. There was something of Fabian about the young Dean Reed.

Dean sang everything: pop, rock, folk music, revolutionary ditties of his own invention. He could whack away at the guitar enough to be convincing. He could orchestrate a musical show. Hollywood made him a professional. And he could perform! His fans loved him and that was his true talent, and so when you walked with Dean in Wenceslas Square, it took an hour to go half a mile.

Everything east of the Wall was relative, of course, and to Dean, Prague was musical bliss, even in the dead middle of the seventies. He called it Music City. In East Berlin there was no tradition for pop music at all. Even when officialdom recognised its inevitability, it did so by establishing an organisation with the chilling title: *Sektion Rockmusik*. As often as not, in East Berlin, a backing band meant a hundred singing strings because, under German socialism, no musician could be unemployed.

In Prague there was tradition. With its democratic history and its bohemian passions, Prague had a life-long love affair with jazz and pop and rock and roll and its technicians remembered. Dean got himself a deal with Supraphon, the state recording label, which lasted the rest of his life. In a good year, what with exports throughout the Soviet Bloc, Supraphon sold a couple of hundred thousand Dean Reed albums.

Dean's first Czech tour was a 'Solidarity with Chile Tour' in 1975. He was living in East Berlin, then, married to Wiebke. Ironically, as Czechs fled West, where they lived off nips of Schnapps and bitter memories of home, thousands of Chileans escaped to Eastern Europe in flight from Pinochet. All over Europe and particularly in Czechoslovakia, many of Dean's *compañeros* from the old days lived in exile.

'Poor bastards, they exchanged Pinochet for Husak and didn't even know it,' someone said, but at least, by and large, no one in Prague bashed your brains out with a rifle butt in a soccer stadium.

And among this free-floating group of peripatetic exiles, émigrés, musicians and poets, Dean was a drop-in star with an American passport.

'Am I popular because I fight for peace?' Dean always asked

Vashek. And because his friends in Prague did not want to hurt him, they said, 'Half like you for that.' He said: 'What about the other half?' 'Because you're American,' they said and were fond of him, although everyone knew he had an American passport and could jump ship any time.

Dean Reed prevailed. On that tour in 1975, Dean sang 'Bye-bye Love' to rock-starved Czechs. He met Vashek Nectar and they became friends. He was sweet with the girls and brazen with the bureaucrats. He stood up for his friends. He spoke his mind. In his white turtleneck, Dean went on television and said: In life you must have love and fun. Fun! It was years since anyone thought about fun, maybe not since 1968 when the Soviet tanks killed fun. Fun was a revolution.

'Meeting Dean didn't help me much. But I don't mind, although it aggravated my problems for the next ten years,' Vashek said, when we were settled in his basement, drinking coffee.

With the obsessive recall of the torture victim, Vashek began the long, sad, intricate tale of his relationship with Mr Hrabal, Master of Power. The road to Vashek's particular hell was paved with good intentions. His life went terribly wrong, and it was full of dark corners and dead ends, like a Czech novel.

After 1968, and already a marked man, Vashek was called by the state to testify against Marta Kubishova, the heroine of the Prague Spring, the girl who sang at the tanks in the streets and was awarded a Golden Nightingale by Mr Dubček.

Frantishek Hrabal, as the chief of *Pragokoncert*, had complete authority over pop music. A former head of disinformation, he was a full KGB Colonel; he was the Master of Power.

'We have people to destroy you,' the Master of Power screamed at Vashek Nectar when Vashek refused to identify Marta Kubishova as the woman in a set of pornographic pictures. Marta and Vashek had worked together in a group called the Golden Kids and they were friends. Kubishova sued Hrabal for slander. Vashek spoke in her defence again, and his career was finished. So fragile was Vashek now, that on one occasion, after he shouted at the Master of Power, his chief torturer, he committed himself voluntarily to a lunatic asylum.

'I could claim I was briefly deranged and had meant no harm,' Vashek said.

On tour in East Berlin, Vashek met Dean Reed.
'Can I come and help?' Dean said.

The Czech regime used Dean: in making him a star, the official press wrote about him glowingly as a 'fighter for peace.'

'The journalists damaged Dean by making him "something inhuman", because it was useful for them to write about a "progressive singer". He was a very brave man, who could say unpleasant things to VIPs,' said Vaclav Nectar. Vashek was braver – he loved his American friend with a touching bravado, even after Dean made his miserable life worse.

Things soured for Dean in 1980. When he signed on for a Czech tour, he had a gentleman's agreement with Hrabal that Hrabal would pay half his fee in dollars. Hrabal refused to pay; Dean went berserk.

Dean wrote to Husak. He wrote to the Minister of Culture. He wrote that Hrabal was the Beria and the Pinochet of Czech culture, a monster, a pig, an idiot!

Husak replied: the matter would be resolved at a meeting with the Minister of Culture. Nothing happened. Dean wrote another outraged letter, but this time, by way of reply, there was only a chilling silence.

It was a gesture that cost Dean. For most of the eighties he was not allowed to perform in Czechoslovakia in person, although he went on recording at Supraphon because there was money to be made from it, and the government was not insensitive to profit.

When Dean was finally allowed to perform in Prague again, he sang 'Give Peace a Chance' and 4,000 people rose to their feet.

'The popularity, doesn't it bother you?' Dean's Czech engineer asked.

'I need it,' Dean would say. 'I can't live without it. It is a drug.'

But most of all, it was Vashek who, because he was friends with Dean, suffered. There were interrogations. Trips were cancelled. Vashek was victimised, terrorised, worked over.

'Hrabal had a memory like an elephant,' said Vashek.

But Vashek never blamed Dean, not even because Dean's righteous outrage was only about money.

'To Vashek, my brother, friend and comrade. I love and respect you very much. You are a very special person in my life. Until death us do part. An embrace,' Dean wrote in the flyleaf of his autobiography.

Vashek showed it to us, and he insisted that the last line was significant. Of this Vashek was sure. Before he spoke, he put a record on the gramophone, to muffle our conversation.

His baby's face was old as death as he whispered.

'With Dean's death my life in fear began,' he said.

The music played dully. Vashek's voice dropped as he spoke of the Czech secret police and an alliance with the East German Stasi and their desire to eliminate Dean Reed because Dean Reed was trouble.

'Dean said too much. He called the officials mafia. He had many friends among the prostitutes here. Many were informants,' Vashek said. Glancing over his shoulder, he added with a meaningful stare, 'One of the girls was called Ophelia.'

# CHAPTER 13

# Schmockwitz

It snowed the day we finally went back to Schmockwitz, to the house on the wrong side of the Wall, at the end of a country road next to a frozen lake. It was four months since we had first come. East Berlin was a city of dead ends: the Wall that kept people in; the badly drawn map on the greasy visa issued at Checkpoint Charlie, which marked forbidden territory; the midnight curfew for tourists; the worthless money which you could not export; the East Germans, noses pressed against the glass at the hard currency Intershop in the Grand Hotel, gazing at leather coats they could not buy from countries they could not visit; doormen who barred the way to hotels; the official reports of Dean's death which yielded nothing much at all except the German obsession with bureaucratic detail; the lonely house where Dean Reed lived next to the lake where he died.

There seemed to be no way forward. The more informants we talked to, the more the mystery jammed up against itself: Wiebke described a massively moody man whose adrenalin rushes left him too drained to turn on a light switch; Victor described Dean as a man of profound political naiveté and great glamour; Vashek thought him a genius as a performer and loved him, even though he ruined Vashek's life. Dictators gave him medals; stunt men gave him kudos; no one could or would talk about his death. A dead end. The wind howled around the Alexanderplatz as we drove out of Berlin towards Schmockwitz. The ear flaps of his Russian hat pulled down over his ears, Victor Grossman sat in the front seat next to Leslie and recited the directions for Schmockwitz. In his lap, Victor held a bag with a couple of avocados. Leslie pretended not to have been down the road before.

As we left the city behind, the snow fell harder. A thick mist came up and the low-lying suburban buildings turned into an endless grey blur as did the railroad tracks on the other side of the road. The dismal little East German cars slid and skidded on the highway: none had chains or snow tyres.

The village of Schmockwitz was shut tight for winter. The pub was boarded up.

At the end of the long, bleak road was the Reed house, with the carved R on a post. We parked and, as we walked down the path to the front door I could see the lake, grey and forbidding. Every time she looked out the window, Renate saw the lake where Dean died.

On the doorstep were two pairs of rubber boots caked with mud. I wondered if they were used the day Dean's body was dragged from the lake.

The house seemed silent. It had been the object of so much effort for so long that I sometimes dreamed about it. Endless telephone calls rang unanswered in an empty house. Suddenly, a light flashed on inside, the door opened and Renate stepped out, kissing Victor's cheek as she came. The scene came to life, as if a figure in a photograph I had been looking at for months put a hand out and pulled me in.

Smiling sweetly, in black leather pants and a white silk shirt, Renate stood in the doorway. She had the anxious, beautiful face of a neurotic angel. She had dark eyes. She gazed at you, a consummate actress, reluctant to let go, as if you were the centre of her world. 'Please,' she said, opening the door wide, tilting her head.

'Thank you,' I said, and gave her some chocolates.

'Thank you,' she said.

In the hall, Renate took my wet boots away and gave me furry slippers. A good *Hausfrau*, I thought. Renate smiled; she knew what I was thinking. Still standing in the vestibule, she lit a cigarette. Her hand shook as she forced a lighter into life. But she grinned with unexpected good humour; she had a wry grasp of the situation, and I liked her.

Victor, who had removed his own boots, was already in the sitting room with the cake. On a table in front of a tan corduroy sectional were blue-and-white cups, a coffeepot, the inevitable cake and a plate of little chocolates. Victor ate a chocolate.

'Decor is Biedermeier Cowboy,' Renate announced winningly.

The house was full of *stuff*: a carved dining-room suite, a cuckoo clock, a sofa, chairs, a big fireplace with a television set, video cassettes, plants, copper jugs filled with flowers, a miniature set of fire tongs and a shovel. Over the fireplace hung Dean's guitar, and there were horse things – bridles, bits – props from a movie. In a picture in a fancy frame on the mantel, Dean and Renate kissed for the cameras. Beside it was a brass carriage clock, with an inscription from Dean to Renate. 'I love you more every hour,' it read.

On the floor lay an animal skin; I think it was a bear. It seemed to have a bear's head.

'Please,' Renate gestured towards the sofa.

I sat down and fell out of the slippers, then I ate some cake.

Renate talked German and Victor translated, although sometimes she slipped into a little English. She was as vulnerable as an open wound. The big dark eyes locked mine into a tremulous gaze. My God, it must have been lonely down the end of that road with only her boy, Sasha, for comfort.

Like all teenagers, Sasha, who was fifteen, seemed to be perpetually on his way out. Ill at ease, he shook our hands, kissed his mother and hurried away, his long, skinny legs encased in black leather pants giving him the look of a big bird.

'He is a good man. He is my little man,' said Renate. 'You would like to see the house, please?'

It was a shrine. On a table were Dean's spurs from Chile. A saddle was tossed over the stair railing. The American flag he washed in Santiago hung on a wall, upside down for irony.

Renate opened a door: Dean's study. The inner sanctum. Through the window was a view of the lake and the woods beyond. On the wall were pictures and quotations from Fidel Castro and Jimmy Breslin. Under the glass top of the massive desk were snapshots. One was familiar.

'Oleg Smirnoff!' I said.

'You know Oleg?' she said.

She was pleased. Oleg was such a good translator for Dean. Dean said Oleg could do it almost better than he could. (I thought of Oleg's vicious hatred of Germany, where they smiled at the dogs and not at him.) Renate was so pleased we knew Oleg.

We exchanged pleasantries about Mrs Brown and Phil Everly. I told her about Nikolai Pastoukhov and Dean's first trip to

Moscow, when he sang all night in the private train that belonged to Deputy Premier Tikhonov.

Lost in reverie, Renate clasped her hands and imagined her handsome husband singing in the train that sped through the Tolstoyan night as if it were a Russian novel she'd read as a schoolgirl. Renate was born to play Anna Karenina. Or Ophelia.

'So what is it exactly that we are here to talk about?' Renate said.

The small talk was over, the cake eaten. Renate wanted to know what the deal was. Leslie talked about the film he wanted to make. He said that he liked to think of Costa Gavras' *Missing* as a model. Renate said it was among her favourite films. This was a good sign. She poured more coffee.

'I speak German?'

She spoke. Victor hauled himself into action and translated.

'Renate says she heard that Wiebke reported to a member of the Central Committee that you were about to offer her $50,000 for her story. If you are going to pay that much, she thinks you are going to focus Dean's story on Wiebke, not Renate, which makes her uncomfortable.'

Wiebke had not lost any time stirring things up. Sitting in her house just down the road, like a spider overseeing her network, she had already phoned the Central Committee. The scenario shifted. How naive we had been.

Leslie took charge and he was convincing. 'We want to work with you,' he said. 'To be absolutely candid, you are Dean's widow. You own the rights to his music. We need you.'

Renate inquired politely about editorial control over the script. Could she see a script when one was ready, she asked.

'I really would like to,' he said, 'but I am forbidden to do so by Parliamentary law.' On the spot, Leslie made up an act of Parliament. What a con artist he was, but then I have known film makers to eat monkey brains raw to get what they wanted.

For the moment, however, Renate was a willing player and she poured out white Hungarian wine into dainty Hock glasses with thin green stems. As she reached out to put a video cassette in the player – it was of Dean's last concert – and as she pulled a large box of photographs towards her, I knew that the ritual had begun. First with Ruth Anna Brown, then with Wiebke, the magic lantern show was offered up. Leslie sat on the edge of his seat; we were eager as children in a toy shop. Looking at the box – it had not been opened since Dean's death, Renate said – I saw the images of the man spill out onto the carpet, as if he were a Jack-in-the-box and only Renate could let him out.

Renate Blume was born in Dresden. She must have been a child during the firebombing that reduced the city to rubble half an inch high, but she did not talk of such things. She was reserved and well bred. Her father was an aviation engineer. Her brother was a mathematician. It was expected that Renate would be a doctor. She wanted to dance, but her parents forbade it. 'We are scientists in this family who do not fool around with such stuff,' they said. Still, she had her way and, having trained as a dancer, she got a place in Berlin's best acting school. Before she had even finished the course she was cast in a film, *The Divided Heavens*.

At the theatre in Dresden, Renate played the tragic heroines. She married a director, Frank Bayer; she worked in films and on television. For her portrayal of Jenny Marx in a Soviet series, she received a Lenin Prize. ('All made-up and beautiful as fat little Jenny Marx,' Wiebke had said, spitefully.)

Renate rose and took a mother-of-pearl box from a drawer. In it was her Lenin Prize, a small, elegantly embossed medal.

'Dean also got one. He got his first, which was right, because he was the bigger star.' Shyly, she produced a scrapbook. In it were fanzine snaps of Renate. 'A fan sent me,' she said self-consciously, giggling over a picture of herself in a miniskirt, her cheeks sucked in, her hair long, her lips white. 'Terrible,' she said.

'I have been so lucky in my work. Then I have had no luck at all when Dean is dead. The man I am looking for all my life and thought I would never find,' she said, piteously.

She first met him on location in a movie called *Kit und Co*, taken from a Jack London novel. 'We were lovers, but only for the film, of course.'

Renate was married and Sasha was still a little boy. Dean was married to Wiebke. But something stirred right away between them. In 1975, she divorced Mr Bayer, but she did not ever want to marry again. 'I lived without my husband and without Dean seven years,' she said. She did not want a star like Dean for a husband – she knew there would be problems.

They were married in September 1981, on the day of Dean's

birthday, and Dean wrote a song for her called: 'On the 22nd of September'.

For her wedding, Renate wore a white dress and she carried white roses. Dean wore a suit. The wedding party was on a boat on the lake. In the pictures, groups of people celebrated, toasting the happy couple, who were radiant: he was fair and handsome, she was dark and beautiful. In one photograph, Dean wore a sailor hat cocked dashingly over one eye. He sat at the wheel of the boat. Renate gazed lovingly into his eyes, and her arms were clasped around his neck in a hammerlock hold. In another, Dean hugged a pig. 'A wedding gift,' Renate said, giggling.

'Three weeks after we are married Dean goes to Beirut,' she said, and did not laugh.

'Dean was an idealist,' Renate said.

Before they were married, she had accepted his need to put himself on the line for his beliefs. She understood Dean because she, too, believed. Like all educated East Germans, she spoke Russian. In working with the Soviets on the *Life of Karl Marx*, she came to understand them. With her whole heart she felt they were a friendly, peaceful race. In the Soviet Union, many people lost their family in the War. The Soviet Union lived war in a way that Americans had never known upon their own soil, and they would never want war again, she said.

'So many women are living alone because of wars, and have never found another husband,' Renate said sadly.

Truly, Renate believed, and she was passionate for Alexander Dubček's Prague Spring, for socialism with a human face.

She showed me the pictures: Dean with Arafat; Dean with Daniel Ortega; Dean kissing little children. In all of them Dean looked luminous. In all of the pictures of Dean with Salvador Allende, Allende appeared to be asleep.

In 1970, Dean went back to Chile to work for Allende's election and later, as he told the story over and over, he became instrumental to it and maybe he was. I remembered the Countess: 'Dean could tell 5,000 miners how to vote.'

When Allende was overthrown, Victor Jara was brutally murdered in the soccer stadium in Santiago. Jara with the dashing moustache. Jara was a hero of Dean's and in 1977, he made *El Cantor*, a film in which, wearing a dashing dark moustache, he impersonated Victor Jara. I had heard that Jara's English widow, Joan, was terribly embarrassed by it.

The bravest thing Dean ever did was to go back to Chile in 1983 when the death squads were rattling around like loose cannon and no one was safe. Renate begged him not to.

'Please, Dean. Don't go. Please!'

He said he would try to be back for Christmas.

Before he left, he got into his car and drove by night to the Czech border to meet his friend Vashek Nectar. There, Vashek handed him the master of a record Dean was to present to the brothers in Chile. In No-Man's-Land at midnight, the two rock stars embraced.

'Promise me you won't sing "Venceremos",' Renate said.

'No, Renate, I cannot promise you. I am not going all the way to Chile to sing "White Christmas",' Dean said.

The secret police grabbed Dean as soon as he arrived in Chile and he was informed that he could not work because he had no permit. But he had not come to play games and he worked for bread, literally, and he strode into the union hall that was filled with his comrades who had paid a loaf, if they could, to see him sing.

Fist raised, Dean jumped onto the stage and the striking workers from the copper mines began to clap for him. Their wives and their kids clapped. Striking his guitar with one hand, the other held in a clenched fist, Dean sang 'Venceremos', the anthem of the revolution. No one had dared sing this patriotic song since Allende's death; everyone in the hall stood. Everyone began singing, raising their fists for Dean and for liberty. Outside the hall, the security men prowled, their weapons ready, waiting for him.

In Spanish, Dean spoke to the crowd and he was euphoric. A woman put a pendant that belonged to her dead husband around Dean's neck, and he could not get enough.

In Santiago the next day, Dean sang 'Venceremos' again, this time to a group of university students who had never heard it before, because they were too young.

Dean was arrested and deported, although there were some who said he bought his ticket out with the American Express card Paton Price had given him for emergencies. And while he was in Chile, a film maker he knew went everywhere with him, to record Dean's bravery. For a moment, as I looked at this piece of film on Renate's video, I wondered if it was all a set-up for the cameras.

The image of Dean singing in Chile faded. Renate was scared when he went, she said, but oh, by and large, they were happy! Dean made her happy. He even whistled at her when she was especially pretty, although in Germany it was an insult when a man whistled at a woman. They had holidays in the mountains together and she helped him prepare his television shows. She coached him in German. They went skiing. Dean adopted Sasha. He offered, but he never pushed.

'I would like Dean to be my father,' said Sasha and, after a while, he took Dean's name.

Looking up at the video, Renate smiled at the image of Dean on a dirt bike which he rode standing up, playing his guitar.

'He really was crazy,' she said fondly.

After they were married, Renate gave up a good deal of her career; she had a more important role: it was her role to be there for Dean when he came back from his many trips, to entertain his friends and comrades. Life was full: Dean performed and he made movies. His friends from America visited, among them Paton Price, who stayed for six months in order to act as Dean's advisor on *Sing Cowboy Sing*, a cowboy spoof he made. It was shot in Romania because Romania was an excellent double for the Old West. There were barely any television aerials in the Romanian countryside, but Paton hated the food. A million East Germans saw *Sing Cowboy Sing*.

Like a fond mother hen, Renate indulged Dean when his Americans came, for she knew that he missed his own language and its jokes. When Phil Everly was at the house, they carried on like little boys, horsing around together. At a concert at Karl Marx-stadt, Dean and Phil played 'Bye-Bye Love' together, just as Phil and Don had once done.

'One thing is sure,' Phil said. 'Renate sure did love Dean. Some mornings, when he got up to go to the movie studio around six, she got up even earlier, drove her car down the road and waited, so she'd be there to wave him off to work.'

*Wounded Knee* was to be their movie – hers and his. Dean was to star, write and direct the film, whose real title was *Bloody Heart*, but which everyone called *Wounded Knee*. A German–Soviet co-production, it was a love story, set against the Indian uprising in South Dakota in 1978, which ended with a violent shoot-out between the Indians and the FBI. It was a perennial favourite of Soviet propaganda and besides, it had everything Russians loved: war; horses; big set pieces. Most of all, it had Indians. In the Soviet Union, a whole population was obsessed with American Indians. Particularly around Leningrad, kids with a taste for exotica joined Indian clubs, wore feather-head-dresses, practised Indian love calls and mourned the death of the great native culture.

Dean and Renate were to star in it as a divorced couple, she as a reporter, he as a photographer. On assignment at Wounded Knee they are reunited, but, in the tragic finale, Renate's character is shot dead.

By and large, life with Dean was idyllic, Renate said, conjuring up scenes of domestic bliss. They had busy lives, but, from time to time, they stole an evening together. Dean would sit near the fire and play the guitar with Renate stretched out beside him on the bearskin rug. They talked about *Wounded Knee* and how they would spend that summer – the summer of 1986 – filming it together in Yalta, and they looked into each other's eyes.

In the fall of 1985, Dean went to America. Nothing was ever the same again.

'Did Dean want to return to America? Would you have gone with him?'

'I would have no audience there. I would have no career, no job. I do not speak enough English, and I am not young,' Renate said.

'After his trip to Colorado he is missing his homeland very much. He is very homesick. He talks of nothing else,' she said.

Dean came back to her full of hope, wanting to live in America which, to her, was a strange land.

Renate loved Dean deeply; she loved his courage, his thinking, his personality, she said. He was the man she had been waiting for all her life and whom she thought she would never find. He was her *compañero*. Now he was dead.

'After Dean dies I have put away all boxes, all pictures, all. For a while, I can only look at the pictures and cry,' Renate said. She wandered to the window; it was completely dark outside. She shivered and drew the blinds against the night.

'Are you hungry? I have some steaks I may fry,' Renate said eagerly.

Looking at his watch, Victor shook his head. He was thinking about his vacation.

Renate would have liked the company, I thought. It was miserable at the end of that road, near the frozen lake in a silent house that was inhabited only by ghosts. When she talked of Dean, she was perfectly loyal, but there was an ambiguous undercurrent; I thought she was angry at him and very lonesome.

We left the house. Leaving Victor and Leslie near the car, Renate walked me to the little cemetery. In her red coat, she put her hand on my shoulder, as if to steady herself. A bunch of wet flowers lay on Dean's grave, where a rough stone was engraved with the words THE COUPLE REED.

'When Dean is leaving for America, I am so unhappy. I think he is never coming back. He got the stone and he shows me. He says, "I love you and I am coming back and some day we are being buried together under that stone." You understand? I think he believes this,' Renate said.

# PART III

✧

## THE DENVER CLAN

# CHAPTER 14

# Loveland

'My God, it's Dean!'

Johnny Rosenburg was sitting in his chair in Loveland, Colorado, watching the TV. It was the summer of 1984.

Johnny's back was giving him some pain as he shifted in his chair, grabbed the remote and turned up the volume. Yes, by God, it was Dean. It was him. On national TV in, where? In Russia. My God.

'Mona. Mona? Mona!' he called to his wife. 'C'mon in here.'

Johnny got out his scrapbook and looked up that last postcard he had from Dean. 1962. Merry Christmas from South America. All those years he had no idea if Dean was dead or alive.

As Johnny waited for Mona, the memories began to flood him and suddenly it was 1959 and he was a kid with an idea about playing some music.

The year Johnny Rosenburg had his spinal operation, his folks bought him a cheap guitar to pass the time. He always had a desire to get into the music business and he found out he could pick out a few chords and had the ability to take what was in his mind and put it into words and music. The first two songs he wrote were 'Lynda Lea' and 'Gonna Find A Girl'. Somewhat later, 'Lynda Lea' did pretty well in Japan.

Johnny hooked up with Ted Lumus from his home state of Nebraska. Ted was a drummer. They got to jamming together and they got a big old bulky tape recorder and went down in the washroom of Ted's parents' motel and laid two songs down on tape to get that echo effect. You got a good echo effect down in the washroom and Ted's parents were OK about them doing it.

About that time Johnny read in the *Recorder Herald* that there was a Capitol recording artist vacationing at Estes Park, at the Harmony Guest Ranch.

'Let's take these two songs up to him and see what he thinks,' he said to Ted.

'We won't get near him.'

'Well, we never will know 'less we try,' Johnny said.

John and Ted loaded up the old tape recorder and drove up to the Harmony Guest Ranch, where they saw Dean out by that pool. So Johnny walked right up to him and told him who he was.

'I've got a couple of songs here. Would you listen to them?' he said, bold as brass.

Johnny figured at that point Dean would say get lost. But Dean just told one of the girls to go get an extension cord for the tape recorder.

After listening, Dean said, 'I like those songs. I'd like to maybe record one.'

Jesus, Johnny thought to himself. I don't want to be a songwriter. I want to sing my own songs. I want some of that spotlight. But what could he say?

'Well, yeah, sure,' Johnny said to Dean.

On Dean's advice, Johnny and Ted cut a demo. Dean said he would take it out to his manager in Hollywood, and a few weeks later, Johnny got a call from Dean; he was back in Estes Park and he had good news. Johnny went up, Dean grabbed him by the hand and smiled.

'Johnny, I want you to know you're gonna be recording for Capitol and you're gonna have the same manager I've got.'

Ted got dumped, but, well, that was the way these things went.

Needless to say, a young kid like Johnny, from nowhere, he was out of his mind excited. Soon after, Roy Eberharder, Dean's manager, flew in to meet with John and his folks and John signed his manager's contract. That was October. In November, he went on out to California and signed with Capitol.

Dean was living out in Canoga Park with Roy Eberharder and Mrs Eberharder and their son, Dale. I had trouble finding Canoga on the map, and, according to Dean's official file, at the time, he was living in Sherman Oaks. Still, as Johnny put it, they lived in one of Shirley Temple's older houses, that she rented out, set on a hillside overlooking Canoga. Johnny moved into Dean's room with him.

Sometimes Johnny found himself alone in the evenings. Other times he'd be gone on the road and Dean'd be there by himself. Most of the time, though they were both there together.

They never went around as a pair, and the only time they were together was at the house, in the evenings, or if, during the daytime, neither one had anything much to do. They'd just lounge around, go out to play badminton, go down to Canoga Park, kick some dust. There wasn't much to do.

Out in Canoga Park, as John recalled, things were going pretty good for both of them, though they never really discussed each other's careers. One evening, Dean and Johnny were at the house alone together. Johnny was thinking about his work, figuring he was getting on O.K. He didn't think it was a bad life. Dean was crazy upset, though.

'I'm never going to get any work if I keep this guy as manager. I don't know about you, but I'm getting out on my own.' he said.

Johnny told Dean he was nuts.

Almost the next day, Dean disappeared. Johnny, who sometimes didn't see him for days anyway, didn't give it much thought for a while. Then he began to wonder. He found Roy.

'Where's Dean?' Johnny said.

'The S O B thinks he can do better for himself,' said Roy.

Johnny let it drop, he was busy trying to keep his own head above water, trying to do his own thing. That was the latter part of 1960, Johnny thought, but in fact, it was in 1961 when Dean left for Chile.

'I sure have had a lot of company since meeting up with Deano again,' Johnny said, inviting me to sit on the two-seater couch in his living room in Loveland.

The road from Denver to Loveland was dead flat; the countryside looked half an hour old. The snow had melted, the sun was warm and it shone on a scatter of wooden buildings set down at random on the raw yellow scrublands. Denver wasn't a mountain town at all; it was the last stop at the edge of a huge prairie, flat as a pancake and barely domesticated. This was the end of the world for the pioneers, the last outpost before they launched themselves with incredible will over the Rockies and on to God knew what beyond. For the early settlers, they might as well have been headed for the moon, so remote was the coast.

Loveland was like an encampment of covered wagons made suburbia in the wilderness: the Rockies were purple and huge in the background; in the foreground was a little grid of streets with small suburban cottages laid out in neat patterns. Kids ran between the houses, or rode bicycles and skateboards.

At Janice Court, Johnny Rosenburg's house was patrolled by big green pines and the screen door, which was unlocked, banged in a comforting way.

The living room had flocked yellow wallpaper and some oil paintings in gold frames. There was a big chair, and a television set. An archway led into a kitchen, where the fridge was dotted with magnets shaped like fruits. On the wall was a precious collection of fancy commemorative plates.

On the table next to the couch was a well-worn Bible, with a brass cross for a bookmark sticking out of it. Johnny, who sat in the armchair, touched it from time to time as we talked. In his late forties, he wore a plaid shirt and jeans and cowboy boots, and he shifted his weight in his chair like a man in constant pain. All his life he'd had a bad back. Or maybe it was just that he was weary of the constant callers who'd turned up at his screen door since Dean died.

But he was a self-possessed man, damaged by disappointment and lost chances, maybe, but with a humorous, long-suffering look and a great talent for storytelling. From the time I met Johnny Rosenburg and heard his stories about how he met up with Dean Reed after a quarter of a century and how Dean came home again to Colorado, I could never get the rhythms of Johnny's speech out of my head.

This chunky, pleasant man in a Denver suburb was what Dean Reed might have been if Dean had stayed home. They had been close as that. In the fall of 1985, a year after he saw Dean on the TV, Johnny met up with him again, and it changed his life. After years of failure and illness, he rediscovered his long-lost buddy, Dean Reed who had become a star. Johnny was illuminated by it.

'This is Mona,' he said, as a well-built woman in jeans came through the screen door carrying a brown paper bag full of groceries.

She had a steady blue gaze and a face out of a Dorothea Lange photograph. Mona was one of twelve children. She had worked three jobs since John's illness and now their eldest girl, Pamela, was in college. She was very proud, but she was quiet. You knew that at the Rosenburg house, Mona ran things, but she always deferred to her husband. We shook hands and Mona went to put up some coffee in what she and John referred to as the 'world's loudest coffee pot'. Mona usually called him John, which was his true Christian name.

After Dean left Hollywood for Chile, things didn't go right for John. He had just signed a seven-year contract with Capitol and was back in Loveland on a visit to his folks and Roy Eberharder called him on the phone.

'Johnny, I got bad news for you. Capitol dropped you,' Roy said.

'What?!' Johnny said, not believing his ears.

'Well, they've got a new policy. If you don't make it big in the first record, that's it.'

Johnny stopped his story to take some coffee from Mona. Then he shrugged some and said there was nothing to explain why he was dropped so suddenly from the music business in the early sixties. He'd been doing O.K. Won a big talent contest in New Orleans. Played Ocean City Park in California, for example, where he did a show with Dirty Stevens.

'She had a big hit out at that time called, "Tan Shoes and Pink Shoelaces". Do you remember her?' Johnny said.

I tried very hard to remember because it seemed so important to him.

'I can't understand why things turned out for Dean and me the way they did.' Johnny said.

I asked what he thought.

'You know, it's really hard to say. I don't know. I don't understand that anymore than I understand why I was treated the way I was,' Johnny said. 'You know, the people that were judges on that panel for that contest, people who are supposed to be able to identify talent when they see it, they picked me and then they didn't want to work with me. There I was on Capitol along with Dean, I had songs that were doing quite well. I don't know why, all of a sudden, I was no longer around.'

'Maybe the business was too mean for you,' I said.

'Maybe,' he said. 'Maybe you had to be mean. Or very sold on yourself, because that's what Dean was. He wasn't doing that great back then. He had to pay his own way to South America where he heard he had a hit with "My Summer Romance".

'He had to pay his own way,' Johnny said again. 'Nobody was sold on Dean more than Dean himself. You know that was it. I mean Dean knew some day, some way, he was going to be a hit. He knew he was going to be a hit one way or the other. I hoped I would be a hit. Hope wasn't enough,' he said.

Johnny crossed his foot over his leg and rested a scrapbook on it. He opened the brittle pages. There were some publicity stills of Johnny Rose, which was his professional name and, as a young man, in his way, Johnny was as handsome as Dean.

Hesitating for a minute, Johnny added: 'Dean disappeared. The first I heard from him was 1962 or '63 more than a year later. He was in South America. He was already a star. I had a postcard. Just like that. Wishing me a Merry Christmas. Then, nothing, not till I saw him on television right here in this room, what, four years ago.'

After he saw him on TV in 1984, Johnny had one hell of a time running down Dean's number over there in East Berlin. He called the TV station in Denver. He called NBC in New York. London said they'd get back to him, but he couldn't wait. Up half the night in a growing frenzy, he called in succession: the State Department; the Russian Embassy, who were not very nice; and the East Germans, who were. Eventually he got a telephone number in East Berlin. When he heard the operator's voice, he just went bananas.

'United States calling for Mr Dean Reed.'

Dean picked up the phone. Just like that.

'Dean, this is an old friend of yours back here in the United States. Does the name Johnny Rose ring a bell?'

Dean didn't remember.

Johnny reminded him they recorded on Capitol together, that his birth name was Rosenburg, but he recorded under Johnny Rose, how they met at Estes Park, how Dean helped him.

Dean remembered. Of course he remembered.

Johnny told him he made the TV news back in Colorado. Dean asked if Johnny was still in the singing business. Johnny told him he underwent spinal surgery in 1981 and couldn't work. They exchanged news about their families and promised to write each other. It was almost crying time for Johnny.

'My God, man, keep in touch, write to me,' he said.

That's how it got started. The renewed friendship got cranked up as they wrote each other, and, a while later, Dean told Johnny he was coming back to Colorado for the Denver Film Festival, fall of 1985. Some fellow called Will Roberts had made a documentary film about Dean. *American Rebel* was its title. It was more than twenty years since Deano'd been back to Colorado.

From things Dean was saying in his letters, Johnny could see he was a big star over there. Big like Michael Jackson. Johnny figured Dean thought people would know him in Denver, but nobody at all knew him back home. It worried John considerably.

You are a a big star over there, buddy, but nobody knows you back in your hometown, Johnny thought. Then he said to himself: 'John, you are a song writer, why can't you work something out here.' So he wrote a song called 'Nobody Knows Me Back in My Hometown'.

'You think he'll laugh at it?' Johnny asked Mona.

'So what? You've had people laugh at your songs before,' said Mona.

Johnny sent it on over and Dean flipped for it. Dean sang it at the Youth Festival in Moscow, the summer of 1985. A couple of months later, he called Johnny to say he was coming to Colorado and would arrive on October 16. It was definitely the 16th. Johnny had all the dates firmly set in his mind; he recorded their first telephone call; he put his memories down on tapes, which he played for me when I saw him in Loveland, and later he sent me other tapes. As a storyteller he was a natural. It was all there on tape. It was uncanny. It was as if Johnny knew that one day someone would make the movie.

Now, in his living room, he shook his head in wonder and despair, because Dean was dead. But that could not erase the pleasure of their reunion.

'When he came back in 1985, I had not seen him, for what? For more than twenty years,' Johnny said.

# CHAPTER 15

# Denver Again

'My God, man, you kept all your hair. Look at me,' Johnny said right off the bat when Deano came off the plane at Stapleton Airport. He just burst out of that plane door like the biggest star you ever saw. He looked terrific. He was forty-seven years old.

Dean was in something of a daze, John could tell. There was some press, but not like John would have liked. Dean had written maybe there could be a horse parade and the mayor could meet him at the capitol. It had happened in Eastern Europe and he was accustomed to the fanfare. John had called a few TV stations.

'Guess who's coming to town?' Johnny said.

'Dean WHOOO?' was what people usually said back.

Johnny had the date Dean arrived engraved in his head: the 16th of October, 1985. Mona was real excited. As boys, they were like the same person: Dean Reed, Johnny Rose, they were two peas in a pod. Their pictures hung together on the wall at Johnny's mom's house. After staring at Dean's mug on the wall at her in-laws' house for all those years, it was real exciting for Mona to meet him for the first time.

Mona got introduced. God, he was a handsome man! she thought when she first laid eyes on Dean.

The first thing Johnny noticed was that, to his ear, at least, Dean had developed something of a foreign accent – which the female race found very sexy, including Mona. But in a way he hadn't really changed all that much.

But then Dean was swept off down to Denver by the film people for a party of the stars, who were in town for the festival.

Mona and Johnny jumped in Johnny's Ford Elite and drove home to Loveland real fast to tape the news coverage. As they ran

into the house, they turned the set on. They saw Dean stepping
out of his limo at the Westin Hotel downtown.

Dean couldn't recognise a thing. Although he had been back to
the USA a few times, he had not been home to Colorado for a
real visit since his high-school reunion in 1963. The thing that
struck Johnny right away was that, when Dean came back to
Denver and went out on his own, he couldn't find where he'd
grown up, and it upset him a lot. The only buildings Dean
recognised were those he had seen on television.

'Dynasty' made Denver famous. It was the perfect soap, the
quintessential fairy tale for the Reagan years: rich people in shoulder
pads doing evil things to one another while having a marvellous
time spending loads of money. It was the most popular show in
the world and its logo, which consisted of shots of Denver's
glittering skyline, gave the city its profile. In Germany, Dynasty
was called Der Denver-Klan, and when Dean came home, the only
map he had in his head of the place where he was born was from
the opening credits of a soap opera he watched in a foreign country
in a foreign language.

Like everyone in East Berlin, he watched both 'Dynasty' and
'Dallas' obsessively. You can't jam television signals and, before
the Wall came down, when there was an East Germany, the
television shows broadcast by the West Germans played in the
East. This was a weapon better than a million Allied soldiers; this
was propaganda you could not buy for a million bucks. Naturally,
the citizens of the German Democratic Republic infinitely preferred
low doings in American cities to lessons in the manufacture of
neon, not to mention dancing girls in animal suits singing 'Winter
Wonderland'.

What's more, because the West German television signals were
too weak to reach beyond East Berlin, the rest of the population
of East Germany made a terrible fuss. It wanted 'Dynasty', too,
and so, in the end, the East Germans were forced to run it
themselves. Now everyone saw the good life: fruit in profusion,
big cars, big blondes. There are a thousand fancy notions about
what finally destroyed the Berlin Wall, but the truth is, it was
Crystal Carrington, the platinum-blonde star of 'Dynasty', who
brought the Wall down.

On the evenings when 'Dynasty' was broadcast, no one went

out. In East Berlin, people pulled down the blinds, not altogether, in fact, because of politics, but because the soaps were *non kulturny*, and all Germans liked to think of themselves as cultured, if nothing else. At the house at 6A Schmockwitzer Damm, the Reeds, more than most, were glued to the television the night *Der Klan* was on.

The Friday after he arrived in Denver, Dean did a radio show with Peter Boyles. Johnny warned Dean not to go on Boyles' show. Communism was not flavour of the month in those days; no one knew much about this Gorbachev guy; Reagan was talking Evil Empire. Boyles was also one angry son-of-a-bitch. The host of the Denver talk-radio station, he could be mean as hell.

'Don't do it, Dean, You're being set up. Don't do it,' said Johnny.

'Johnny, I have played my songs in thirty-two countries and I have risked my life for the things I believe. You don't think that I am afraid of some guy on a radio show, do you?'

'It's seven after the hour of nine o'clock on a Friday, the 17th of October, in Denver . . . you heard it through the grapevine,' said Boyles' voice from the Fairmont Hotel lounge, where he was broadcasting.

The music switched over from Martha and the Vandellas to Dean Reed singing, a ballad thing about Sacco and Vanzetti. Dean called them Nicola and Bart . . .

In Loveland, Mona and John listened to the radio as the music faded fast and Boyles' voice came up again.

'That was the voice of Dean Reed,' Boyles' voice said. 'And this is gonna be a difficult interview. Dean Reed . . . was born right here in Colorado and now lives in East Berlin. He's back in Denver for the première of a documentary film about his life at the festival, and he's a major star in the Eastern Bloc and parts of South and Central America.'

Johnny could tell from Boyles' voice that he wasn't real convinced. He got him confused with John Reed, too, that American who helped the Russian Revolution way back when.

'Do you consider yourself a defector?' Boyles said.

'Not at all, Peter. I consider myself an American patriot,' Dean said, his voice real firm and cool. 'I'm a good American, Peter. I can take a sword 360 degrees around my head and cut no strings. I'm a puppet of no one, Peter.'

Boyles kept egging Dean on, implying he was a traitor, a communist, a defector. Dean started getting mad.

'Peter, I resent that. Dean Reed is not what you say. Dean Reed believes in equality for all mankind. You sound like a fascist . . . ' He just ploughed right on in. 'There's a worldwide famine. You're talking just like the neo-Nazis that killed Berg.'

'Don't you ever accuse me of that,' Boyles screamed.

'That's the way you're talking.' Dean stuck it to him again.

'Get out of here! Get out of here! Take a walk . . . '

Johnny listened to the radio and thought: Jesus, man, I told you Boyles' best friend was Alan Berg, the talk-radio guy who was murdered by the neo-Nazis. Johnny knew those old Nazi boys were gonna be sitting up there in Idaho now, watching for Dean. He thought: Man, if you stick around here, you had better get yourself a bullet-proof vest.

'Take a walk . . . ' Boyles said.

Boyles threw Deano off the air, but what startled Johnny was, in the background, along with the noise of scuffling, he could just about make out Dean's voice. He was whistling.

That night, because of the Boyles affair, when *American Rebel* premièred, a squad of police cars cruised the Tivoli Center in downtown Denver.

Jesus, Johnny thought. But in the end it went O. K.

Johnny had bought about twenty-something tickets for the show and inside the Tivoli's movie theatre, he and Mona and the others settled in their seats. The lights went down, the film came on and *American Rebel* opened in a black-and-white, rain-streaked Moscow street. In the next sequence, Dean was mobbed by fans in Red Square. The film maker, Will Roberts, described how he was visiting Moscow when he came across the scene and asked his interpreter what was going on. His interpreter was Oleg Smirnoff.

'That's Dean Reed,' Oleg said.

'Who's Dean Reed?' said the film maker.

'Why, Dean Reed is the most famous American in the world,' said Oleg.

Johnny just laid back and enjoyed himself, although he wondered how Dean could expect anyone in America to reach out with open arms to him when, in the next sequence, he was sitting there in that film singing 'Ghost Riders in the Sky' to Arafat.

'You must be kidding me,' Johnny said to himself, as he was prone to do. Arafat just sat there with that checkered tablecloth on his head, tapping his fingers on the table in time to the music, while his boys danced around with their guns held aloft, like they were toy guns.

Considering the adverse reaction to the Boyles business in the Denver press, not to mention the Arafat thing, there wasn't much trouble that night at the film festival. After the show, folks gathered to welcome Dean, and pretty soon he was inserted into the Denver life, as if he had never been away.

Except that Dean never heard from Barry Fay again. Denver's big rock promoter, Fay got in touch with Dean when he arrived, but after the Boyles business he dropped it. Fay and Boyles were thick as maple syrup.

That was Friday. On Monday, Johnny went down to Denver to pick Dean up and bring him to Loveland for a stay. He had all the details of Dean's visit clearly recorded in his head and on tape, as well, and he sent me the tapes faithfully.

'Is that all motor?' Dean said appreciatively, when he saw Johnny's Ford Elite.

'It sure is,' said John.

'It's a typical American car, lots of power,' Dean added.

'I wouldn't have a small car, they scare me to death,' John said.

'Renate is the same way,' said Dean.

As John drove through downtown Denver, Dean went on just ranting and raving about how wonderful it was.

'Well, Dean, you call yourself a country boy but you like this sort of thing. A town that has more than one stop light is too big for me,' John said.

'Johnny, you just don't know how to live.'

'So how come you left Hollywood?' Johnny wanted to know.

'They sold out my contract to some guys from the Mafia,' Dean said.

'Are you sure about that, man?' Johnny asked, because he considered Dean's response pretty paranoid. 'I don't remember it like that. I thought they were just a couple of guys from Abilene Kansas with a Cadillac dealership who bought you out,' said Johnny.

Dean didn't answer.

In Loveland, Johnny pulled into the driveway in Janice Court. Everyone in the neighbourhood was hanging around. Johnny had explained in no uncertain terms just how big Dean was in the entertainment business.

When he just leaped out of the car and said 'Hi' and shook their hands, they nearly dropped dead of shock.

Mona came out to greet Dean. He put his stuff in the house and, grabbing his camera, climbed the ladder at the shed in the back yard and began taking pictures. The mountains were exceptionally beautiful that fall. Every time Mona Rosenburg looked out of the kitchen window, she felt glad to be alive.

'You just know that when Dean looked out of our west window and saw those mountains, his heart must have had a flutter,' Mona said to Johnny later on.

In the week in Loveland, Dean rode a neighbour-boy's motorcycle, threw a football – he forgot how hard it was to throw a spiral and how much fun – ate Mona's pecan pie, gave her little love bites on her neck, left his room a mess, and spoke German with Pamela, the Rosenburgs' daughter, who was studying the language.

Dean sang for the kids and juggled and walked on his hands for fifteen minutes at a go. He admired the way Mona and John kidded each other – they had lost a child once and joking kept them going through the hard times.

The sun shone all week long. Dean and John drove over to Collins to buy cowboy stuff that was on sale and Dean thought the 'fifty per cent off' sign was a capitalist trick. He bought a belt buckle, but did not have Dean Reed put it on because they did not make a big thing of personalities over there. Instead he had L O V E put on it.

He gave interviews to the local press. He took Mona and John to a party given by *Denver* magazine, which pleased them since they didn't ordinarily brush shoulders with the type of people who went to those parties, such as the deejay, Gary Tessler. Mona saw how Dean held all those people spellbound with his baby blues.

Nights, after supper, John and Dean sat up late and talked. They talked religion and Johnny thought Dean was more an agnostic than an atheist, although he did some research and found out Marxism is a religion and Marxism is atheism. Dean told Johnny *Michael* Gorbachev was going to make big changes; John had the idea Dean had a talk with Big Mike. Dean always called him Michael.

They batted ideas around.

'Over here we have a tough freedom. A lot of people might run back to Russia.' Johnny said. 'Anyhow, how come you only talk politics. You're an actor, aren't you?' Johnny added.

'Why can't I be both? It worked for Reagan,' said Dean.

Dean laughed and so did Johnny, but Johnny had the feeling Dean meant it.

But, sometimes, Dean would be laughing, kidding and feeling he could be the first one hundred per cent genuine international superstar, then he would drop way down. Johnny found him one night, reading an article that was pretty tough on him. Dean's mood fell apart.

'It's just one article, Dean,' Johnny said.

'You just don't understand, Johnny,' said Dean.

But in the mornings, Dean would straddle his chair backwards and eat his Wheaties.

'Breakfast of Champions,' he would say and hug Mona.

Dean was a big hugger and it made John uneasy, but Mona loved it. So did Pamela and her brother, Eric, who went by the nickname of Bull. After breakfast, the phones began ringing off the wall, people wanting to talk to Dean.

'Let's shut down the telephones, Dean, and go up in the mountains,' Johnny said.

'Johnny, I'm not vacationing here. I got to lay the groundwork for when I come back.' It was already in his mind.

'I am coming back. I am coming back, and one day we will be buried together under that boulder,' Dean had told Renate before he left home for America, because she was so scared of his leaving. And when Dean took her call early one morning at Johnny's house, she was more scared than ever. The Boyles radio show bust-up made the news in East Berlin and it was reported that Dean's life was threatened. Dean reassured her over the phone.

'I am not being buried under that boulder, Johnny,' he told his friend late that night. That was the night that Dean told Johnny socialism let him down. He told him he was not proud of having been married three times and that he loved Renate a whole lot. He was very firm in that, although she was awfully jealous, he said.

'Before I left, she thought I was not coming back. I got a boulder and I said, Renate, I love you and I am coming back and you and I are being buried under that boulder. But, Johnny, I am not being buried under that boulder. I do not want to die in a country that is not my own,' he said.

There was a party on Dean's last night in Loveland and Johnny made a video. At sundown, everyone danced in the Rosenburgs' backyard to Phil Collins on the cassette player. Dixie was there. She came up to Loveland for the party.

Dean did the Twist and everyone laughed at him because he was so old-fashioned. Dixie showed him how to dance 1985. 'Pornographic dancing,' Dean called it.

He quit dancing at one point, and walked on his hands for a while, then he grabbed Johnny and arm wrestled him.

'That's the first thing I always had to do with my dad every time I came to see him. We could never really talk, so we did this stuff,' Dean said.

Afterwards, in Johnny's basement with the upright piano, Dean gave a concert. As it turned out, it was his only concert in America. He was wonderful. He sang practically his entire repertoire. He told jokes. He did political schtick. He kidded the little kids.

Kids, old people, toddlers, Johnny's neighbours and friends sat on chairs or on the floor. A little apart, crouched against the wall, was Dixie.

All that night, Johnny was aware of Dixie, some woman Deano met down in Denver. She was some kind of rival for Dean, although Johnny did not put it that way. 'I want to let you know that I've told Dean, when he comes back, I've got a place for him to stay,' Dixie said.

'That's real nice, Dixie. That's really nice,' Johnny said, although Dean always had a place with him and Mona. Johnny would always be there for him.

At the end of the concert, Dean scanned the room.

'Now I want to thank someone here. I want to say thanks to Johnny. I helped Johnny Rose back in Estes Park, then he came to Hollywood and I left.'

'Couldn't stand the competition,' Johnny called out from the back of the room, ducking his head with delight.

'Right. Anyway, John got in touch after almost twenty-five

years. He wrote this song for me,' Dean said. 'John, do you want to sing this with me? Come on up here.'

With a diffident shrug that did not conceal the thrill he felt, Johnny ambled up to the front of the room. Together, he and Dean sang 'Nobody Knows Me Back in My Hometown'.

After the concert, there was ice cream and cake, and because they knew Dean was leaving the next day, people were reluctant to go. Johnny's neighbours were taken with how nice he was and one, a woman called Fran who was a devout Christian, later told Johnny that Dean was the most Christ-like man she had ever encountered. As the party broke up, Dixie remained behind; she was the last to go.

Plunking himself down on the Rosenburgs' sofa, after Dixie left, Dean said, 'She is in love with me. There is nothing that she wouldn't do for me.'

Looking at Dean, Johnny thought: If Renate was here and she looked into Dixie's eyes, and she is as jealous as you said, you'd be in a whole heap of trouble, boy.

The next morning, Dean left Colorado.

Mona couldn't bring herself to go to the airport. 'That was a sad day,' said Mona. 'They had been apart so long and we didn't know when he'd come back and, as it turned out, he never did come back at all.'

Mona said this on one of the tapes Johnny sent me. At the end of it, Johnny added: 'Dean was a confused man, and after he left Colorado he was even more confused. How can I convey what I felt about Dean, what my family felt. We loved him and he loved us, but we're not the only ones of this planet that he loved, I know that. If anybody ever got to know Dean, a piece of them died when he died. He did what no other American did – Dean became a superstar in a part of the world we call our enemy.'

In exquisitely recollected detail, the taped accounts Johnny sent me conveyed his memories of Dean's week in Loveland. If Dean had stolen away a piece of Johnny's life when he left for South America all those years ago, he had given it back.

Letters from Johnny followed. We had discussed the casting for the Dean Reed film, joking around about who would play Johnny. If it was Robert Redford, Mona wrote, she was going to play

herself, and she sent along a jar of her pickled beets, which I had
enjoyed in Loveland.

'We're pleased to hear the tapes were acceptable. Gotta tell you
it's crazy how we remember even more as the days go by,' wrote
Johnny.

Johnny also enclosed a note from Dean, which Mona forgot to
put in with the beets.

Dear Johnny,
   Damn. Why didn't we take the time to go fishing for a week, and
in the evening we could have built a fire and with the stars for a
roof we could have discussed so many things.

# CHAPTER 16

# Wheat Ridge

Outside the Tivoli Center, Dixie passed the time waiting for Dean by eavesdropping on a couple of police radios. Dixie could read police code. She had been to the Miami Convention in 1972 with her husband, who was big on Nixon and had FBI protection. To pass the time, the FBI guy taught Dixie to read the codes.

Because of Dean's bust-up with Peter Boyles on the radio the morning before, there were plenty of cops at the Film Festival. On the warm September evening, they cruised the center, their windows down, their radios on. The second showing of *American Rebel* was on Saturday night and Dixie couldn't get a ticket, but she figured, what the heck, she'd go along and if she couldn't get in, maybe she'd run into Dean.

Half in the shadow, Dixie watched people going to the show. She let her mind wander on the subject of Dean, recalling how there weren't many cowboys around Wheat Ridge, let alone an older one that even talked to them. Once, Doug Dana gave her a 1955 *Wheat Ridge Annual*. It had a picture of Dean in the play, *Pistol Pete*, serenading the girls. Then he went to Hollywood; she was just a kid and . . .

She saw him.

Bounding out of a car, Dean strode up the steps of the Tivoli Center. Without thinking, Dixie darted out from the shadow into the light.

'Dean? Hi, I'm Dixie,' she said eagerly.

Dean was nonplussed.

'We used to ride and swim together. Don't you remember?' she said.

He didn't know who this woman was. People were always

waiting for him in the damnedest places – outside his house, at concerts. Being nice to people was what he did. It made his time on the planet count for something.

'Little Dixie! Of course, I remember. *Ja,*' said Dean effusively.

It was weird how he had that little German accent, Dixie thought. It was kind of nice. Dean introduced Dixie to his mother, Mrs Brown. Mrs Brown didn't remember Dixie either, but why would she? As a kid, Dean had lots of friends she never particularly met, so she greeted Dixie and smiled.

After the show, Dean invited Dixie back to visit with him at the Westin Hotel. In her own words, she thought it was so unique that Dean would be her friend. He was the same slim cowboy she had seen as a child. He spent the evening with her and sang her three songs so gently. In public he told the same three stories over and over, as if he'd memorised them, but, alone with her, he opened up. When he told her he wanted to think about coming home, he cried.

They met again in the week he was in Colorado. He told her that he loved Renate, but that he did not want to die in East Germany. It would be hard for Renate to work in America. Dixie said she would help find Renate a job. He talked to her about his need for America, about the movie he was making, about peace and love.

During the week, she met Johnny and Mona and their friends; it was so special: Dean let her be one of their group. And before he left Denver, she was already at work for him, thinking about his career in America, looking for the props he needed for the movie he was going to make that summer. For *Wounded Knee,* as he called his movie, she sought out Indian artifacts and she found a vintage Marlboro sign that was exactly right for the period.

'You're fantastic,' Dean said to her over the phone from Loveland. 'Would you like to come up here? We're having a bye-bye Dean party.'

She said she would love to come and asked if she could set up a fan club for Dean in America.

For the party in Loveland, Dixie wore slacks, high-heeled boots and a white silk blouse. As she danced with Dean in the Rosenburgs' yard to a Phil Collins tune, she was a very pretty woman. The next morning, Dean left for Los Angeles.

★

As the memories escaped from Dixie, her face had the same adrenalin glow I had seen during the mad ride in the pick-up truck. We sat in her small house in Wheat Ridge. She held a large grey cardboard box of Dean's letters in her arms. It was winter again. The pick-up truck was parked out front. The dog, called Bear, sat in the window, licking the pane.

'Say hello to Bear,' said Dixie.

I said hello to Bear.

Dixie looked in the fridge.

'There's orange. There's cola,' she said.

'Orange, thanks,' I said.

It was Dixie's father's house, but she rented it out and kept only a room for herself. Most of the time she lived in the mountains at Grand Junction. Her few possessions were crammed into the box she held.

Dixie looked older than when I first met her a year earlier. Thinking about Dean's death had worn her down. His letters were all she had, except for a few ballpoint pens with the legend: 'Colorado is Dean Reed Country'.

'Have some,' she said. 'I guess you could say they're a rarity now.' She gave me a few cheap pens and tried to smile.

In the box was a jumble of audio tapes. She taped all of Dean's telephone calls. She put one in the telephone answering machine and I heard the recording of a telephone ringing. Then Dean's voice came up, nice and sweet, as if he lived in that plastic box, waiting only for Dixie to give him life. They exchanged salutations between Wheat Ridge and East Berlin.

'Is that me calling you, or you calling me?' Dean's voice said. 'Are you just waking up? Did you have nice dreams? Are you a member of the Denver Klan?' he joked. Dean seemed to be entombed inside the scratched plastic cassette case and the tapes had the creepy vitality of relics, as discomfiting as a saint's toe-bone in a glass box.

'Why did you make tapes of Dean's calls?' I asked.

'I just like hearing his voice. Not just then, but all my life.' Dixie said, giggling like a geisha.

That night we had dinner at the Rattlesnake Club inside the Tivoli Center. Dixie showed me the steps where she and Dean first met.

The restaurant had fat copper brewing vats – it had once been a brewery – pushed halfway through the floors like unexploded bombs. The distressed walls looked like the consequence of a tasteful war. The waiters wore Topsiders and pink Ralph Lauren shirts, as if they were Yalies or yachtsmen. Only a few tables were occupied. Dixie, thin in her short white fur jacket, looked bewildered, as if she did not know whom to trust.

We talked about Dean and she offered me the cardboard box with the letters and the tapes. The next day, I went back to the little house in Wheat Ridge and, with a kind of obscene speed, I took the box and left town as soon as I could, as if she might change her mind about the treasure. In the box, in the tapes and letters, lay the details of Dean's desire; after the wonderful week in Colorado, he wanted to come home to America so badly he could taste it, and Dixie conspired with him to make it happen.

When Dean left Colorado, he went to Los Angeles to look for a manager, but he spent most of his time talking into answering machines. Everyone Dean knew was out of town: The Everly Brothers were in Australia making a video; Jane Fonda was away. No one answered his calls and he hated the smog.

A fellow named Levinson was interested in working for Dean, but Dean did not trust him; he felt Levinson would sit on his ass and wait for Dean to perform, then come in for his twenty per cent. He told Dixie this on the phone, told her this was the America he hated, said that Hollywood was worse than the killing fields of Cambodia, because you never knew who your friends were. As soon as things went awry for Dean, he stiffened up his morale with the political rhetoric he could wrap around him like a familiar blanket.

Ramona was the other reason Dean went to Los Angeles, he told Dixie. Ramona was his daughter by Patty and he wanted her to take his name. Mrs Brown said it was true that Dean was keen on Ramona, who visited him in East Berlin. Ramona wanted to make Dean's life story as a Hollywood movie.

I saw a snapshot once of Dean's children: Ramona, Natasha, Sasha, and they were an oddly assorted bunch: Ramona, the hefty, self-possessed American teenager; Sasha, the only boy in the group, the East German who wore his privilege as uneasily as he wore his skinny black leather pants; Natasha, the pale little girl, left out in the middle.

All his life, Dean put his back into getting the hard currency he needed to send money to Patty for Ramona. But, according to

Dixie, Ramona would have nothing to do with Dean before or after that trip to Los Angeles and it nearly broke his heart. In the spring of 1986, he sent Dixie a copy of a letter he wrote to Ramona to commemorate her eighteenth birthday.

He called her his 'Dearest Daughter' and told of his sorrow that he was often not there when she needed him. He told her life was not black and white. He passed on the many homilies Paton Price had preached to him. The letter, full of political sentiment so syrupy you could spoon it on, was couched in the most intimate terms. Nonetheless, Dean sent Dixie a copy. I guessed everything felt more real to Dean if there were an audience.

In Los Angeles, Dean stayed with Tillie Price, Paton's widow. For Paton was dead now. Dean went to visit his grave and was terribly sad. 'Oh Tillie, how I miss him,' he said. In the house where Paton Price once taught his students the meaning of life, Dean sat on the bed in his room, wondering if anyone would ever call him back. A second Hollywood career seemed a pipe dream. Sure, he'd amassed $300,000 in a West Berlin bank from residuals on his movies, but in L.A. he discovered $300,000 wouldn't buy a chicken coop. Tillie's house looked like a chalet in the Austrian Tirol, where she was born – all cuckoo clocks and dark wood. Dean wished he was back in Colorado.

Tillie gave a little party.

'Don Murray and Kent McCord came,' Dean told Dixie. 'I asked Kent if he could get me an agent and he said only Jack Fields, who is Ed Asner's agent, is brave enough politically. For the last five years, Kent has only worked ten days because he led a strike against a studio. Haskell Wexler – I know him from Chile and Nicaragua – said the same thing.'

At the party was Maura McGivney, an old girlfriend of Dean's from Hollywood days. Of the old gang, only Maura still came by to see Mrs Price, who was old and unwell and called herself 'Silly Tillie'. Maura McGivney fussed over her because it made Maura important. Dean's coming was a huge event in that dark little house of women.

'When Dean was here, he used to leap out of bed in the morning and run out to the pool for a swim, naked, with a huge erection, singing "Oh What a Beautiful Morning",' Maura told me when I visited. Tillie was embarrassed.

★

All the time Dean was in Los Angeles, Dixie was looking for props he needed for his movie. She was looking to buy a South Dakota police car.

'I went to South Dakota,' Dixie said on the phone when Dean called her.

'My daughter wants to become a singer,' Dean said.

The conversation had the dreamy quality of two people dawdling down different paths, but hoping to meet up.

'Nothing much is happening. It's not as nice as Colorado. The smog is terrible,' he added.

There was some talk about *Wounded Knee*. Dean said he was down in the dumps.

'I'll be leaving on Monday to go to Minneapolis. I'm not having as good a time as I did in Colorado,' he said again. He was flirting with Dixie, wanting her to say she'd come on to meet him, without having to ask.

'Would you fly out and spend some time with me in Ohio?' he said finally. She said she would come to Minneapolis.

The bravado evaporated. 'It gets on my nerves. I've been calling people in Hollywood and I haven't talked to anyone except recorders,' Dean said. Dixie was sympathetic. It must be awful for Deano out there.

'I would love to spend the night with you tonight,' Dean said suddenly.

'If I thought that was true I'd trip over my own two feet,' Dixie said.

Dean went on tour with *American Rebel* across America. In Minnesota, where he had friends, he met Dixie. It was there they agreed that she could be his manager and help pave the way for his triumphal return to America. She would be Dean's Colonel Parker. Dean had fallen in love with America.

Dean wrote to her from Kennedy Airport in New York on November 15, 1985.

Dear Dixie,
I am sitting at John F. Kennedy Airport . . . and would like to write you a couple of my thoughts and emotions. I have spent five weeks in my homeland this time more than at any other time during the last twenty-five years. The trip was the happiest trip I've ever made to America. I've seen my blue skies again and my battery was recharged.

151

I saw my mountains and remembered my boyhood years. I saw so many faces of my homeland: Denver, L.A., Minneapolis, Columbus, New York; so many people, so many histories and past experiences. But all, I believe, must have a common future, a future of peace . . . I believe I have a role in bringing these changes about. It is time I returned to my own land and try to do what I have done in thirty-two other countries.

First I shall make *Wounded Knee* the very best movie that is possible, in the hopes it can bring laughter, inspiration and knowledge. One step at a time . . . I shall be back soon. Bye–bye for now.

He signed it Dean. Dixie sent Dean a bumper sticker that read 'You can't hug children with nuclear arms.'

When Dean left America, Dixie feared losing track of him again. She feared he would hate them all for the actions of a few. She tried to call JFK Airport the afternoon Dean was to leave, to beg him to know not all Americans were Peter Boyles. But she could not reach him.

After that, Dixie spent a lot of time with some friends trying to reach a righteous decision about how to help Dean. The afternoon she received his first letter, she was so relieved she cried for six hours. 'I am very happy to be part of your Colorado world and eager to make Colorado another home for you, again!' Dixie wrote to Dean, adding if ever she stepped on his toes, or Renate's or Sasha's, he was to tell her plain.

Dean returned to Germany in the middle of November. It was a busy winter for Dean, what with the film and an album in the works, but they talked on the phone frequently and exchanged letters. With Dixie at the end of the line, America was never out of Dean's head; he was forty-seven years old; he wanted to go home.

Often, Dixie's letters ran to six or eight pages, single spaced. In January, Dixie wrote to Dean seventeen times. He was astonished and delighted. All the letters were about him.

Almost as soon as Dean left Colorado, Dixie went to work as Dean's Colonel Parker, paving the way for his return. She set up a fan club and had nifty membership certificates printed; Mrs Brown was made an honorary member and so was Renate; Dixie got bumper stickers printed that read SO WHO'S DEAN REED? She wrote to classmates at Wheat Ridge High; she called record companies and checked out which songs had been hits; she commissioned record finders to locate copies of Dean's old records, including one titled 'Cannibal Twist'; she drove across the South-west, looking for props for Dean's movie, and had a lengthy correspondence with the South Dakota police department on the pretext that she was a schoolteacher whose class was interested in such things, and so obtained pictures of South Dakota police uniforms, badges, cars.

Along with her letter, Dixie sent Dean a package that included postcards showing the Denver Mint and panoramic views of Denver. She shipped the props, via Czechoslovakia, to the DEFA Film Studios in Potsdam. She sent: turquoise jewellery she purchased in Santa Fe; a denim jacket from Johnny; an Indian necklace.

Dixie wrote out shipping lists and in one case, at least, she painstakingly translated it into German: three music video tapes, one red bandanna, three copper medallions, twelve boy scout pins, one pack Skoal (chewing tobacco), one plastic ring, one 1986 calendar, one empty milk carton from the Wheat Ridge dairy (where Dixie and Dean worked after school as kids) for a joke; one box liquorice for Renate – just for fun. For St Valentine's Day, she sent a cubic-zirconia heart-shaped pendant for Renate.

Dixie wrote Dean of her progress: she picked up material on music videos; their production, the costs, layouts, directors in the Denver area; she sent away for copyright laws; she ordered the *Songwriters Market* book; she ordered a Nashville yellow-page telephone directory; she spent hours in the library getting a list of universities and colleges in America.

Her letters were full of good advice and jokes; she was coy, cute, smart, flirtatious, sassy. She chided and chastised, instructed Dean to be good to himself. When he was down, he was to look in the mirror and say 'I love me.' She was bossy, sweet, provocative, spirited, determined, and greedy, but only for love.

'You are truly fantastic. Why aren't you President?' Dean wrote.

Dean said her letters were 'jewels' and exclaimed on how many she had written. He complimented her on her humour. 'I tried to translate some of the jokes to Renate,' he wrote, 'but it is difficult to translate jokes – that is my problem living in Germany . . . Humour must be in the native tongue, *ja*?'

His letters were typed on a portable typewriter, and he noted his spelling was terrible, but blamed it on the fact that he spoke four languages. He enclosed the address of Mr Oleg Harjardin, the President of the Soviet Peace Committee, because a friend of Dixie's had requested it.

That January, as he shuttled between the film studio in Potsdam, his recording studios in Prague and Moscow, where he was still negotiating the deal on *Wounded Kneee*, he continued to write. You could read all of the events of their lives – which were the same now, for Dixie had surrendered completely to her own passion for making a home for Dean in America – and all of the events taking place in the world. In the early winter of 1986, the Challenger Space Shuttle blew up and Dean took it as a bad omen. They discussed Cory Aquino and Dixie referred to her as 'that gal in the Philippines'. Then Dean wrote to say that the box of props Dixie sent had arrived. What a shot in the arm it gave him and his crew, he said.

Dixie began German classes and she signed one of her letters 'Chow' because it was a word Dean often used. Then she asked him what it meant, anyhow.

Dean wrote her, 'It's an international word in Italian for hello and goodbye,' and she said that was 'neat' and was relieved to know, because she could not find it in the German dictionary.

He also wrote to her about the Sandinistas and about his dog, which bit him one Sunday. And she wrote back about the minutiae of her activities and her long letters were interspersed with philosophy, sly asides and little drawings – moon faces of herself, smiling or pensive. There was such longing in all of them, and poetry, and the sense that she was blossoming, that her world was enlarged, embellished, lit up by Dean Reed. They wrote and called each other about life, work and friends; they told jokes, they bantered. You could feel the intimacy build, as if they were locking into some fatal two-step to the exclusion of everyone else.

In the house in East Berlin, Dean taped portions of *Der Denver Klan* in German for Dixie, just for fun. But Dixie couldn't understand German, in spite of her classes, and, in any case, the videos were incompatible. The difference in video machinery on the two sides of the Berlin Wall was a perfect metaphor for the collisions between East and West, between desire and reality, between Dixie and Dean.

Still, Dixie wrote to Dean to say maybe she could send him

some money to buy her an East German video machine so she could watch the tapes he made for her.

'Why waste your money?' he replied.

Dean's letters to Dixie covered a lot of territory and revealed a man with an enormous appetite for work, for movement, but also a man who, in between the lines, was growing weary of it all. The letters careened between revelations of his philosophy of life, the determination to better the lot of all mankind, and the steely practicalities of the performing life: copyrights, arrangers, engineers, producers, contracts, deadlines.

She wrote him that if everything failed, he had a home in Colorado, literally. Both Dixie and a friend had 'rental homes' that could be his when he visited, but that was only if everything else failed, only after they 'punched out the street lights of America'.

Dixie wrote to Dean of her feelings for Colorado: 'the inky blue darkness of the star bedecked night', 'the light blue cloudless sky of morning'; of a delicious Mexican meal she had eaten; of her snowmobile, which was a delight. She tempted him with the pleasures of an American life and wished him 'beautiful blue-sky days'. She said she hoped Renate would 'like our weather, our little towns and our big towns, our massive shopping centres filled with people who are rude, kind, happy, sad, little, big, young and old!' In her own way, Dixie was a poet of the banal.

'In case you haven't figured it out, getting a letter from you, or a card, is better than home-made chocolate cake,' she wrote to Dean.

The next time I saw Dixie, we had brunch at the Brown Palace Hotel in Denver. As white as a bone, she looked as desolate as Denver without the snow, its glamorous skyscrapers all up for sale.

Dixie had promised me more tapes. She had tapes of all her telephone conversations with Dean, she said, right up until his death. Interesting tapes. Telling tapes. Weird tapes. She had them at home at Wheat Ridge, she said. She changed her mind. She had them at her other house in Grand Junction, up in the mountains. Her safe house. She teased with promises of information, but it was not intended as a tease and her heart wasn't in it. She seemed

frayed and worn with sorrow. The robust bacon and eggs Dixie
ordered were at odds with the frail memories of Dean that deton-
ated in her endlessly, like tiny land mines.

In the huge dining room, large people cruised around the tables
with thick china plates in their hand, slapping on mounds of
scrambled egg, smiling at dollops of corned beef hash, stacks of
pancakes, and bacon and sausage, all of it lavished with butter or
drowned in maple syrup, their thick cups of brewed coffee awash
in heavy cream.

A jolly Irish band played and sang folk songs with an insistent
disco beat. It was St Patrick's Day and the bagels were green.

Small in her chair, Dixie ate her breakfast.

The calls and the letters continued on into the winter of 1986. The
manic reporting of every detail in their lives continued, but Dean
had begun to focus seriously on his return to America. There was
an ecstatic mention of the possibility of *60 Minutes*. The biggest
show on American television was interested in Dean! And Dean
fixed his return to America for October, 1987, which was only a
year and a half away.

His return, he said, would be based on the distribution of
*American Rebel*, and the release of his new 'Long Play' in America,
which he also intended to call *American Rebel*. In a letter to Dixie,
he discoursed on the meaning of the word 'rebel'. Dixie looked it
up in her Funk and Wagnall's Dictionary and also in her Reader's
Digest *Family Word Finder*.

But how to present himself to America, he wondered. There
would be a personal tour; his film must be shown in the universities. He, Deano, would appear on television and radio talk-
shows and there would have to be an advance man to handle
Deano's publicity.

With Dixie, by letter, he discussed the autobiography he intended to write, for the other one was incomplete. Maybe Dixie
would write it for him. Yes, why not, and perhaps they could
get an advance from a publisher, although maybe that was too
optimistic.

She pooh-poohed all that, and told him he should be nicer to
himself. He would soon be rich, she kidded, which was just
as well, because she might be wanting a new Rolls Royce in
1987.

And Dean wrote of his dream of founding a social democratic party in America. If there were 260,000,000 Americans and only two per cent voted for him, that would be considerable, and so you wondered if the poor boob was too beset by arrogance to know that no socialist, not even Norman Thomas, ever got two per cent of the American vote.

'My dedication in my life has been to use my fame and talent to fight against injustice wherever and whenever I found it,' Dean wrote, then added, 'I believe that there is a great commercial hole to be filled in the USA. There is a need for a new singer to fill the void which Pete Seeger used to fill.'

Now Dixie had a real purpose. She called Mrs Brown; she called Tillie Price; she talked to Phil Everly on the phone and Phil did not have the heart to tell her that she had no idea how to be a manager. There were pitfalls everywhere, Dixie saw, as she toiled to put Dean back on the American map. But she had, at last, found a community.

And then relations in the community soured. There was bickering about who owned what bits of film – Mrs Brown had given Will Roberts money to accompany Dean to Chile; Will mortgaged his house to make *American Rebel*. Writing Dean's biography, Dixie thought maybe she would write to Yassir Arafat.

'Wouldn't that fritz Johnny?' she wrote to Dean, and asked Dean to release her from her promise to work with Johnny. His views were on the hard right, she said.

Dean said 'Johnny was a religious and conservative guy, who, if he did not love Dean, would never be a fan of his life.' But Johnny did love Dean and Dean would not release her. To cheer her up, he sent her Yassir Arafat's headscarf for a present. She showed it to me, and I wondered if Arafat handed out headscarves to distinguished visitors as the White House might give away cuff links.

To protect Dean (in case he hit it big), Johnny had Dean sign a deal with him for residual rights. It would stop people making spin-offs, such as Dean Reed dolls, without Dean's approval. The contract ran until the end of 1988. Dixie didn't like it one bit. Dean said he made the deal because Johnny was 'sick and didn't have much of a future,' explaining how much it meant to John and Mona when he, Dean, came and gave them his love and trust. Anyhow, Johnny promised when the day came that Dean signed on with the William Morris Agency in Hollywood, he would tear up that contract right in front of Dean's eyes.

Dixie didn't put much stock in that, but Dean left her no choice, so she majored on Will Roberts' duplicity instead. Will was no friend of Dean's, she wrote; Will was reluctant to part with his material. Dean wrote to Will that Dixie was his partner now.

For months, I tried to contact Will Roberts in Ohio, but he was elusive and his answering machine only played an endless version of Greensleeves whenever I called.

With Dean's visit to Colorado barely at an end, the quarrelling started. It went on, in the calls and letters, in the accumulation of the infinitesimal details of a life that would never be led. It continued even after Dean died. The conspiracy was not the KGB's nor the CIA's, but that of his friends, born of the best intentions, for his own good.

There were insinuations and suspicions; the various factions took differing views of Dean's future in the United States and how it should be effected, and no one agreed. Dixie took some friends up to Loveland to check Johnny and Mona were not agents of one kind or another.

'God, Dixie, can't you see we're just poor clods,' Johnny said.

They dissected every letter Dean sent, as semioticians might do; they taped his telephone calls, and sent the cassettes round in carefully made packages. They copied the video cassette of Dean's farewell concert in Johnny's basement. They wore his bumper stickers on their cars and his heart on their sleeves.

In the way that Dean's American friends operated, it was just like a network in an East European underground: there was the hope; the desperate desire for information; the coveting of news; the fear. Cassettes of his songs and even his telephone calls were copied over and over, like the *magnetizdat* which Soviet kids made of rock music, passing them along, their amateur quality – where you could hear the laughter in the background – making them more potent. Videos were copied, too, until they were too grainy to look at. Letters smuggled from one partisan to another were cherished and re-read. There were also the aspersions cast on those who seemed to have defected. There were the relationships degraded by desire and need. At one point along the Dean Reed trail, I heard from a musician who had known Dean in Moscow that someone – perhaps it was Mrs Brown – had received rumours that I worked for the CIA.

In Colorado, Dean's friends were not hicks. But they had no idea of what Dean's standing really was in the Soviet Union, in East Berlin. They could understand only that their friend had become a star. By the time Dean came home, for different reasons – Johnny's bad back, Dixie's longings – they inhabited a world that was as flat as the yellow scrublands on the way up to Loveland from Denver. Dean's presence as a star animated it and they could not bear to let that go.

Their delight seduced him; he was homesick; he saw an opportunity to move on one more time and he was determined to take it, one more time.

In trying to solve the mystery of Dean's death, I made a kind of sodden progress. Every time I turned up on what I thought was a fairly substantial dock, I sank back into a peculiar swamp. There were times I felt that Dean had existed only in the desires of his friends, that he was putty in the hands of his rememberers, who could do whatever they wanted with him, and that I was the last in a line to hear new versions of what had become a kind of folk tale in a very odd network of believers.

Dixie saw his return to America in grandiose terms. It would be the return of a great star, of a prodigal son. Dean wrote that he did not want her to be disappointed, that there were people who would be afraid of him because of his politics, and who would not answer her calls or letters.

Buried in Dean's own letters was a hard, cold, little core of realism, a chilling premonition that none of it was going to happen. I think Dean knew the truth, but he was a patsy for hope.

At the Brown Palace Hotel, Dixie refused another cup of coffee. The Irish band packed up its band boxes. Dixie was absorbed in some private despair.

'Dean was going to have trouble making it back here in the music business. It was all run by Jews. Deano didn't care what a person was, of course, he didn't care if a person was pink, white, black, green, purple or even a nigger.'

I wanted the rest of her tapes very badly. There were telephone calls from Dean right up to the end, weird calls from phone boxes in West Berlin. She came forward, then withdrew. I could feel my own frenzy grow. I had never wanted anything as much as I wanted those tapes, but Dixie was off on another tangent.

Dean had money in a bank in West Berlin. Emergency money. 'Can you check if there have been any withdrawals since Dean's death. If there haven't, I'll give you the tapes,' she said.

'I'm not sure I understand,' I said.

'I've been getting strange phone calls. I think someone is speaking Spanish. I think the calls are coming from South America.' She tried to drink some coffee, but her hand shook and she put the cup down. 'I want to know if there have been any withdrawals recently because Dean may need that money. If there have been withdrawals, it will prove that . . . '

Dixie did not finish her sentence, but looked up expectantly at the entrance to the restaurant. Then she finished her sentence. ' . . . that Dean is alive.'

# CHAPTER 17

## *60 Minutes*

'Why are you a communist, Mr Reed? Why do you believe in the Berlin Wall? Call yourself an American? What about Afghanistan?'

'Well, Mike, you see . . . '

'Yeah, you call yourself . . . '

'For Chrissake, Oleg.'

In his big fur hat, Dean trudged around Red Square with Oleg Smirnoff, who was playing Mike Wallace. Oleg was in his nerd's cap and spectacles. *60 Minutes* was coming up and Dean wanted plenty of rehearsal time. It was the winter of 1986.

Hit me harder. Ask me another question, he told Oleg. Pretend you're Mike Wallace.

Oleg had no idea. He was more like a bad actor playing a KGB hood than a veteran American journalist.

'Hit me again,' said Dean, obsessed with *60 Minutes*. It was his passport back to America. He told Oleg he was going home – he was remembered after all at home. He could go back. They did remember Deano in Denver!

'Hit me harder,' he said.

That winter, Dean was always on the move – Prague, Moscow, Schmockwitz, East Berlin, Potsdam, where the DEFA Film Studios were located. He could barely stop to think. Still, there was always time for Dixie.

From the house at Schmockwitz, he phoned to tell her about his trip to Moscow. He sat at the big desk in his study, the portable typewriter in front of him, his spectacles on his nose. In the window, he could see his reflection. He found a few grey hairs. He tried to focus on *Wounded Knee*. He could think of little else. Along with *60 Minutes*, the film was his ticket back to America. The telephone rang. He answered it eagerly.

'Hi, Deano, I'm just reading all of your letters,' said Dixie.

'In four days in Moscow I spoke only English. I was getting ready for Mike Wallace. Johnny has begged me, "Please don't do *60 Minutes*," ' Dean said.

Renate was worried. She got on the phone with Dixie. 'I am afraid about the meeting with Mike Wallace. He is clever and intelligent. I will be silent. I will learn from you and Dean positive thinking,' she said.

'Johnny says *60 Minutes* goes deep into the past,' Dean told Dixie on another phone call.

Back in Loveland, Johnny was frantic with worry. Dean just did not understand the type of people at *60 Minutes*. He did not get that America had no love for communistic people.

Johnny sat awake nights. He worried about Dixie down in Wheat Ridge, leading Dean a merry dance. She had a way with her, even telling him, Johnny, that she wanted to get him inserted back into the music business along with Dean.

When he heard about *60 Minutes* coming up, Johnny went on out to the shed in the back yard where he sometimes worked. 'I went out there and made a tape. I wanted to talk to Dean, not to write to him,' Johnny said.

'I said, these people go deep in your background, I said. 'Stay away from *60 Minutes*. They're gonna cut you to pieces.' Johnny said.

He sent the tape over to East Berlin.

Renate was outraged. 'What kind of a friend is this that comes down on you so hard and tells you not to get this publicity?' she said.


It was not clear how *60 Minutes* came about. The confusion about its origin made people suspicious.

In London, Bill McClure claimed it was his idea. McClure, a London-based producer for CBS, was a large man who did not like Dean Reed. An old Europe hand, he knew his way around the continent. Having once lived in Berlin, he seemed to have cast himself as a character in a Len Deighton spy novel and said, knowingly, that Dean Reed exploited his position.

'A very big fish in a very small pond,' breathed McClure. 'Renate was a *bona fide* star, but the son, Sasha, was a strange guy, a kind of half-caste.' McClure's neck bulged over his collar; he loosened his tie.

The original idea was to do a piece for *60 Minutes* on American defectors. It was to include Victor Grossman, Dean Reed and Harrington, a black political cartoonist.

McClure thought Dean was a hustler, an opportunist without political conviction, a self-aggrandising old crooner with an ego the size of the Berlin Wall. 'Dean Reed was approaching fifty and he was frightened,' he said. 'Dean Reed was a fake.'

McClure's dislike emanated from every pore. His animosity, however, I discovered, was mostly to do with Dean's last-minute decision to defect from the show. McClure had set everything up. He flew Mike Wallace into East Berlin. Then Dean backed off. McClure sat in East Berlin with a crew, with Mike Wallace ready to go and this putz, this cowboy, this fake said he didn't want to do it. McClure's job was on the line.

'Whose version would you believe? Mike Wallace, who gets maybe a million a year, or Bill McClure, who gets maybe fifty grand?' said Erik Durschmied. 'Anyway, the show was my idea.'

I met Erik Durschmied at the Intercontinental Hotel in New York and we went out to Murphy's Irish Pub on Second Avenue. He liked the cheeseburgers there.

Durschmied worked for CBS News in Paris. He was a tough little Viennese of about sixty, a legend in his time, who went alone, on foot, into Indo-China as a reporter-camera man – with a return ticket, of course – and made his reputation. He made no apologies for his lingering shots of the dead and dying during the Iran–Iraq war. He had thinning hair and a good tweed jacket.

Durschmied's Danish wife, Annalise, was Dean's friend from the old days on the radical circuit, and the couples saw each other frequently. In Schmockwitz on a visit, he and Annalise were invited by the Reeds to watch television. It was the day's main event, although Durschmied could not remember if it was 'Dallas' or 'Dynasty' that they saw that night.

There was a knock at the door. It was late. Everyone froze. Durschmied went pale and he felt his palms sweat. The Stasi had come to arrest Dean. Dean answered the door. Renate smoked. There was a muffled conversation in the hall, but Durschmied could not make it out.

Grinning, Dean bounded into the room. In his hands was a

package wrapped in blood-soaked paper. The butcher had smuggled them a piece of meat. 'There are only two good days in East Berlin. Tuesday, when we get 'Dallas'. And Wednesday, when we get meat,' Dean said.

Erik Durschmied ordered a beer and a cheeseburger. At Murphy's Irish pub, there were checkered cloths on the table, and at the bar, a crowd of men with their ties at half-mast. In unison, the crowd of drinkers craned its neck to catch snatches of a football game on a television set suspended from the ceiling over the bartender's head. Durschmied ate. While he ate, he talked.

'Dean hated East Berlin,' he said. Chomping methodically on his hamburger, he swallowed some beer and looked satisfied.

'Did you like Dean?' I said.

'Yes, and I'm a black and cynical bastard,' he said. 'Dean was a feather in the wind. He was naive. But he had enormous charm. whatever his talent as a musician, his talent for charm was never in any doubt at all.'

According to Durschmied, Dean also had a sense of humour, at least about his own films, and he laughed about casting Ukrainians and Bulgarians as Indians in cowboy pictures shot in Romania. 'He knew his films were garbage', said Durschmied, 'but Dean himself had no taste. He gave us some of those vulgar porcelain statues. We were touched, of course, so we kept them. But they were junk.'

Durschmied had his own blind spots. We talked about Dean's womanising. There was plenty of it he agreed, but he confided that Dean was capable of real friendship with a woman – his own wife Annalise, for example. Durschmied must have had his head in a sack. It occurred to me, that, like Dixie and Wiebke, Annalise Durschmied was slender, small-boned, sexy, blonde and feral.

'Would you have gone to bed with Dean?' Durschmied said.

His accent grew more Viennese with every beer, and a friendly leer spread across his face. There followed an exchange about whether or not I would have slept with Dean Reed, or, indeed, with Elvis Presley. The crowd had grown noisier in the front of the bar. I edged my chair away from Durschmied.

'Would you have gone to bed with Marilyn Monroe?' I said.

'You bet! Just think of telling the boys in the locker room next day,' he said, wiping mustard from his chin.

Leaning over the table, Durschmied whispered his self-aggrandising scenarios. He was big on hush-hush stuff, it was his best product. He belonged to a network of informants, witnesses and hacks, and all of them traded bits and pieces of information like hard currency in an East European stronghold. It was the stuff they survived on; it gave them power. Durschmied cooked his tit-bits into a meal.

'Remember, it was the American Embassy that got Dean free in Chile when he was arrested there in 1983,' Durschmied said. 'Why would the Embassy bother with some commie type who'd gone over to the other side?

'Ask yourself why,' said Durschmied.

Was Dean a spy for us? Was that what Durschmied was saying? Was he CIA, the ultimate mole, the American version of Kim Philby? It was a tantalising idea: the corn-fed blue-eyed boy with his crew cut and Chevy, his mule races and his silly songs. Did Paton Price run him? Was the sudden move to Latin America exquisitely planned? Was the socialist rhetoric a perfect cover for an agent? In his tight pants, with the guitar slung over his shoulder, with his merry antics and goodwill, he had converted plenty of Russians to America. Was Dean Reed the Tab Hunter of the secret world?

It was a great scenario. I didn't believe it for a second. Durschmied had just been to Lapland to photograph reindeer irradiated by the fallout from the spill at Chernobyl, and that sort of thing got to you. Erik Durschmied was the kind of man who heard voices coming out of his cheeseburger.

For the hell of it, he tried out the notion that Dean Reed was still alive and living in the Soviet Union, but it seemed unlikely that a six-foot American rock star had gone to ground so easily in Gorbachev's Soviet Union with news crews constantly on the prowl. Durschmied giggled. He was just trying it on. It was provocative, but it was small talk.

'The whole thing is a jigsaw puzzle, and you're looking for a bit of sky when the sailboat is right in front of you,' said Durschmied mysteriously.

He clamped his mouth around some french fries and would say nothing more about the sailboat, what it was, where it was. It was clear he didn't know much, but his urgent whisper had a persuasive conviction and, although I was by now inclined to accept that

Dean Reed's death might have been just an accident, Erik Durschmied's spy stories were tempting. In any case, when he swallowed, he had something interesting to say.

'Dean Reed was a man without a language. Without a language. *Ja*. Like me.' he said.

In the tapes I had with Dean Reed's voice on them, his English was stilted, as if something essential was missing.

'Look, I was only fifteen or so when I left Austria. All my vocabulary for subjects before fifteen is German. Everything else, which means my entire professional life, my political life, is in English. The same with Dean. His American vocabulary was 1961. Everything else was in a foreign language. Spanish. German. His musical life, his political life, his married life, his whole adult construct was foreign,' said Durschmied.

Dean spoke English, German, Spanish, a little Russian, all of them badly. The gaps in his languages matched the gaps in his experience. The old-fashioned English was meshed in the smiling countenance and the belief in peace and freedom. It was always 1961 in Dean's world. The clock in his head stopped when he left America.

In a letter to Wiebke he once wrote that being in America made him happy because he could speak his own language. It was so astute it turned my head. Dean was not a subtle man, but he had poignantly diagnosed what ailed him: he was a man without a language.

Durschmied got up. I got up. The cheeseburgers were finished and so was the beer.

'Of course, you know Dean and Renate were planning to go to live in Rome,' said Durschmied.

Rome? Rome! No, I didn't know about Rome; there had been no mention at all of Rome. But Eric Durschmied was half a block ahead of me, singing a Tom Lehrer song in counterpoint to the noises of the New York night.

'They're rioting in Africa, they're starving in Spain . . . ' he sang and disappeared around the corner.

In his office at CBS News, Mike Wallace at first appeared to be performing for the cameras. That was the way I saw it, not necessarily the way he played it. His face had been famous all of my life. In the corridor of the *60 Minutes* offices on West 57th

Street, I could already hear the utterly familiar voice, that, coming out of my television set one Sunday evening had got me here in the first place. Mike Wallace was talking on the telephone.

He looked up and raised a hand in greeting. He looked just like Mike Wallace.

It was as if the cameras stopped turning and Wallace relaxed and was himself, although perhaps that was the best performance of all.

At first, Wallace said, he thought Dean was a bit of a fraud. A few minutes later, as if he had given it a second thought, he said that was an unjust assessment and that Dean probably did believe the things he talked about. He was naive maybe, but he had conviction and he was charming. Wallace did not object to Dean's playing hard to get. Unlike Bill McClure, he found it neither objectionable nor manipulative.

'The guy was scared. Many people on the verge of an interview try to back away and then come back again. I harboured no hard feelings about that,' Mike Wallace said.

Wallace was deeply impressed by Renate. He felt in her a profound solidity. She was a considerable woman.

'Was Dean intelligent?' I asked.

'Intelligent enough. He was certainly no dummy, though he had a learned rhetoric and could do the communist number; but he adjusted his view as we went along. It wasn't merely a kind of parrot repetition; there was some real involvement. Of course, he had done this interview plenty of times and he knew the words and knew how to express himself in those terms,' Wallace said.

'Did you like him?'

'Yes, I did. He was a political naif, but he was honest. He was honest,' Mike Wallace said.


On February 9, 1986 Mike Wallace flew into East Berlin. Bill McClure was already there wringing his hands, wondering if this putz, this cowboy, this commie, Dean Reed, intended to do the interview.

Dean had tentatively agreed to the interview, but he did not like Bill McClure much so he changed his mind. Wallace was at the Palast Hotel, where you had to be a V.I.P. to stay.

'Please come,' said McClure.

'Please help me to say no,' Dean said to Renate.

They got to the Palast Hotel, where they met Mike Wallace, Bill McClure and Anne de Boismilion, the associate producer who worked for CBS in Paris. A woman from East German television was with them.

The three women went to the restaurant. Half an hour later, Dean came in, grinning sheepishly. 'I've agreed to do the interview,' he said.

In the end, Renate was impressed. They shot a huge amount of footage: in the Alexanderplatz; near the Berlin Wall; in the woods beyond Schmockwitz. They shot film of Renate; of Dean; of Sasha.

Generously, Wallace let me look at the out-takes and read the transcripts. It was compelling stuff.

Towards the end of the three days during which he interviewed Dean Reed, Wallace and his crew were in the house at Schmockwitz. With great passion Renate spoke to Wallace about Dean and his causes.

'You are just as eloquent and just as much an idealist as your husband,' said Wallace.

He turned to Dean Reed. They talked about Germany. Dean insisted that travel was not a priority for most people. Wallace asked why he thought so many East Germans wanted to go to the West. Dean was silent. Wallace told him that ten to fifteen thousand East Germans emigrated every year. That a million more wanted exit visas. That the East Germans traded political prisoners to the West for hard currency every year, like cattle, at between $15,000 and $40,000 a head. Dean said he was unaware of it.

Dean asserted that there was freedom to worship under Communism and said he was confirmed in the Church, and so was Renate. But that was long ago.

They talked about his career and Dean grew a litle contentious.

'I don't like being called the Johnny Cash of Communism. I'm Dean Reed.'

'But you know what it means.'

'I know that it means they're trying to say that Dean is as famous there as Johnny Cash is here . . . They call me the Red Sinatra also. Er, it bothers me because I'm not the Red Sinatra . . . I'm Dean Reed and I'm a very very popular man.'

Dean told Wallace how much he missed America. He said he stayed in East Germany because he loved Renate.

'. . . Why do you become the captive of the women with whom you have spent your time?' Wallace asked.

'Aren't we all captives of our women, Mike?'

'The main motivation of your life is . . . ?' Wallace asked.

'Love,' said Dean.

'We've heard your cowboy songs. We've heard various songs. Would you sing "Yiddishe Momma"?' Wallace asked.

'This is one of my favourite songs in my life, Mike. I've sung it in every country of the world, for my mother. My mother is not Jewish but I think this song is one of the most beautiful songs of all time for a mother,' said Dean.

'I understand you had some difficulties with that song in the Soviet Union,' Wallace said.

On Dean's second tour in the Soviet Union, a little man, who said he was from the Ministry of Culture, told Dean it was forbidden to sing 'Yiddishe Momma'. Dean told him that Lenin would roll over in his grave if he had heard him say that because no Marxist could be anti-semitic and, though he, Dean, did not agree with Zionism, he loved the Jewish people. He even told Arafat.

'Yassir,' he said, 'I always include "Yiddishe Momma" . . . ' And Arafat said, 'That's O.K., Dean, I have nothing against the Jewish people.' So, if it was forbidden to sing it in the Soviet Union, Dean would leave and never return.

'Dean, it was all a terrible mistake, of course, you can sing anything you want to in our country,' said Mme Furtseva the following Monday. Mme Furtseva was the Soviet Minister of Culture who once tried to get the Beatles a Soviet concert date; with Donovan she very nearly succeeded; she was not a woman who stood for any nonsense.

'If anybody ever tells you to change something that you say or do, you come to me and I'll hit them over the head,' she added.

'You sang it?' said Wallace.

'I sang it. And I continue singing it,' Dean said.

'There,' said Wallace.

'I do it a cappella.'

'Oh, perfect. Do it a cappella,' said Wallace.

'Can I sing it "Yiddishe Poppa" and sing it to you?'

'You could,' Wallace said.

★

'I sang "Yiddishe Momma" to him and he cried,' Dean said to Dixie that night when they had a long conversation.

'Mr Mike Wallace left today,' added Dean. 'I got him very upset. I'm not going to do the show, I said. I have nothing to sell in America. I have no guarantees. Then Mike comes. He is very full of compliments. How good-looking one is; how great one is. I said, we will make a contract. First, if we do it, you will buy the material of me singing from the film of Will Roberts. Second, you will do a complete portrait when I'm filming in August in the Soviet Union.

'We did three days' shooting. Then he came into the house and we shot for four hours. "You know, Mr Reed, I wasn't expecting a man as intelligent as you," Mike said. "We're going to do the portrait of you now, twenty minutes from Dean." Everyone in the GDR is very impressed,' said Dean to Dixie.

She thought it was neat.

In his office at CBS, Mike Wallace scanned a letter from Dean.

'He concludes by saying, "And maybe we can also solve the problem of the 'Yiddishe Poppa'." ' Wallace said.

'What does that mean?' I said. I wanted to hear Wallace's version.

'I'm a non-practising, non-religious Jew. A bad Jew.' Wallace smiled. 'I was incredibly moved and I nearly burst ino tears . . . After that, frankly, the piece was really a Valentine. Sitting there in East Berlin with this cowboy from Colorado . . . there was this terrific yearning to come home . . .'

In the six weeks that followed Mike Wallace's visit to East Berlin, Dean was increasingly busy. In March he stayed at Vashek's in Prague. When Renate went to bed, the two men talked all night about women. Why didn't I marry a Czech girl? said Dean. Wiebke was making trouble, he said. He didn't mention Dixie. But he wrote her he was depressed.

The telephone calls and letters travelled between Schmockwitz and Colorado in a never-ending stream. Dean was tired. He wrote to Johnny in March: 'Sorry if I don't write. There are TV shows and films. I'm damn tired and I feel old at times . . . Fifty will be coming along . . . Keep your fingers crossed for Mike (Wallace), ex Mack the Knife.'

'*60 Minutes* is not finished yet. Did I tell you? I spoke to Mike

Wallace. They're gonna hold it 'til fall until they have the biggest public,' said Dean. It was early April.

'Beautiful,' said Dixie.

As usual, Dixie and Dean bantered and giggled down the phone.

'You have a beautiful day,' Dixie would say.

'Have a nice week,' said Dean.

'Say, I love me,' Dixie said, signing off.

On April 20, 1986, *60 Minutes* went on the air with the piece about Dean Reed. Although it had been scheduled for the following fall, as Dean told Dixie, for one reason or another – probably because there was an empty slot – it went out in April.

At home in New York, half-watching the television, I stirred from my Sunday lethargy to listen to Mike Wallace.

Johnny and Mona Rosenburg sat in their living room in Loveland, glued to the TV. The title of the piece on Deano came up. It was called 'The Defector'. Sweet Jesus, thought Johnny. Dear God.

The sonorous voice of Mike Wallace began talking out of the box. There were shots of Dean's concerts. Nice shots of Dean walking hand-in-hand with Renate in the woods, walking with Mike Wallace. Some of the material sent Johnny into an almost uncontrollable rage that made his knuckles white.

'You equate Ronald Reagan with Joseph Stalin?' Mike Wallace asked.

'I equate the possibilities of Ronald Reagan with – with Stalin,' said Dean.

Johnny could feel himself wanting to be sick as Dean said he thought Mr Gorbachev was a more moral man than Reagan. He denied that East Germany was a colony of the Soviet Union.

'Why was the Wall put up in the first place?' asked Mike Wallace.

'The Wall – the Wall was put up to defend themselves in the first place,' said Dean.

Johnny just sat there and listened to Dean defend that wall and it burned his butt so bad! He was also scared silly for Dean. He figured if Dean ever came home now, he better get himself that bulletproof vest. Dean talked about maybe bein' a senator from Colorado . . . if Gary Hart was goin' on to the Presidency, why not? Dean smiled.

Half blind with fear and rage, Johnny made his way to the shed in the back yard. Johnny thought to himself: He is gonna be shot. He honest to God believed Dean would have died right here in America . . . There's too many hate groups.

In Moscow, it was the middle of the night and Dean was fast asleep and, in any case, it was weeks before he would see a cassette of the programme. But in his shed in Loveland, Johnny began to figure how to communicate this with his friend in East Berlin. 'You cannot defend that Wall in this country,' he said to himself.

# PART IV

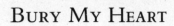

## Bury My Heart

# CHAPTER 18

# Mosfilm

In May, while Johnny sat in his shed in Loveland chewing his liver and trying to tell Dean how angry he was, Dean was eating his heart out over *Wounded Knee*. The start date for the movie he had been working on for five years was the 24th of June and it was coming at him like a train down a track: there was no stopping it.

*Wounded Knee* was going to change Dean's life. It was the crossover picture that would make him a real contender as a director in the East where, so far as movies went, he was just a good-looking crooner. Having been to America, he was obsessed with making a real movie instead of a piece of garbage where you could punch your fists through the sets. 'Sing Cowboy Sing' had been an enormous hit, but he was fed up with playing an idiotic singing cowpoke dressed up to play a part that was already his own. Renate would star with him in *Wounded Knee*. They would be together all summer long. They would have a chance to patch up the quarrels they'd been having that were nagging at Dean like his ulcer. Dean would show his movie in America. He was convinced that it would be his ticket home.

In the spring of 1986, the deal began to come apart.

For the whole of the spring, Dean led a chaotic life – the film, concerts, albums, television shows. He was always on the road – Potsdam, Prague, Moscow, Berlin. He sat up late in Schmockwitz, reworking the script. He wondered when his voice would fail; his age was creeping up on him. He was too old to be a pop star. His glasses slid down his nose. He was forty-seven.

In Potsdam, Dean struggled with the changes at the DEFA Studios. Resources were drying up. Erich Honecker still ruled East Germany with a rusty iron hand, but the producers at DEFA dreamed of the hard currency that deals with the West would bring. Maybe Dean thought *Wounded Knee* was the perfect vehicle, but the smart money at DEFA, such as it was, knew the West wasn't interested in a movie where the FBI were the bad guys. A Moscow, oiled by Glasnost, knew it even better.

*Wounded Knee* was cut back. At almost 700 shots, it ran more than two hours and 500 was the norm. There were two and a half metres of film per shot. Everything was painstakingly planned. Everything was expensive, even the lousy film stock.

'I must tell the American life with all the details. There must be lots of short scenes,' said Dean, who, like all movie directors, dreamed of a thousand extras. He was forced to scale back from a cast of 600 to a cast of 60.

'Sasha doesn't like my music,' he wrote to Dixie. 'He calls me "old man".'

Then Dixie's letters stopped. In the middle of May, Dean wrote to her: 'My God, has it been a long time without a word from you!'

In May, the nuclear power plant at Chernobyl blew up, but Dean was preoccupied with Dixie's sudden silence; he sent her a black-and-white copy of a colour photo of himself and said he thought he looked rather young. 'Oh it is nice to have a baby face!' Dean wrote. The letter was full of the bravado of hope, but it was permeated by anxiety about the film.

Real dread crept into his soul when Dean discovered that Moscow was losing its enthusiasm for his movie. For five years, he had negotiated the deal; half of the money for the movie was Soviet; the Russians held the trump card. In spite of his terrifying schedule in the winter and spring after he came back from America, until the week before he died, Dean shuttled to and from Moscow regularly, as if his life depended on it.

All movie making has a surreal quality: Jewish actors play Nazi generals; day becomes night; designers rebuild the Sistine Chapel in Slough. *Wounded Knee* was more surreal than most.

In Alma Alta and in Uzbekistan, Dean cast his 'Indians'. Others came from a collective farm that was populated entirely by North Koreans. American police cars, jeeps, sedans, like the Chevrolets of Dean's youth, were selected from the vintage car clubs that flourished in Riga and Tallinn. In Yalta, the spring before he was to begin filming, Dean's crew had a perfectly credible American church under construction with wood shipped into the Crimea from Riga because, in the Crimea, wood was scarcer than gold. Yalta was the principal location for *Wounded Knee*; but the studio at Riga was Dean's base.

In the Soviet Union, the production of every movie was assigned by Moscow to a regional studio. *Wounded Knee*, a German co-production, was given to Riga in part, at least, because in the Latvian capital, everyone spoke German.

'Dean felt we were Germans, that we were too polite, too reserved for his taste,' said Lilia Liepine, his good-natured production manager, when I met her in the Soviet Union in 1989. In her pink angora sweater, Lilia looked like Mrs Brown and she mourned for Dean like a mother.

At Riga, in the studio, the boxes of props which Dixie sent from America were stored. So was the footage which Dean shot on Denver's skid row, when he was home on his visit. It would give the movie the real feel of America and the tale of the filming on skid row had already been added to the 'Annals of Deano'. He loved telling it: how he found himself in the middle of a burglary that day on Larrimer Street where the bums lived; how a real American cop stopped him with a big riot gun; how he bravely kept the cameras turning and got the real goods; how frightening America sometimes was, with its hundred million handguns. Dean was frightened by the gun, and exhilarated.

So far as Lilia knew when we met her, years after Dean was dead, the piece of film and the box of props were still in the studio, the cracked Coca Cola sign a little memorial to the movie Dean never made.

Obsessed with detail, a man possessed by a vision of a professional Western film but doomed to make it in a country where every piece of equipment was forty years out of date, Dean himself saw to the casting, the sets, the make-up tests. He chose a horse for himself at a collective farm where wild horses were broken. Month after month, he travelled the whole of the Soviet Union with Lilia Liepine, restless, anxious. In Yalta, mobbed by fans, Dean gave an impromptu concert at the end of a long hard day and Lilia said to him 'How can you stand it?'

'I like it,' he said. 'I need it.'

When the arrival of his American Army tank from North Vietnam was late coming to Moscow, Dean fretted horribly.

Hanoi was the only place you could put your hands on an American tank, if you were filming in the Soviet Union. I remembered that I had seen a photograph of Dean with some North Vietnamese generals. He appeared to be joshing them, making jokes and maybe that was how he finagled his tank, or maybe they just gossiped about Ho Chi Minh's days as a pastry cook at the Parker House in Boston.

Wouldn't people be frightened by an American tank trundling down the road to the Crimea, I asked Lilia. She shrugged.

'USA, USSR, there isn't a lot of difference between tanks,' Lilia said.

'Of course, in the end, the Russians cancelled the money for *Wounded Knee*,' said an American diplomat who had known Dean. The man, who did not like Dean, was retired and bored and he insisted on anonymity, because it made him important and gave his story authority.

'The Russians killed the movie,' he said with absolute certainty. 'Everyone knew,' he said, 'the movie was kaput.'

If it was true, the emotional spill for Dean would have been like Chernobyl.

I came back to Moscow to try to find out what went wrong with *Wounded Knee*. Leslie had come, too, because he was beginning to think about setting up the film. It was the end of 1988 and Perestroika had oiled up the movie business. At the studios, in the beehive of offices that made up the network of the bureaucracies that ran the business in the Soviet Union, no one asked to see your script. No one asked about your politics; they only asked how much money you had to spend.

All film studios smell alike.

Mosfilm smelled of celluloid, make-up, hot lights, cigarette smoke and ego. In the Lenin Hills, on the outskirts of Moscow, the studio had offices, sound stages, prop shops, costume stores and a huge back lot where vintage trams lay rusting in the snow. Outside the stained stucco office building was a parking lot and, except for the snow and the lack of Porsches, it might have been Warners.

'Film is our most important art,' Lenin said.

'I have worked for Roland Joffé,' Vera said. As we drove up to the gates at Mosfilm, Vera, who was our interpreter, said that she worked mostly for film people and that her last client had been the director, Roland Joffé. Leslie said we knew Roland, and Vera lit up. It made us all friends.

The lobby at Mosfilm had the silvery, stylised feel of an RKO set; Fred Astaire might have danced Ginger Rogers down those Art Moderne corridors. Black-and-white photographs of great Russian movie stars lined the walls. I couldn't find Dean anywhere on the wall of stars.

The man in charge of foreign co-production had a very good suit and an office big as a conference room, with a map of the world on the wall. He looked like a producer. I never knew his name and I thought of him as Mr Big. He addressed himself entirely to Leslie.

Mr Big was not interested in a conversation about Dean Reed. He wanted to talk deals. He wanted to talk to Leslie about the prospect of making Dean's life story in Moscow: how much of it was to be shot at his studio, what lights, sets, costumes and crew he could flog. Production at Mosfilm was way down. Times were tough.

Movies were big business in the Soviet Union. Russians went to the pictures all the time – as much as nineteen times a year some people said – largely because there wasn't much else to do – their flats were crowded, the restaurants were disgusting. The cinemas were warm at least, and you could neck in the back row.

Even before Gorbachev took office, the kids were fed up with the drivel that came out of the Soviet studios. State censorship, the yes men of the Brezhnev era, and the decades of stagnation meant that movies ran largely to provincial romance and costume drama. The Russians were crazy for costume drama: the Russian version of *Mary Poppins* was the biggest cinematic event since the *Battleship Potemkin*; *Sherlock Holmes* ran a close second.

Within months of Gorbachev's ascent, the director, Elem Klimov, was elected head of the cinematographers' union, and it was massively symbolic. Klimov's films had been banned for years. Now, censorship crumbled. Movies once thought irreverent were screened. Sexy movies. Political movies. Soviet film stars appeared in *Playboy*.

In 1987, Juris Podnieks made *Is It Easy To Be Young?* and it was a watershed because, in his dark, tough picture, he portrayed hostile punk kids and their passionate desire for money above all else, money and good times.

But where once the film business was heavily subsidised by the state, Perestroika meant every studio had to turn a profit. Top executives offered themselves up to potential investors – especially investors from the West – like high-class hookers. The Soviet movie business was beginning to look a lot more like our own.

In Moscow one night I had dinner at Dom Kino, the Film House, which was a cross between Groucho's in London and Spago's in Hollywood, except that the food ran to burned *shashlik* and the decor to nylon curtains. Still, it was a stylish, animated crowd of actors, directors and writers, well-dressed by Moscow standards, who welcomed us and kissed the air beside each other's cheeks.

'Just remember,' one cynic said, 'these people who now dance to the Gorby Gavotte, used to do it to the Brezhnev Boogie and before that, in some cases, to the Khrushchev Carioca.'

Eating ice cream at Dom Kino was Nikita Khrushchev's grandson. A balding and plump young man in jeans, he had a placid smile on his face as he ate.

In his office at Mosfilm, Mr Big called for coffee. I wanted to talk about Dean Reed, but he produced only the usual official pap and I yawned and drank my coffee to cover the boredom. Mr Big was not interested in me and I did not like him. He offered Leslie a cigar. Leslie was a producer in a good suit. A Western co-production was a juicy prospect.

'You'll want to see a script, of course,' Leslie said.

For years, Leslie had been sneaking around Eastern Europe in order to make highly political drama-documentaries. Posing as a tourist, watching his back, he hob-nobbed with dissident generals in back alleys, took illegal photographs of Party Headquarters in Prague and of the shipyards in Gdansk. Suddenly, in the heart of Moscow, all anyone talked to him about were below-the-line costs and exchange rates.

Hopefully, Mr Big held out his box of Havanas. 'A cigar?' he said.

'Can we film in Red Square?' Leslie said.

Sure, you could film in Red Square, although the Kremlin was heavily booked years in advance. All Mosfilm required were the relevant pages of the script, and this only in order to provide the necessary crew and equipment. Everything and everyone at Mosfilm was for rent.

'What about Dean Reed?' I said.

Mr Big shrugged. It was Dean's ambition to play John Reed. Around 1980, the Russian director Sergei Bondachuk planned to make a Russian version of John Reed's life and Dean promoted himself for the part. Bondachuk went to California and, the language notwithstanding, offered the part to Warren Beatty. Later on, of course, Beatty made his own version and called it *Reds*.

'Directors were interested in Dean as an actor, but only up to a point. Dean would only work for hard currency . . . "We'd love to use you," directors would say, "but currency is what we lack." ' said Mr Big.

As I pushed the conversation in the direction of *Wounded Knee*, and as Mr Big watched Leslie, trying to decipher his intentions, the door opened and an old man ambled in. He wore a shiny blue suit, a greasy yellow shirt and a tie that must have come from a Soviet production of *Guys and Dolls*. He looked like Harry the Horse.

Harry slumped into a chair. His back permanently curved, as if he'd spent too much time shooting craps, he held his cigarette between this thumb and his forefinger. In preparing *Wounded Knee*, Dean came to Mosfilm to look for costumes and Harry the Horse was his minder.

Harry accepted a Marlboro and talked: 'Dean wasn't such a big star, but the young girls were crazy about his looks,' he said.

'He was a little bit yesterday's man. Many actors are gifted, but stupid. He saw what was going on. Dean was not stupid,' said Mr Big.

Realising that no money would change hands that day, Mr Big lost interest in us and looked at his watch. Harry the Horse took charge.

'You like to see studio?' said Harry.

Mosfilm was big as a mausoleum. We traipsed across a cardboard set for a fairy tale which was in production. Mismatched green plastic leaves dangled from styrofoam trees and a few actresses in pink tulle smoked cigarettes. The cameras were big as dinosaurs, the lights as big as tanks.

In the make-up department, in smocks and hairnets, a group of women worked silently at pots of paint and powder. Like everywhere else in the country, there were shortages. Good blood was hard to come by, for example. The youngest girl in the room had a Walkman on and she jiggled a little at her task. Across the room, displayed in a glass case, were a pair of false limbs, the exquisite work of the prosthetics team; in another case, was Rasputin's wig.

The costumes were stored in a separate warehouse. In one section alone there were military uniforms and at the end of every rack a detailed diagram of the uniforms it held, including the period, the size, the rank and order of the soldier or officer in question. The Nazi uniforms were crowded together and, in this country where so much was invested in remembering the defeat of the Germans, I had the feeling that these were not costumes at all. German caps were piled on a shelf; black and brown leather gloves lay in tidy pairs in a carton on the floor. In another, larger box, jackboots, tied together by their laces, were stacked shoulder high. It looked like the anteroom to a concentration camp.

I had to get some air. We went out into the snow where, clutching his pack of Marlboros, Harry the Horse escorted us to the back lot and left us there underneath the gallows.

It might have been the set for *A Tale of Two Cities*, although I supposed in that case there would have been a guillotine; there was only a rope dangling from a post and a spectator's stand, but next door was the London Street. Quaint shop fronts and nineteenth-century signs were half obscured by the snow and Baker Street had begun to rot.

In winter, no one worked outdoors and most of the sets were in disrepair. I looked for the Battleship Potemkin, but there was only a section of an old green train – I think it was American – and the rusted tram.

Our car and driver were waiting at the front gate of the studio. The driver looked like Karl Malden. Each day as we parted, I gave him some Marlboros.

'You know what? You look just like an American film star,' I said.

'So what are you giving me tomorrow?' the driver said.

★

Sasha Surikov was the chief at Sovinfilm, the organisation that fixed foreign co-productions. The contracts for *Wounded Knee* were somewhere inside Sovinfilm.

Fat Sasha, as we came to think of him, was a fixer. He had an office in the centre of Moscow with cut-velvet wallpaper an inch deep. The door to the office was padded leather, tufted and buttoned. The furniture was heavily upholstered and so was Fat Sasha.

Sunk in an after-lunch torpor, he was a young man whose weight made him middle-aged. He smiled mournfully from behind his desk. Getting to Fat Sasha had eaten up days, but he was said to be Moscow's best fixer. As it turned out, however, it was not Fat Sasha who knew whether Dean's contracts had ever been signed. Only the man Fat Sasha referred to as 'the Lawyer' knew. The Lawyer was, of course, unavailable until the end of the week.

'What can I do?' Shrugging, like Mr Big, Fat Sasha talked directly to Leslie. Then Fat Sasha said what Harry the Horse said. 'Dean wasn't stupid. Dean and I talked about *Wounded Knee*. Once he said, "I don't think it will ever happen." '

Once more I thought a tiny knot of reality must have lain inside Dean like a gallstone. Like his ulcer, it ate him up a piece at a time.

Although there was a cooperative loo in downtown Moscow, with piped-in muzak and toilet paper, where for fifty copecks you could have a peaceful crap, Perestroika, at the end of 1988, had not yet made itself felt in Moscow's hotels.

We had begun at the Hotel Budapest, where my room had a drain in the middle of the floor and indolent cockroaches lazed in a puddle in the bathroom. Something unspeakable discoloured the sheets, and the only amenity was a green plastic radio beside the bed, which bore the mysterious sticker: Inspected by Mildred.

Leslie's room wasn't much better. It had a large refrigerator that did not work. The orange paper curtains, that did not meet, fell on his head. Vera, who had become our unofficial fixer and friend, was determined to do better, so now we stood in the lobby of the Rossiya Hotel, which had 3,000 rooms and a concert hall. When John Denver came to Moscow in 1985, he played the Rossiya as if it were Caesar's Palace, except that Caesar's lacked the stagnant slush on the lobby floors. Dean was a fan of Denver's.

'Why can't I be John Denver? I'm from Denver, too,' he often said. In Russia, Denver was much admired for his music and his politics, although people made fun of his pimples. When Denver played the Rossiya, Dean flew in from East Berlin on an impulse. He had no visa but he was Dean Reed, after all. It didn't work out and the officials at Sheremetyevo Airport kept him waiting. By the time he got to the Rossiya, he had missed the show.

For a moment I fantasised that Dean was, in fact, alive, and would come striding into the cavernous lobby. Laughing, he would make the dreary crowds laugh too. But Dean was dead, and it was all just idle speculation to help kill the time, and all there was in the lobby of the Rossiya was a sign for Diner's Club that read: RUNNING OUT OF ROUBLES?

Even in her tiny high-heeled leather boots, Vera Reich was very short. She was curious about everything. She had a genuine smile and she was completely incorruptible. As she bartered with the reservations clerk at the Rossiya, rue and outrage crossed her face. It was a brilliant performance.

'Everything is fixed,' Vera said, wiping away her make-believe tears.

'How do you do it?' I said.

'I just keep talking until they can't stand me anymore,' she said, and we all went upstairs.

The Rossiya was so big you needed a map to get around, but, having navigated the corridors, which were like Kafka's version of a vacation, we found my room and sat down there and drank a lot of Scotch.

At Vera's language school in the early 1970s, rumours began to make the rounds: Dean Reed was coming. The girls began to whisper it. All through the school you could hear the whispers. Along the corridors, before class began, in the recess, at lunch, they whispered it: Dean Reed. Dean Reed.

'Dean Reed is coming.'

'Like the Pied Piper,' said Vera.

'Was he good? Was he a good singer?'

Vera grinned. 'Who could tell? Who cared! He was so handsome and he was wearing very tight pants. He sang rock and roll. He brought us this gift. He was American.'

'I guess Dean was popular because he espoused socialist values,' Leslie said.

Vera chortled politely. 'What you must understand is that we believed exact opposite of propaganda. If the television said, America is slums, poverty, crime, we believe exact opposite. I may ask you something?' Vera inquired delicately.

'Sure.'

'How it is that some people in United States are joining the Communist Party?'

I told her that everything was not quite perfect in America. I said that there were many people who were illiterate. Kids with AIDS. Guns. I gave her the old leftie's rap: the hungry, homeless.

'But, surely, they are just bums,' said Vera.

For the time being, I left Vera to her dreams about the streets which were paved with gold.

A few months later, Vera visited the West for the first time. She didn't care about the supermarkets – the variety of goods made her hyperventilate, in fact. What she loved most about England was that relationships were not degraded by need. Vera loved the West for its friendliness.

'I guess Dean's problem going home to America was that people in America weren't too keen on socialism,' Leslie said.

'They're not too keen on it in the Soviet Union either,' Vera said. She pulled on her knitted hat. Vera was going home to some remote corner of Moscow and would collect us in the morning. I thanked her for fixing the rooms and tried to give her a box of fancy soap, but she shook her head and refused. 'This is my job,' she said politely. She smiled and was gone.

# CHAPTER 19

# Leningrad

We went to Leningrad to see Boris Grebenshikov play. It was a hot ticket. Grebenshikov was the first authentic Russian rock star, and in Leningrad, the Russians were playing with Western musicians in public for the first time. It was my first rock concert in the USSR: AQUARIUM AND FRIENDS '88. Fifty roubles on the black market.

'Guess what Aeroflot doesn't have,' said Leslie.

'I'd just as soon not know,' I said.

'Go on, guess what Aeroflot doesn't have,' he said again.

'Forget it.'

'What they don't have is oxygen. No spare oxygen supply,' he said cheerfully, and then tapped the window pane with his knuckles, pleased with himself.

'And very, very big windows. One crack and . . .'

Leslie smiled at the stewardess, who did not smile back, but delivered a tray with a cup of water that tasted like swimming pool and a single toffee, which passed for lunch. Several drunks, cans of beer in hand, roamed the aisle. How dull travel in the Soviet Union would be without the terrors of Aeroflot, the drunks, the horrible hotels, the listening devices. Small talk would dwindle drastically, dinner parties would grind to a halt. Already in Moscow, yuppies talked real estate and laptop computers and almost no one looked at the ceiling before launching into an attack on the system. Dull, very dull.

The plane shuddered. I closed my eyes and thought of a photograph of Dean's first trip to Russia: the arrival at the Finland station in Leningrad; the laughing American, packed into a tiny plane, surrounded by comrades in big fur hats. I thought of Dean standing on top of a big Russian express train, riding backwards, strumming his guitar, singing 'Bound for Glory' for the cameras. He had travelled West, to Siberia. 'This train . . .' he sang astride the moving cars.

On that train, travelling west, Dean gave his passion, his moral support, his enthusiasm to BAM. BAM was Brezhnev's campaign to open new regions for development. It was a sham, a façade, a hollow endeavour run by corrupt politicians who used Dean. To this Potemkin railway, bolstered by the heroic antics of a movie set, Dean gave his time and hope. A decade after BAM was begun, nothing had changed; workers along the railway lines still lived in shacks with open sewers beside them.

In a blinding snow-storm, we arrived at the Pribaltiskaya, a modern hotel on the outskirts of town. Drunken Finns lay in the corridors. Because in Helsinki the drinking laws were draconian, Finns flew into Leningrad for the weekend, hired a girl, got laid, drank themselves into a stupor, threw up and fell down in the hotel corridors.

Art was waiting for us at the hotel. He had just returned from London, Paris, New York, Los Angeles and Graceland. Art Troitsky said that he had enjoyed the West, but wished he had escaped in a balloon instead of buying a ticket on a boring jet. But life had grown altogether boring for Art. Where once rock and roll was a dangerous game, now, in 1988, the *apparatchiks* were listening to the *Metallisti*.

'Hmm, Metal,' they said, stroking their chins. 'Very interesting.'

'My Father is a Fascist' was the biggest hit in Leningrad.

On the stage, half a dozen British musicians in leather pants, shades, and ear studs, lolled among the lights, amplifiers, guitars, trunks, and Perrier bottles, all of it trucked in overland from Helsinki in the snow. Half a dozen film crews had come in to Leningrad to shoot a rock documentary. There was enough equipment to furnish a small planet, lights, sound gear, but there was no black paint with which to paint the stage. In Leningrad, in this industrial city of four million people, there was no black paint.

Leslie had ordered in yet another crew, because he was hoping to grab some footage from the concert for the Dean Reed film. His production manager wandered the stadium looking for a potential Dean Reed look-alike as a stand-in. Under his arm was a bag with a pair of cowboy boots in it.

Fat Lev was the local promoter and he scurried every which way, like a beetle in a jar, grinning. 'All you need is Lev, eh?' he said to everyone he met.

As always, the Russians were late, except the cellist, who sat on the stage, sawing at his instrument like a dentist trying to get at a difficult tooth.

Keeping order, more or less, was Dave Stewart of the Eurythmics. A tiny hirsute man, Dave had produced Boris Grebenshikov's first Western album. The percussionist was Ray Cooper. A big man in a fine suit with a shaved head, Ray kept his drumsticks in a silver champagne cooler. It was Ray's second trip: he had been on tour with Elton John in 1979 – the first Soviet tour by a Western superstar. From time to time, Ray went to the Kirov Ballet with his roadie.

There appeared at the back of the stadium a group of tiny gymnasts, twirling, spinning, tossing Indian clubs. They projected their perfect baby bodies into outer space like tiny sputniks, oblivious to the music. Maybe rock and roll was already unremarkable to them.

Ray Cooper hit his gongs; he resembled the man from J. Arthur Rank.

Slim, pale, with big Slavic lips and long blond hair, Boris Grebenshikov appeared. He was four hours late. Boris was thirty-five and he could look incredibly plain, or light himself up and be unspeakably handsome. He had the smile of a star. While Dean was promiscuous with his smile, Boris saved his up, waited, watched, held back, letting it come very slowly. I introduced myself; we had almost met in New York. For a second more, he calculated the smile, then he gave it all away. 'Yes, I know your name quite well,' he said.

It was hard not to compare Dean Reed with Boris Grebenshikov: the daring, uneducated boy from Colorado, the child of the fifties who became an official superstar in the Soviet Union; the Russian boy whose earliest memories were of the illicit crackle of the Beatles on the Voice of America, the mathematics student who became the first authentic Russian rocker. Grebenshikov's band was called Aquarium and they played in every style, but it was the lyrics that made him a hero. Next to a good tune, which is what made the Russians love the Beatles, they were crazy about a good lyric. Grebenshikov believed in the Beatles, he believed in the spiritual. People wrote asking him about his karma. If you were oppressed, Boris said, you could sing the blues.

The songs Boris sang were his own; religious, sentimental, satirical. They were a long way from Dean's simple platitudes.

Boris was a rebel because nothing else gave him peace. If Dean became a star by joining the mainstream, Boris became a star in the underground. In the years when Dean drank toasts with officialdom, Boris, like a character out of a Dostoevsky novel, wandered the Leningrad streets after dark, looking for trouble and finding it. In 1980 at a concert in Tblisi, he lay down with his Telecaster and got up a legend.

'Aquarium looked like rebels. When Boris lay down on the stage holding his Telecaster on his stomach, the entire judging committee stood up and left the hall,' Art said. 'The officials said, why did you bring those faggots here?'

Kids crossed the continent to see Boris. They climbed the stairs to his sixth-floor squat on Sofia Pereovskya Street in Leningrad, where he kept a picture of The Beatles on the wall as a shrine. The kids wrote poetry on the walls.

Boris was the perfect hero for his generation, for whom the significance of rock and roll was religious. Break the rules, it said. Keep the faith.

Boris' underground album was copied on cassettes a million times. Across the Soviet Union, kids cherished them because Boris' music was unofficial and hard to get hold of, and, therefore, in Soviet eyes, more valuable. Perhaps Dean's popularity declined because he had become too easy.

In 1987, Boris went legit. Melodiya issued an album by Aquarium made from the underground tapes. 200,000 copies sold out in a couple of hours. Boris signed his own contract with CBS Records; no Soviet had ever signed a contract before.

Boris went to America, where he was enthralled and confused and sat in a closet in a flat in the East Village, listening to music, and by a pool in Hollywood. His fans despaired. Perhaps he, too, had become easy. Boris and Art were friends, but Art was angry at him and he was cynical: within a decade you would hear Boris' music in the elevator of the Moscow Hilton, he promised. Even Art's mother liked Boris.

★

Like most Muscovites, Art despised Leningrad and I could see how he felt. The 'City of Bad Memories', he called it. It made me feel imprisoned.

A port city blasted from a swamp by slave labour, it was a provincial town, invaded incessantly by foreigners, its *fartovshiki*, the two-bit criminals, hustled you relentlessly.

Still, it was a Georgian wet dream of a city with its matched sets of pastel buildings and the gilded griffons on the bridges and the pale green Winter Palace iced with snow.

What I remembered best in Leningrad was the freaky wax statue of Peter the Great, with his own hair, in a glass case at the Hermitage. And the waiter at the Metropole Restaurant who stood in a puddle of brown water, jars of caviar shoved in his pockets under his tailcoat. And the fact that, under siege by the Nazis, Leningrad's people ate wallpaper paste.

Snuffling into his coat sleeve, our guide shifted his feet. It was cold. All day he listened to us as we abused his country – the bureaucracy, the food. He refused our Marlboros.

'Are you with the rock concert,' he said.

Everyone knew that Boris was in town.

'Yes,' I said.

'I met Boris once about eight years ago, but he's very famous now. He wouldn't remember me.'


Before the concert began, I wandered into a dressing room where tinted photographs of heroes of Soviet sport – ice skaters in spangles, footballers in jerseys stiff with sweat – were on the walls. A member of the Russian band was there. His hair draped over his ears, he stared into the mirror, reciting his mantra. The room was sweet with pot. It smelled like 1968.

'Sing it in Russian!'

Boris sang in Russian.

12,000 kids clapped and wept. The hard core who stood at the edge of the stage, linked arms and lit candles. Kids rushed to the stage and a pale young girl, turning her face up to him, held up a picture of Boris, an icon in a plastic sleeve.

'Sing it in Russian!'

But Boris took charge. He introduced Dave and Ray. These were his friends from the West, he said, and they were going to sing some songs in English.

'Sing it in Russian!'

Film crews in running shoes raced around backstage, recording it all. News crews were there. Foreigners loved rock and roll in Russia. It was the sexiest image of the decade. The revolution had come and it sounded good. It sounded great. It was noisy. It was vivid. It seemed to tear up the monolith of seventy years and throw it away with wonderful abandon.

Kids punched the air. The girls with the pale lips swooned. In the best seats, officials clapped politely and tried not to wish they were listening to Tchaikovsky. Kids threw flowers. Kids unfurled Russian flags, and the hammer and sickle waved to the sound of Ray Cooper's chimes. A boy in a yellow satin jacket turned his back so everyone could see the slogan on it. It read: GLASNOST '88, as if Glasnost were this year's Woodstock.

In the middle of the swaying sea of bodies, a young Russian soldier in uniform got on his girlfriend's shoulders and loosened his tie. He made a V sign. Seeing me standing backstage, next to Leslie, he gestured wildly. He wanted Leslie to take his picture. Then the boy whispered to his friend, who got on his girl's shoulders and the two of them made V signs and laughed like crazy.

'Take our picture,' they mouthed.

Boris sang his anthem: 'Rock and roll is dead, but I'm not yet.'

'I'm from Sunderland, Boris is from Leningrad. We meet. It's just a tiny thing. But it's better than killing each other,' Dave Stewart said.

'All you need is love.'

We sang it, wishing it were true.

The revolution looked like a rock concert. It made you cry in the way that singing 'Imagine' made you cry. It was the best thing since peace and love went out of style. How Dean would have loved it! Oh, how he would have crowed at its arrival, this delicious goodwill, this noise, it was everything he wanted. Or would he? Maybe this world would have passed him by, in its spandex mini-skirts, its boys in ponytails with stubble on their chins and sedition in their hearts and an ambiguous Russian mix of sex, politics and religion. Maybe Glasnost '88 would have left Dean on the sidelines with his acoustic guitar and bell-bottom pants, an old man. Maybe Glasnost would have left Dean Reed dead in the water.

'Sing it in Russian!'

# CHAPTER 20

# The Blue Bird Café

'The sixties are alive and well and living in Moscow,' Jo said.

At the bar at the National Hotel, at a small table with his big bag, I found my friend Jo Durden-Smith. It was the day we got back to Moscow from Leningrad. Jo had on his high-heeled cowboy boots and a hat. His tooled leather shoulder bag was open. He never went anywhere without it: Jo was a writer.

An Englishman who spoke in whole paragraphs, he dripped with charm, in spite of his ruined face and hooded eyes, or maybe because of them. He and Leslie were old friends. When Jo left London for America in the sixties.

'I have to commit myself to the revolution,' Jo said.

Twenty years later, Jo had discovered the Russians, as he had once discovered America. It wasn't just that Jo liked to be where the action was – which he did – there was something about the Russians that touched him in the way that America had once done. Unlike the cosy, comfortable, middle-class England he came out of, where everything was known, in Russia, Jo could lose himself. And he could claim it as his own at exactly the moment when you could actually feel history happening – I suppose that's how the American sixties were, too. Here it was all over again: the politics; the rock and roll; the drugs; the clothes; the wild nights.

And as Jo shuttled in and out of Russia, it grew more and more exhilarating. Westerners flooded in: movie producers did deals; Western comics did stand-ups in Red Square; businessmen grabbed what they could – I knew one who felt salvation for the Soviet Union lay in potato chip factories. In Moscow, at least, Glasnost had also begun to liberate the Russians, not so much from fear but from nothingness, from those blank faces in the subways. Their natural melodrama was prised out from under the anxious surface and people bellowed with rage and sometimes with laughter. Even the women who guarded the floor at the Rossiya Hotel were moved and they smiled shyly and hoped you would offer them some lipstick.

Joe was crazy about all of it and he had a real writer's tolerance for it all and for the Wispys – the poets and musicians who played Bach on the *balalaika* until early morning; for the hoods who could get you diamond earrings cheap; for the famous pianist whose main interest was the relative merits of seven-star brandies. Jo knew his way around Moscow: he could get you into the Bolshoi Ballet through the back door, where a man waited to ply you with cakes and sweet champagne; he knew where to buy a good steak; he knew everyone in Moscow and everyone knew Jo. He met Yelena, who was an interpreter, and they fell in love and, a year later they got married and had a baby. Jo did not believe in your ordinary souvenir.

Like any number of Westerners before him – the folk singers in sandals and the spies and the Jewish lefties, like my mother who went to Moscow once and danced in her nightgown with a naval officer at a nightclub ('It looked better than any evening dress *they* had!' she said), above all, like Dean Reed, Jo was seduced by the Russians.

'The sixties are alive and well and living in Moscow,' I repeated portentously to anyone who would listen.

Jo's girl, Yelena, lived with her momma and her daughter in a flat in the centre of Moscow. Yelena's momma wore a headscarf and bedroom slippers. She took messages for everyone and made wonderful eggplant and chocolate cake. I gave her a box of scented soap and later, through a half-open door, I saw her perusing the label carefully, decoding the legend of this box from New York City.

Like everyone in Moscow with access to the West, Yelena's family hoarded stuff, and the kitchen where we ate supper was strewn, in profligate disarray, with shortbread, Scotch, and Chanel nail polish.

We ate stroganoff, kasha, pickles, eggplant, cabbage, cookies, chocolate cake, bread and butter, beer and wine and whisky and soda. And while Jo poured more beer, Yelena's daughter took me to her bedroom to show me the Dean Reed poster on the wall.

She was sixteen and it had been there nearly all her life. It was inscribed: 'I thank you for your love and friendship and for your tears as you watched *El Cantor*. Be brave and happy and truthful.'

As a little child of five, Zenia saw *El Cantor* on television. 'I saw Dean Reed in a film about Victor Jara on Soviet TV and they killed Jara and I cried. They were such humble people and I have such an image of them and their ponchos.'

'What do you want for your birthday this year,' Yelena asked her daughter.

'I want to meet Dean Reed,' Zenia said.

'My momma dressed me up like a little doll and took me with her to the Rossiya Hotel where Dean was performing.'

'Do you want me to dance with you?' Dean said to Zenia when they met.

'What do you think of me?' he asked her next.

'In my kindergarten, some people think of tables, some of chairs. I think of you,' said Zenia.

Showing off, she began counting in English for Dean and he laughed and she nearly died of embarrassment.

A lifetime later, in the winter of 1986, Zenia saw Dean again. It was in Krylatoskoye at the Olympic Velodrome, which was Stas Namin's old discotheque. Stas was at the peak of his popularity and it was a big disco packed with kids, lights, music and smoke. Suddenly, the door opened, Stas Namin appeared, and clapped for attention.

'We have a friend here. We have the famous Dean Reed,' Stas said.

There was an uncomfortable silence and, half a beat too late, the crowd obediently rushed towards Dean, who strode into the spotlight.

From his pocket, Dean took pictures of himself and began signing them, handing them out to the dancers in the club, who took them politely.

Sitting on a box that held the equipment that made smoke for the disco, Zenia watched, a little aloof.

'Dean was all frozy and had snow on his coat,' she said.

'His music was not interesting. Once he was handsome, and he was trying to keep his romantic American image,' she said. 'But he realised the game was over. It reminded me of an F. Scott Fitzgerald story, *The Last Beauty of the Self*.'

An intense feeling of sadness came over Zenia. That night in the discotheque Dean reminded her of her grandpa who could not face the truth.

'Grandpa grew up under Stalin. Grandpa was a spy during the War. When he worked for the KGB, he felt it was real and virtuous. If you take their work away, men like this have nothing. In the end, he had nothing to live for. He was just like Dean Reed. 'Grandpa used to say "My eyes can see 180 degrees," ' Zenia said.

'You can take a sword 360 degrees around me and cut no string,' Dean would say.

'Grandpa was a true believer.'

That same night in the discotheque Dean talked to Zenia. 'What do young people really feel?' he asked. 'Will you write to my daughter, Ramona. She only wants to marry a millionaire and I am unhappy,' he said, and she meant to write, but there was never time.

'My attitudes changed of course,' Zenia said. 'We are the small brothers and sisters of Boris Grebenshikov. We had all our principles changed. We have none left.'

'Why did you keep Dean's poster?'

'He was a hero created by publicity and I understood all the power in this country is shit, but I believed he believed. When I heard he died, I was not surprised. I thought: everyone has to pay. But the poster was a bright impression of my childhood. Dean was our first American.'

As Zenia sat on the box in Stas Namin's disco, the terrible sadness of fifteen weighting down her skinny shoulders, she thought to herself that, in 1986 when she last saw him, Dean Reed seemed like a man surprised by the passage of time.

'Time had passed quickly and he had not noticed and now it was too late. I thought he was the saddest man I ever saw.'

At the Blue Bird Café, the musicians, in their wide-boy pinstripes, like visitors from the past, produced the poignant ripple of 'Autumn in New York'. It had been a famous rock venue and was now a jazz club and the smoke was thick. Crowded around the little tables in the cellar, the jazz fans, like jazz fans everywhere, bobbled their heads knowingly into their black turtleneck sweaters.

The introductions were in English. 'English is the language of jazz,' said the manager.

'Jazz is the language of democracy,' said the tenor sax player, who called himself Alexander Mouscou and whose hero was Charlie Parker. Mournfully, he returned to the stage, where he played 'Moonlight in Vermont' for us.

From the next table, a man with a hard face hailed us and said that he had been to jail once for listening to Willis Connover's Jazz Hour on the Voice of America, and not for the first time, I thought ruefully about my own adolescent contempt for the Voice of America. The arm of imperialist 'Amerika', we said it was. In Moscow, I discovered that jazz and rock and roll on the Voice of America kept people alive. Like Dean Reed, I had been a sucker for an ideology.

'Dean bloody Reed.' Art was mumbling into his glass of Avocat.

From the moment Art said, 'Come to Moscow, I will introduce you to those who knew Dean Reed,' he was the perfect guide. He had stage managed everything, producing girlfriends, rock stars, information. He played the good reporter, objective, impartial. He was intelligent, selfish, cynical and smart and, always surprising, very tender. Cosmopolitan, urbane, Art was a metaphorical New Yorker, one of the dispossessed. Art didn't need some crummy clod of earth to claim as a home; he rarely went on about roots; his home was his friends, wherever they were, and he could work the city. Any city. Rock and roll was his revolution. Now, he raised his glass, drank it dry, and a stream of venom poured out of him.

'Dean Reed was a bastard,' Art said quietly. 'At first everyone welcomed him. He looked like an American and he sang like one. In the early seventies, drastic changes happened. The generation of young Soviets split into the Stupids or Rednecks and the Non-Stupids or Underground. For another decade Dean was cheered by the Rednecks, for whom he remained the only real star.'

'Rednecks?'

'The working class and peasant young people who took what culture they were given by the state. Dean Reed was like a token American on Soviet TV. Dean Reed was all there was.

'The Rednecks believed what they were told by the Soviet media: Dean Reed was very big in America but he sacrificed his popularity in the US after discovering communist ideals. We understood he was nothing in America . . . I personally realised that quite well, I read books, I followed the music charts. A fucking American Soviet traitor.

'I shared the 100 per cent ironic and despising view of him which existed in the Soviet underground. We simply could not understand, how can a person who represents the Western culture which we loved so much, which for us meant freedom, how can a person who comes from there be such a bastard?

'He shakes hands with Soviet officials, appears in concerts with the most hideous Soviet pop stars, singing patriotic songs, awful patriotic Young Communist singers . . . For most, he was young, he played the guitar, he occasionally did something like "Blue Suede Shoes". For us, it is a betrayal. How can he be on the same base with all these small Communist Soviet bastards? He was on the one hand rock and roll, on the other hand for everything that we were opposing. We couldn't understand because he was a person who digs rock and roll, wears cowboy boots, who was born in the USA, the land of the free, home of the brave and Chuck Berry. He was perceived as the ultimate bastard. It was weird. It was just weird.'

On May 30, 1986, Art Troitsky organised a concert to benefit the victims of the nuclear disaster at Chernobyl. Held in Moscow, it was the first event of its kind. Rock and roll went legit. The bands were all Russian. Everyone signed on, including Alla Pugachova, the biggest pop star in the Soviet Union.

With her red hair, her skinny legs and big bosom, she was their Bette Midler. Her face was mobile, fleshy, intelligent and well travelled. She lived in a large flat in Moscow with a tufted leather bar, a maid, a melon-coloured bathtub and a bodyguard who was really a poet. Pugachova had given millions of Russians permission to be vulgar, and her records sold thirty million copies a year. She had been official for twenty years, but she was her own woman. She did not like Dean Reed, but she was polite.

'Dean was a man who checked his own talent, who never developed,' Pugachova said, but then the conversation moved on, as if Dean had not really mattered for a very long time.

With the Chernobyl concert, Soviet rock came of age. It had given a generation an identity. As Art put it, it meant: fight your parents. It meant: you are free to do what you want, no matter what the seniors say. It was a form of fighting back, a reaction to oppression, a catalyst for change. It taught people how to be themselves and how to oppose the rules.

'Rock was a concentration of all the good things in life,' said Art.

Tens of thousands turned out for the Chernobyl concert. There was a rumour that Dean Reed was there, at the concert, but nobody asked him to play. It was less than two weeks before his death.

In the same conference room at Sovinfilm where Dean negotiated his deal for *Wounded Knee* that spring in 1986, sat Boris, the Lawyer. He was the legal advisor to Sovinfilm and he wrote the contracts and witnessed them. A nice man with a good smile, he had a head like a skull. He was fond of Dean.

'Was the contract for *Wounded Knee* cancelled?' Leslie said. 'Was *Wounded Knee* shelved?'

But Boris the Lawyer wanted to reminisce.

'I have a friend who is very similar in appearance to Dean Reed – my friend and I were buddies in the Army – so I felt friendly towards Dean,' said Boris.

'Dean was always enthusiastically welcomed, a permanent friend of the Soviet Union. Yes, he always had photos in a bag ready to deliver when asked. He behaved himself. He was a good guy.'

'Completely?'

Boris was a lawyer and he shifted into a moderate gear. 'Dean was temperamental. He scolded, he shouted. But he was a good guy all the same,' he said.

Boris reiterated what we already knew: how important *Wounded Knee* was to Dean; how he was obliged to take a co-director; how the co-director got cancer a few months before filming began, leaving everyone in the lurch and the film companies nervous.

But what about the contracts?

The first script was approved as far back as the 15th of November, 1984. Boris the Lawyer had the piece of paper.

'But the final contracts, no . . . I think not. I think these were never signed . . . '

Boris dived into his lawyer's bag. Leslie and I waited, not looking at each other. If the contract had not been signed, if *Wounded Knee* had been shelved, it would have been the end of the road. It would have given Dean a motive for dying and us a motive for an end for our movie. Leslie and I, on the road now for two years, sat in our chairs while Boris the lawyer knelt down to open the bottom drawer of his desk. For a moment, he shifted some paper.

'I have found it!'

Triumphant, Boris emerged with a sheaf of papers. On the 10th of June, 1986, the final contract for the co-production on *Wounded Knee* had been signed, or so it seemed, by a Mr Gerrit List, a representative of the German film studios at Potsdam.

I stared at the bits of paper written in languages I did not understand, signed less than forty-eight hours before Dean died, and wondered if the two events could have been connected.

Or was it Yalta? Rumours circulated that filming had been cancelled because Yalta was devastated by the fall-out from Chernobyl, when it blew, in May.

Boris shook his head. Yalta was clean, he said. Other film makers were at work there, but it was years before the horrors of Chernobyl were revealed.

Boris shuffled more paper. Shooting was to have begun on June 24 in East Germany and on August 11 in the Soviet Union.

'Everything was set,' he said. 'Even the music director, who was from Prague. He was called Svoboda. Everybody in Prague is called Svoboda. Unless they are called prisoner,' he added with a straight face.

I didn't get it.

'Svoboda means freedom,' Leslie whispered.

'When Dean died, everything was cancelled,' Boris said. 'Without Dean there was no movie. He was the movie.'

Boris the Lawyer handed across a termination contract for *Wounded Knee*. It was dated July 15, 1986. The contract for the picture was declared null and void. Dean's body was discovered on June 17. They hadn't wasted much time.

Boris the Lawyer looked sorry. He sat perfectly still for a minute, lost in some impenetrable Russian reverie. Then he smiled cheerily and packed up his lawyer's briefcase.

'Things change,' he said.

# CHAPTER 21

# The End of the Road

You could see the barbed wire from the telephone booth. It was a hundred yards from the Berlin Wall. Even on days when Checkpoint Charlie was jammed with cars, the crumbling stretch of West Berlin had a doomed, uninhabited appearance and it was a frightening, desperate place.

Dean called Dixie.

Things got worse and worse for Dean. Anxious and exhausted over the contracts for *Wounded Knee*, he and Renate fought more and more often, and his letters to America were punctuated with expressions of fatigue. He felt old. Incessantly, he looked for grey hairs in the mirror.

He called Dixie every Tuesday from Schmockwitz and every Friday from the West. He was scared to death.

On one occasion at least, Dean went into West Berlin wearing a false wig and a moustache. Dixie told me this and she said he used a phony name. What name I had asked, what name? Dixie fumbled some papers and pulled out a brown envelope and pointed to the name on the return address: Manfred Dorniok, it said and I knew Dixie must have misunderstood. Why would Dean use a disguise? Why would he use the name of a distinguished West German film producer who was his friend? Why did he really cross the Wall to call Dixie? It was the stuff of melodrama, but it was driven by real panic.

Perhaps he crossed to get to the Berliner Bank, a branch within spitting distance of the Wall, where he kept his hard currency account. Someone else said it was to get away from Renate.

Renate had been unhappy about the calls and letters from Dixie all through the winter and spring.

'She's so insecure,' said Dean to Dixie.

'She's a little girl, Dean. Don't blow it.'

'How's your love life?' Dean asked.

'I don't have one. I haven't been looking,' Dixie said.

'Paton used to tell us you can't look for that.'

The tension grew. When Dixie called, it was often Renate who picked up the telephone. She was always polite.

'He is home, but moment, please,' said Renate and went to fetch Dean.

'I had some problems with Renate today,' said Dean.

'Pick yourself up,' said Dixie.

'It's a little bit more difficult. It was your telephone call. She said we talked for one and a half hours. I said it couldn't be like that. She's jealous sometimes. She's crying now.'

'I want to be her friend,' said Dixie.

'I know she's scared,' said Dean. 'She's not accustomed to someone sending so many letters back and forth. I tell her very often, but it doesn't help.'

'You go on down and put your arm around her, go tell her we want her,' said Dixie.

But Dixie stayed on the phone.

Dean had asked Dixie to write to Renate and she had written. She wrote about American customs and how everyone would hug Renate; she wrote how Renate would like the climate; that she must not cut her hair because American men liked women with long hair; that she must not be sad.

In March, Renate replied.

'Let me try to explain how the conflict between Dean and I arose. I don't know you, and I don't know whether you have any feeling for my predicament.

'My husband travelled in his homeland . . . My thoughts were with him and yearned for him but I couldn't form a picture in my mind because I didn't really comprehend . . . He came back full of hope, wanting to live in America, which to me was a strange land. He had got to know a beautiful, intelligent and rich lady – you.

'He cannot remember you as a young girl but all of a sudden you're in his life. Since he came back he only thinks about you and not us. He is so aggressive and unjust against my homeland, which has given him every chance for professional development. He is only happy when he comes home and finds there is a letter from you or America. For good or bad he has completely changed . . . I am no longer a partner to him. Do you understand him, Dixie? I can no longer develop ideas with him. I can only listen to him. I dread the day when Dean will no longer need me. Love can only grow when people need each other. Now there is still only Dixie, the friend, the manager. He would have abandoned me if I had obstructed your contact with him . . .

'I understand his great yearning for his native country. The older one gets the more intensely one yearns for the country of their childhood. But I confronted him about our conflict; how it would carry on if I were to find a young director who was particularly interested in me, who stuck closely by me and gave me big presents . . . He would not be able to bear it . . .

'I want your friendship and I promise that my nerves will not be torn to shreds . . . One evening, a lovely evening by the fire (and this kind of evening is rare in our eventful lives) Dean spoke to you on the telephone for half an hour. I was once again forgotten. Before, I was the most important thing in his life – and vice versa. Now, I was once again forgotten. My insecurity grows and grows and then I cried and screamed. It will not happen again . . .

'With us artists, we are a mixture of inferiority complexes and over-estimation . . . When Dean and I are low together it is complicated because it leads to a bad outcome. And a bad outcome is only recognised when it is too late.

'I have known Dean since 1973 . . . I love Dean most deeply . . . ' She asked Dixie for a photograph of herself and said she wished only for her friendship.

A week later Renate wrote again, a short cheery letter, thanking Dixie for her friendship. Renate noted she had a cold and could not kiss Dean.

The two women never met.

I knew that whatever happened to Dean happened inside the last few weeks of his life. After the trip to Moscow, I had come back to Berlin to talk to Renate at the house in Schmockwitz. Once more, I sat in Checkpoint Charlie. It was summer, and the sour, pale guards were in shirtsleeves, but nothing else had changed. Nothing, nothing would change here, I thought. It was the summer of 1988.

I looked at the telephone booth that was within sight of the Berlin Wall. Maybe it was here that Dean called Dixie.

He told her the movie was coming unglued. Someone was following him, he said. He had plans to 'flee to the West', she said, although it seemed odd, because he had an American passport and no need to flee.

'I don't know my status here. I'm frightened,' he told Dixie from the telephone in West Berlin. 'I am frightened.'

Dean talked a lot about America late that spring – the special smell of Colorado, its blue skies – his longing was endless. He could always pull himself up, though. He was all over the place, like a man cleaning up his life. He visited Wiebke in the little house with the swimming pool, where on a hot day in spring she sat in her bikini in the garden, typing translations. Smiling, Dean pushed open the gate.

'I've been thinking things over and I want to leave a present for Natasha,' Dean said.

He gave Wiebke 3,000 Czech crowns.

'That's very generous, Dean,' Wiebke said.

He said he wanted to see Natasha more often because he was going to the United States.

'I want to come back and talk. Maybe I shall come back on Monday,' he said.

'He never came back,' said Wiebke. 'I wish I had just wrapped away my typewriter and said, "This is a good time, why don't we talk now?" But the moment passed and we didn't. That's the last time I ever saw him.'

Doggedly, Dean continued his work on *Wounded Knee*. On June 1, 1986 he wrote his classmates at Wheat Ridge High: Dear Friends, 'Wheat Ridge-ites' and countrymen – lend me your ears. Hey, I miss you all and feel that it is not especially fair that during the school reunion I shall be directing and acting in a film that I wrote . . . I would much rather be with you all at the Old School House in the Ole Gym – we could play some basketball and my team would lose . . . I also hate missing the Ole-Fashioned Picnic, because I love to eat hamburgers and potato chips, and we don't have that here in East Germany where I live!!! We have a lot of

German hot dogs, but I happen to be a hamburger fan (One always wants what one doesn't have!)'

He wrote of his destiny and how it had taken him to thirty-two countries, that he spoke four languages (English the worst!), sat in prison, fought injustice, made his mistakes, favoured the human race over the arms race. He wished his friends much peace love courage and happiness, and signed it, with an embrace, 'Dean "Slim" Reed'.

*Wounded Knee* was scheduled to begin on Tuesday, June 24. Tuesday, because it was bad luck to start a picture on a Monday, Gerrit List told me.

On my way to Schmockwitz, I met Gerrit List in East Berlin. He was a production manager at DEFA who had worked with Dean in East Berlin almost from the beginning and I got the impression that he had considerable power inside the film business.

I met him in the lobby of the Grand Hotel, which had become my refuge in East Berlin. He was a middle-aged man in an anorak and the grey leather shoes of the East German smartset. He smoked Camels. He was almost certainly a Party member. With Dean, he had made *El Cantor* in Bulgaria and *Sing Cowboy Sing* in Romania. List could effectively manage the complicated life of a location: he could work in Soviet Karelia in winter and in Cuba in tropical heat, and, once, he waited patiently in a Cuban port for a ship that was three weeks late because he did not have the hard currency to expedite the baggage by air – that was sometimes the price of working in movies. He had a nice time in that sunny Cuban port, though. 'The Bay of Pork,' he called it.

It was Saturday morning when we met, and although he refused even a coffee – I think he wanted to get on with his shopping – he talked freely about *Wounded Knee*. By June there were already ninety people at work in Yalta and List looked forward to a complex three month shoot. 'The Crimea looked a hundred per cent like South Dakota!' he said with the tidy pride of a good production manager who has accomplished the impossible and reinvented the world: Bulgaria for Chile; The Crimea for Dakota.

'Riga was a very fine studio and I have developed very hearty friendships in the Soviet Union,' he said.

It was true. Everyone in Russia liked Gerrit List.

Crossing his plump legs, he exhaled some smoke and I asked him if the trip to America changed Dean. He nodded. 'He was filled with impressions. "My country is so great. People are so good. Politics are so bad," ' Gerrit counted them off. 'He tells me Dixie will organise a concert tour. "I want to do it. People are now knowing the truth," ' he tells me.

Dean was a bad singer, said List, who confided that he was a fan of Dixieland. But it didn't matter.

'Dean just played himself,' said Gerrit. 'In the beginning, some people said, "Why does he stay?" I think, only my opinion' – Gerrit put his hand lightly on his breast – 'he stayed for love. For Renate.'

Things had changed for Dean in East Berlin.

'In the Soviet Union Dean was like God. Here it was no longer so. A lot of people felt he wasn't so big.'

I didn't tell Gerrit List that things had changed for him everywhere, that in the big record store on Kalinin Prospekt in Moscow, you could not find a single Dean Reed album or that at Supraphon in Prague, by 1986, production on Dean's albums had dwindled almost to nothing. In 1979, 1980, 1981, 90,000 copies of his records were issued. With 'Country Songs', the 1986 album he set so much store by, there were only a couple of thousand. After that: nothing.

It was not a thing his friends in Colorado knew.

I remembered that Dean told Mike Wallace that he espoused the socialist way because it offered, above all, security. He did not have to worry about a job or about medical care, unlike his father who died for the lack of it. Not even the security of socialism could protect him from the defection of his fans or from his own middle age.

Renate knew.

At the house down the country road, she waited at the front door, smiling. It was a lovely day in early summer and the house and woods looked as they must have looked on the day Dean left. Boats bobbed on the lake. There was the sound of lawn mowers and the smell of new cut grass. A large man in short shorts and Scholl clogs appeared. Hans produced and conducted Dean's television shows and he lived across the lake.

Just then, throwing themselves out of the boat, Sasha and his friends clattered up the walk into the house, and Renate smiled and went to get them a meal. In summer, crowded with children, the windows open, the house was much less lonely, but it was in summer, of course, that Dean died.

Renate cooked for the giant, gangling kids who gorged themselves. I talked to Hans.

Yes, he said, Dean's popularity as a singer was going and he was sad about it. He knew tastes were changing. His voice was fading. He was nearing fifty. He wanted to act.

How sad?

But the kids skidded out to their boat and Hans went away with a basket of strawberries to his red Peugeot that matched the fruit, his Dr Scholls' clogs going 'clock, clock, clock' down the garden path.

At first, Renate told me little things. She told me how, when Dean's co-director on *Wounded Knee* got cancer, the blow was enormous. She showed me Dean's own copy of *Wounded Knee*; the script was painstakingly annotated in English in his schoolboy handwriting. There were notes about casting, but also notes about the best place to buy plastic cups in West Berlin and you could feel Dean's immense weariness. He was the star, the director, the writer of *Wounded Knee*, and still, he had to get the plastic cups. Real directors did not buy their own plastic cups.

Renate sifted through the boxes that lay half open. After Dean died, she received a telephone bill for 2,800 marks. A thousand pounds. Most of the calls were to Johnny in Loveland, she said. I thought they were to Dixie and that Renate knew it. Her voice was bitter.

'It was *60 Minutes*. The letters,' Renate said suddenly, lighting a cigarette, tossing back her luxuriant black hair.

She began to talk. Renate was a realist. She knew that on the university circuit in America, with a few songs and the story of his extraordinary life, Dean might have made a small go of it. Dixie and Johnny wanted to turn him into a commercial pop star and take the politics out.

'He was not good in that way,' said Renate simply.

*60 Minutes!* The night it was shown, Renate was frantic. America had just bombed Libya, and with the anti-Arab feeling in America and with Dean dancing around with Yassir Arafat . . . My God, she thought. It was a disaster. Dean was in Moscow. She could not get through. He came home after the day *60 Minutes* was transmitted, and, when Renate told him, he was crazy. His mood went black. Everything was over, he said.

'Kaput,' she said. She used the word 'kaput' and put her head in her hands.

Miraculously, it turned out for the best, or so it seemed. Miraculous, but things change. In May, CBS sent a video tape of the show to Schmockwitz, and Dean watched it and was happy. It was fair minded. Dean was quite chipper. Mike Wallace sent on a few nice letters which viewers had written. Dean wrote to Wallace to thank him and suggest they work together for world peace.

Dean didn't hear much from Dixie for a while, or from Johnny, and that worried him some. He wrote to say he hoped the show had not changed their relationship.

Why was Dean worried enough to write to Dixie? Did he suspect that Dixie was losing heart and Johnny was sitting out in that shed, his butt burned over Dean's betrayal? Dean whistled a lot and made plans. It must have been in the week or two before Dean's death that the rest of the mail was forwarded to Schmockwitz by the CBS bureau in London.

Renate shuddered, as if death had come into the room, and, chilled, she wrapped herself with her arms. The letters! Oh, God, Renate remembered, the letters.

Every night, spectacles on his nose, Dean sat up in bed, reading the letters. Over and over. Over and over he read the letters to *60 Minutes*; the letters which called him a traitor and a terrorist and a fraud; which said, in effect, keep out of America, no one wants you here – go home to Russia, they said. No one wants you here.

And still Dean kept reading.

Not all of the letters were inarticulate. The cruelest letters did not despise Dean for his politics, but for his hypocrisy, his ego, as an opportunist, a man of little talent who could only make it east of the Berlin Wall.

Dean read them again. Renate snatched them from him and tore them into little pieces. After that, Dixie and Johnny started phoning him: You blew it with *60 Minutes*. You'll never work in this country, they said.

Even Victor Grossman knew.

'Did Dean plan to defect?'

207

'He didn't have to defect. He had an American passport,' said Victor. 'But he wanted to go home. *60 Minutes* was going to change his life, but it all went horribly wrong.'

'What went wrong?'

'What went wrong with what?' Victor said.

'With *60 Minutes*. You said it went wrong.'

'Dean thought he'd done so well on it. Then Dixie – you've met Dixie?'

I said I knew Dixie.

'Dixie wrote to him to say: you blew it. You fucked up. It's over. You can't come home again. You did so badly on *60 Minutes*, you blew your chances. Dean lay on his bed in a darkened room unable to function. His movies were less popular. This is a country of twelve million people. Dean said "I've given concerts in every single bloody town." He was a big star, then his star began to fade. The kids wanted to stand by the Wall and listen to Michael Jackson. He heard the doors shutting one at a time,' said Victor.

The wraps were coming off. There was something horrible and bleak in the middle of this story.

Renate listened in to the calls from Colorado.

'What kind of friends were these?' she said.

Dear Johnny,

I realise the problems that are now going through your mind, Johnny. You are in a pickle, as the cowboys would say. You and your friends and family met a guy named Dean Reed after twenty-five years of absence. You and your friends liked what you saw and heard. But then this guy named Deano goes and declares himself a Marxist or Socialist. By his enemies he is called a commie!

Dean never gave up trying. And Johnny, who felt himself to be Dean's friend, according to his own lights, worried for Deano. He was convinced if Dean came back to America after *60 Minutes* he would get his head blown off. Which was why Johnny spent a whole lot of time out back in his shed, trying to tell Dean what was what.

The last time I visited the Rosenburgs, Mona said that, just before his death, Dean phoned very early one morning. She took the call. Dean asked if everything was all right because he hadn't heard a word.

Mona said they had bad flu.

Dean said if they were in any kind of trouble, he would come back there and fix it, and during the whole conversation, early that morning, Dean acted as though someone was listening in, looking over his shoulder. Something was wrong, Mona felt, but she could not say what.

What did it mean? Mona did not know. Maybe Dean was looking for a reason to come back. But it was early in the morning and she was feeling lousy and the line was bad.

Johnny went out to the shed where he worked and came back with a cassette in his hand.

'I wrote a song for Dean and here's a kind of mystery: I've been accused of foreseeing Dean's death by writing this song. But after the *60 Minutes* episode, after how shook up he was and how shook up I was, I sat down and wrote a song called "Yankee Man". It's about Dean. I sent it, I think it was about two days before he died, and of course he never got to hear it. I've often thought who over there got to hear it? Has Renate heard it? Have the authorities heard it?'

Johnny put the cassette in the player and turned it up.

Yankee Man you say you're proud to be an American
But you can turn around and you tear your country down
If you can't find nothin' good to say about the USA
Then you'd better stay right where you are,
In the land of the big red star
But still I'll always call you a friend,
I guess I will until the end,
I only wish you'd turn yourself around
For if you don't change what you say, your coming home could be the day
Someone will place you six feet under ground.
Yankee man you've walked upon the wrong side of the world for just too long.

The package with the cassette was postmarked June 11, 1986 the day before Dean disappeared. It arrived in Schmockwitz after he was dead and only Renate heard the terrible song.

'Shall we eat?'

It was dinner time and Renate was looking for a word in English.

'I am missing this word,' she said, grimacing, balling up her fists, opening a package of cigarettes, crumpling the cellophane.

'Damn. A word. What is the word? I am thinking.'

We went to a little restaurant at a camping site, a few miles from the house at Schmockwitz, down a bumpy lane near the lake. Kids in shorts ran and played among the chalets and tents. Their parents sat outside and smoked and called them in to bed.

It was a fine summer evening, humid, soft – the way it must have been the night Dean died. Renate apologised for the restaurant, but I liked it. It had piney walls and checkered tablecloths. The waitress smiled. I had beer and Renate had champagne. We both ate dainty little steaks with mushrooms.

I asked her if she could talk about Dean's death at all, and it was as if a dam burst. She talked and talked, and the first thing she said was something she had hinted at before: that she had to believe his death was an accident because otherwise she could not bear the pain, because otherwise it was . . . what was this word she was missing?

There was no acting, no mannerisms, no performance. Just a woman talking about loss. Her hands were steady when she lit her cigarette.

In the last week of Dean's life, he had what she called a heart attack – I could not know how serious for we had no interpreter. She told the story in a flat, matter-of-fact voice. Renate and Dean were at home in Schmockwitz. Dean was reading his script and making notes when he clutched his chest and sat back suddenly. He would not let her call the doctors. He was one week away from the biggest film of his life, which would have been stopped if a doctor was involved. They argued. Finally, he slept. The next morning, he would not talk about it, but it was in the same week that they had the fight about the lawn.

It was how such things happened, Renate said. I said I understood. It was a very hot day. The lake was filled with boats. The sound of the lawn mowers all across Schmockwitz gave off an insistent buzz. Renate asked Dean to cut the lawn. He refused.

You know how these things are, Renate said again. I said, again, that I knew.

A terrible fight ensued and Dean was enraged. He had a bad temper, she said, and she, too, had a temperamental side, but usually she could balance things, but on the day of the grass cutting, she could not – how shall I translate? – hack it. And so there was the fight, that was about cutting the grass and about not cutting the grass.

Dean stormed upstairs to his study. A few minutes later, she followed. To her horror the door was locked. Dean never locked the door. Never! Renate knocked.

'Please Dean, please let's talk,' she said. 'Talk to me!'

There was no answer.

'Please!'

As if in slow motion, he opened the door and she saw him take a machete – a prop from one of his films – from the wall where it hung, and he took it down and raised it and began to slice his arm. He sliced his arm fifty times.

'My father was brave enough to kill himself, but I can do nothing,' he said to Renate.

Dean stood in the door at the top of the landing and then slowly sank to the bed; Sasha raced up the stairs to see what was wrong. Renate barred the door. 'Go back downstairs,' she told Sasha. 'Go downstairs! Go!'

Dean only nicked himself, she said. The cuts were no more than scratches and there was no real blood. But there were rumours a doctor was sent for. Rumours that he cut himself fifty times. The 'Canuto's Trial Cuts' in the autopsy report I'd read in the winter of 1987 at Denver Airport in a snowstorm, waiting for my plane home.

At the pub in Schmockwitz that same day that Dean cut his arm, was Wiebke. With her was Natasha. The pub was only a few minutes away from Dean's house in Schmockwitzer Damm. Her hand around a beer glass, Wiebke leaned back to catch the sun.

'Why don't you go round to Papa's and say hello,' Wiebke said to Natasha. Natasha shook her head. She was angry and hurt: on her birthday earlier that spring, she had waited for Dean all day long by the garden gate. He never came to see her.

Then, Wiebke heard the wail of the police sirens. They were coming from the direction of Dean's house. Within hours, the rumours spread: Dean had slashed himself fifty times. Odd, how Wiebke always seemed to get news about Dean Reed before anyone else.

★

At the lake-side restaurant, Renate sipped her champagne and lit another cigarette. She should have . . . what? Called for medical attention when Dean wounded himself? Should she have halted work on *Wounded Knee*? But Dean . . . he, what was the word she was looking for?

That Thursday – in the aftermath of Dean's disappearance and death, there was some confusion about the sequence of events and the accounts varied by a few hours or even a few days, but this was definitely Thursday, June 12. Dean and Renate had dinner. Dean took a sleeping pill, as he had every night of his life since he was twenty. They argued again, bitterly, but not violently as on the day when Dean slashed himself.

At about ten in the evening Dean talked to Gerrit List on the telephone. Gerrit had just returned from Moscow. He had news of the contracts for *Wounded Knee*; it was the news Dean was so anxiously waiting for and, unable to wait until he saw Gerrit next morning at the studio, he said he was coming to sleep at Gerrit's house. Gerrit lived in Babelsburg only a few minutes from the DEFA film studios, whereas Smockwitz was a forty-minute drive. So Dean and Gerrit could talk that night and then make an early start on Friday morning.

At about half past ten or just after – Renate could not say – Dean left the house in Schmockwitz. He got in his car and drove away.

On Tuesday, June 10, 1986, Gerrit List signed the contracts for *Wounded Knee* in Moscow and flew back to East Berlin. He went straight to the studios because there were preparations to make for the film. Because Dean was the director as well as the star, there would be tests made on video, and there were also special effects to arrange. Among the first sequences to be filmed for *Wounded Knee* was a night-time scene shot during the day. *The American Night*, Gerrit called it.

That Thursday evening, as he remembered it, Gerrit telephoned Dean at home in Schmockwitz, although the police reports record that Dean phoned Gerrit. In any case, they exchanged greetings and Dean said he was coming to spend the night with Gerrit.

'We can speak and I can sleep and tomorrow I am already at work,' said Dean.

'My wife was away so I make up the bed in the sitting room. It was not good manners of Dean to ask. He didn't sleep at my home before. My family is in holiday. But he wanted to hear news and start early and it was forty minutes from Schmockwitz to the studio in Potsdam. He never arrived.'

When Dean didn't show up – after Gerrit had gone to the trouble to make up the bed in the sitting room – Gerrit was furious. Still, he figured Dean changed his mind again and gave it no more thought. Or perhaps he did not want to phone Renate, thinking Dean had gone off somewhere else – one of his escapades? A woman? It was hard to say, but Dean had pulled plenty of stunts in his time. Gerrit went to bed.

Next morning, Renate drove herself to the studio.

'Where is Dean?' said Renate.

Dean is not here, someone said.

Gerrit told Renate Dean never arrived at his house, but he was angry rather than upset. Once, on another film, Dean had disappeared, into the mountains on an impulse.

'This is not good to suddenly make a holiday when everybody at the studio was waiting to work,' Gerrit said angrily. He was quiet, but he was angry.

When Renate completed some make-up tests, Gerrit sent her home to Schmockwitz because, as he explained, in these things he was Renate's producer, too.

Growing angrier and angrier, Gerrit phoned around, looking for Dean. We must know where is the director, he said. It was Friday.

Renate called Gerrit. She was upset. Maybe there has been an accident, she said. Gerrit drove to Schmockwitz.

Although Gerrit did not admit it at first, they did not call the police. It would cause a scandal and Gerrit remained sure there was an explanation.

He always drives so fast, Renate said. Maybe an accident. Maybe, she said after a while, another woman. She became frantic. Please let it be another woman. Gerrit picked up the phone.

He called Prague, where he talked to Vaclav Nectar. He called around Berlin, to Potsdam, to Dean's Baltic island hideaway. No one knew anything. Gerrit's heart sank. He had begun to think it was an accident.

On Friday evening it was impossible to leave Renate alone. Gerrit got some clothes from his house and went back to stay with her. The next day he called a girlfriend of Renate: she must have a nurse he said. Then the English journalist telephoned. My God! An English journalist!

'Did the guy from the *Sunday Times* get to you?' Dixie had written Dean.

The guy was Russell Miller. On his way through Denver earlier that year on a book promotion tour, the *Sunday Times* journalist appeared on a radio show. He was looking for good ideas for his next book, said Miller casually. Dixie said it was she who phoned him to talk about Dean Reed, although Johnny said he called the station first.

Miller arranged to interview Dean for the *Sunday Times*. The interview was scheduled for Saturday, June 14, 1986.

Miller arrived in West Berlin on Friday afternoon. He called the Reed house and Renate said Dean had been taken to hospital that morning. In the evening they spoke again and she said the doctors thought Dean had an infection and he was not at all well.

In the middle of the conversation, as Miller later reported in the *Sunday Times*, the telephone was taken from Renate. A man came on. He told Miller he was Mr Wieczaukowski, the co-director of the movie Dean was due to start in a few days. He confirmed Dean was in the hospital and might have to stay several days.

On Saturday when Miller called, Renate said her husband was to be in the hospital until Tuesday. Miller said he'd come back to Berlin later and went home to London. When he read Dean was dead, Miller called the number Mr Wieczaukowski had given him in Potsdam. A woman answered. She said it was a private number and no one called Wieczaukowski lived there.

Gerrit took the telephone from Renate.

'I was for these things Renate's producer, too,' he said again.

The last thing he needed was an English journalist. My God! Dean is not at home, he said. He is lying ill in the hospital.

He told Mr Miller the interview would be rescheduled. He said the first thing that came into his head. In his heart there were forebodings and he had to get rid of Mr Miller, the English journalist. He gave Miller a phony name and telephone number.

'I said the first thing that came into my head. I was Mr Wieczaukowski,' said Gerrit List.

★

On Saturday they continued to look for Dean, but Sunday was the worst day, Gerrit said. It was on Sunday that employees of the lifeguard station at Zeuthener See and Schmockwitzer Damm informed the German People's police that a model A WAS 21061 automobile, licence plate number ILT 8-05 had been standing about twenty metres behind the lifeguard station since at least Friday morning. It might have been there earlier, but they would not have seen it until the morning of the 13th when they came on duty. It was Dean's car.

On Sunday Renate informed the police that her husband had been missing since the night of June 12.

She alternated in her moods. She thought Dean was alive. She knew he was dead. She said it over and over: He is dead. He is alive. Gerrit was frantic.

Increasingly distraught, Renate trembled a lot, smoked cigarettes and was white as death, Gerrit said. On Monday a neighbour phoned. She had seen a lot of police cars near the lake. She had seen the Red Cross. Maybe Dean was drowned, she said. No, no, said Renate, Dean was a good swimmer. It was a shallow lake. It was high summer. He was a good swimmer. Please let him come back. Please. Oh God!

'I am missing this word,' Renate said again.

We had finished our steaks. It was still light out, as we left the restaurant. You could smell the pine from the woods and as we walked, Renate told me a story she said she had not told before.

Some years earlier, Renate and Dean took Sasha on a skiing holiday. It was a lovely holiday Renate said. One afternoon she and Sasha were doodling about in the snow, skiing, playing, laughing, when Dean disappeared.

He had gone inside to take a telephone call. It was the news of Paton Price's death, but Renate didn't know and she and Sasha kept playing and throwing snowballs and laughing. After an hour she said they ought to go back to the chalet. She wondered what was going on.

When she got inside, she found Dean fast asleep. An open bottle of sleeping pills was beside the bed, and it was empty.

Renate ran to another chalet where she knew there was a doctor. He looked at Dean and at the pills. He said Dean hadn't taken enough to kill himself. Just let him sleep it off, the doctor said.

Be watchful, the doctor added. Dean may wake in the night. And Dean did wake up. Naked, he stumbled toward the door; it was twenty degrees below zero. He was full of sleeping pills and he would have frozen to death if he had gone outside, said Renate.

'If you go out there you will not only kill yourself, you'll kill Sasha and me,' Renate shouted, pulling him back into the chalet with all her force.

It would have been a betrayal.

That was the word she had been looking for all day. Betray. Yes. Betray. That was it.

She had to believe Dean's death was an accident. If it was a suicide, he had betrayed her. Just before he died, in spite of everything, he told her how much he loved her. If he then went and killed himself it was betraying her trust. She was very fierce about it. But it was something that had been preying on her mind for a long time.

We walked together for a few yards, along the rural lane near the lake. It was two years since Dean died on a summer night like this. I looked at the lake. I said I hoped Renate would meet someone else nice some day.

'No,' she said violently. 'I hate men.'

It would have been a betrayal.

Early on the morning of June 17, 1986 at 8.20, a body was discovered in the Zeuthener See. 'It was approximately 300 feet from the lake side,' noted the police report.

Renate's neighbour came across the lawn to Renate's house – Renate could see her from the kitchen window. The neighbour smoothed her apron awkwardly.

'I think they've found Dean,' she said.

# CHAPTER 22

✧

# Who Killed Dean Reed?

In Wheat Ridge, Colorado, the telephone rang in an empty house. A machine with Dixie's voice on it answered.

'Dixie, this is Ruth Anna Brown, Dean's mother. Damn this machine! You never call me back, but I guess you've heard the terrible news about Dean? Call me this time, Dixie,' the voice said.

'Hi, Dixie. This is Johnny. Call me! For God's sake, Dixie call me!!'

A reporter in Leipzig telephoned Vashek Nectar in Prague. Vashek said his life in fear began with that call. In Moscow, Oleg Smirnoff heard the news on the television.

'Dean first, me next,' Oleg thought.

In Paris, Erik Durschmied was in the Metro, reading the *Herald Tribune*. His wife, Annalise, was with him. Durschmied turned so white, he looked like a man in the middle of a heart attack. When the train stopped, he pulled Annalise onto the platform.

'What is it?' she said urgently.

'Dean is dead,' he said.

In the little house with the dead leaves in the swimming pool, Wiebke told Natasha as best she could that her father was dead. Natasha had seen Bobby die on 'Dallas' and she knew that Bobby wasn't really dead. 'Maybe Daddy is not really dead at all. Like Bobby on "Dallas",' Natasha said.

Gerrit List was in charge of the funeral. Renate was drugged like a stone. He sent her to a sanitorium where she slept and slept. He organised everything. He notified the relatives. He received Mrs Brown. He collected Ramona and Patty from West Berlin. At Checkpoint Charlie, the daughter from Dean, as Gerrit called her, was weeping like Michael Jackson.

'My father is dead,' she kept saying.

Originally, the authorities refused to let the body be viewed, Patty told a Denver journalist. It had lain in the water for four days, was not fit to be seen and would cause distress. The body had been partly devoured by fish and was shocking. The officials were correct, but they were not forthcoming. Mrs Brown could get nothing.

The policeman she met with was mightily pompous.

'In the GDR we do not have crime,' he said.

The officials relented.

Eleven days after Dean died, Patty went to the morgue. Renate could not bear to go.

In the morgue, in order to get a good look at the body, Patty knelt down beside it, as if she were praying. It was Dean's body, she said. She was sure. Later she talked to a reporter from the *Denver Post*.

'My daughter has his toes. They were Dean's toes,' she said.

The body was cremated.

Mrs Brown had questions: if Dean meant to defect, why did he take his important papers with him on the night he disappeared, but not his passport? Why was he wearing two coats on a warm June night? Why was he cremated so quickly?

Gerrit gave the order for the cremation. It was the seemly thing to do, once the autopsy report was complete. Will Roberts arrived in town and went a little nuts from grief. He said that Dean was murdered.

The night before the memorial service there was some wrangling over the disposal of the remains: Will Roberts wanted to have parts of Dean sent to places he loved – Chile, Nicaragua. The women were horrified. Things were so tense in the house at Schmockwitz that Mrs Brown could not stand it and went to a hotel. The memorial service was held on Tuesday June 24 in East Berlin, the day scheduled for the start of *Wounded Knee*.

All of the Reed women were there: Ruth Anna Brown, Patty, Wiebke, Renate. They declared themselves sisters. They were all Reed women, they said and held hands.

All of the children came: Ramona, Natasha, Alexander, whom everyone called Sasha. Friends came from abroad. Vaclav Nectar came from Prague.

It was like a big Hollywood funeral: the bereft beautiful women;

the famous faces behind the dark glasses; the concentration of power; the titled dignitaries who packed the hall: The Deputy Minister of Culture, the Director-General of the DEFA entertainment film studios; a member of the East German Communist Party Central Committee; the First Deputy Chairman and General Secretary of the German Democratic Peace Council; the President of the Committee for Entertainment.

There were pink carnations everywhere. The service had been arranged by Gerrit List and by DEFA and everything was correct. Dean was a hero in East Germany, honoured, officially approved, supported, generally loved.

The overwhelming smell of the flowers and perhaps of the concentration of power, made Wiebke sick. She had never been so queasy in her life, but she thought she might faint. Renate was drugged like a stone. She used the expression over and over. She was up to six Valium a day.

Unbidden, Will Roberts got up, faced the crowd and delivered a funeral oration: Dean's ashes ought to be tossed across the oceans of the countries he loved, said Will. At the last moment Will said everyone should stand up and give a big hand for Dean. Will stood and clapped alone.

Gerrit List was mortified. It was not the way things were done in Germany. It ought to have been a sombre occasion. There was a form to these things. But he rose, too, and began clapping and everyone joined in and it was surreal and a little macabre: the sober Germans in their dark suits, the Party officials, the Americans, all clapping for a dead man at his funeral.

As the service ended, Dean's peppy singing voice came over the loudspeaker. He was singing: 'Gimme me a guitar . . .' Again, many of the family stood and applauded. Mrs Brown rose. Dean must be buried in East Berlin, she told the congregation. Here were his friends, she said.

To himself, Gerrit said: Please God, no more applause.

A hundred people went to the house at Schmockwitz for coffee and cake. It was like the Last Supper. Patty was nice to Renate. Renate said later that Patty helped her and was truly a sister. Patty helped her understand Dean's moodiness. All the wives embraced. 'We are all Reed women,' they said again to one another.

Mrs Brown wondered why there was no candlelight parade for

219

Dean through the streets of East Berlin. She couldn't understand why no one held a big parade, a vigil, for Dean.

'Like they did in New York for John Lennon,' she said.

When there were just a few people left in the house near the lake, Gerrit went home and slept in his own bed.

'All is over,' he said and slept.

DEATH IN BERLIN FOR DEFECTOR WHO CHANGED HIS TUNE . . . MYSTERY OF AMERICAN POP STAR IN LAKE; IT WAS MURDER SAYS MANAGER.

It wasn't over.

In his last will Dean left everything to Renate, except for the 5,000 marks each that he left to Natasha and Sasha.

There were a dozen theories that grew into a hundred conspiracies. On June 18, an Associated Press item appeared on the obituary page of the *New York Times*. It was short and uninformative, noting only that the East German press agency said Mr Reed died from a 'tragic accident'. On Sunday June 22, five days after Dean's body was pulled from the lake, Russell Miller published the article in the London *Sunday Times* that chronicled his conversations with 'Mr Wieczaukowski'.

The mystery that he reported became the basis for a scatter of articles; so little news came out of East Berlin, that it became the centrepiece of a web of theories. Mike Wallace had a stab at a follow-up story, but he abandoned it after a couple of phone calls. For *60 Minutes* it was only another story. Until I met Gerrit List in Berlin two years after Dean died, no one identified him as the disappearing 'Mr Wieczaukowski'.

'Accidental death by drowning,' said the official report. No one accepted it. It was the most intolerable scenario of all because it had no meaning. Only Gerrit List clung to it, insisting, when we met, that Dean went out on the pier in the lake to look for a set for *Wounded Knee*. There was a bungalow on the other shore – you could only see it from the end of the pier – and the way was barred by a corrugated metal gate. The gate was locked. According to List, Dean tried to climb it, flipped over, fell and drowned, looking for a bungalow that looked like home.

No, said Renate firmly. That gate was always open.

★

Questions were raised about the autopsy. There was a Valium-like substance in the blood. Enough to kill? It depended. The liver was as big as an alcoholic's, said the report, but Dean never drank.

Clive was a British stringer for *Time* in West Berlin. He crept into the frame. 'You knew about the reports,' he said.

'What reports?'

'They were pretty convincing, the reports I read about Dean having treatment for cancer the last months of his life,' said Clive.

There was nothing about cancer in the autopsy report. The ground turned into a swamp. The dead ends had mirrors at the end of them.

Why was Dean wearing two coats on a warm June night? The body was found clothed in a jeans jacket Johnny Rosenburg gave Dean, as well as an overcoat.

Because he planned to flee? But he did not have his passport. Was his passport stolen? Wiebke said it was stolen, but how did she know? Did Dean leave home, discover he had forgotten it, then fly into a panic, a rage and slam his car down towards the lake?

A theory about the extra clothing ran like this: obsessed with detail on *Wounded Knee*, Dean wanted to break in his costume. There was a kind of precedent for it back in Loveland, where Johnny once found Dean banging up a brand new camera bag in the back yard.

'What in the name of . . . ' said Johnny. Dean said he was breaking it in. You could not have brand new gear in a movie. It looked phony.

In Dean's car were copies of *Mother Jones* which Ruth Anna sent him. Dean also had his Dad's last letter.

How could it be an accident? How could he have drowned? Dean was a great swimmer. Everyone said so. As a kid he was a lifeguard at Estes Park. At forty-seven he was in top shape and could walk on his hands, Phil Everly said.

Mrs Brown had 2,006 scenarios, she told the *Denver Post*.

Everybody had a scenario. There were those who believed that Dean was killed by the East German Stasi or the KGB because, having lost faith in the system, he wanted to go home. But why had he lost it now, in 1986, when Glasnost was delivering hope for change and Gorbachev, in whom Dean passionately believed, was in power. And why would anyone bother? He wasn't important enough to kill, said Vladimir Pozner.

Leslie could just imagine a scenario, however, in which a police official made his displeasure with Dean unofficially known to an ambitious – or drunken – underling who took it on himself to get rid of Dean.

'Unlikely. It would be too big a risk for any policeman without explicit orders from his superior,' said Georgy Arbatov when I eventually met him in Moscow. Arbatov, Dean's highly placed minder, also assured me that Dean was not assassinated by the KGB. 'The KGB did not go in for assassination at that time, you see,' said Arbatov who, in telling me this gave me to understand that, at times they did indeed go in for assassination, and that although he, Arbatov, was currently in his laid-back post-Cold War mode, he was a tough cookie. His only criticism of Dean Reed, whom he liked and thought a talented man, was that during a certain period Dean had become a Maoist(!) But he, Arbatov, had written to Dean trying to show him the errors of his ways.

But did Dean know some awful secrets about Honecker's lavish life style at Wandlitz, about the smuggled gold and the corruption, which were not revealed until the end of 1989. Was he going to tell? Or was he part of it? The Countess said Dean did errands for the king-pins, took money to Swiss banks, drove a Porsche – but there were no signs of it, and anyway, the Countess had her own axe to grind.

Others said it was a screw-up, a blurry East German version of a Mafia hit. Dean knew important men. Once you were in, you couldn't get out, they said. Everyone cut his theories to suit his politics. I remembered Mrs Brown had whispered the CIA were on notice to do a 'wet job' on him if he got out of line.

Vashek Nectar believed it was the Czech secret police and the Stasi. He said Dean had come to fear for his life in the East and once, on his way to Prague, a wheel came off his car when he knew it had just been screwed tight.

After Dean's funeral, Vashek, who could not forget how Dean had antagonised Czech officials, sat on a bench in East Berlin, talking to Gerrit List. Although in public Gerrit insisted it was an accident, he told Vashek he believed 'someone helped Dean die'.

I even heard a theory that the KGB and the CIA had a beer and, deciding Dean was a nuisance, acted in concert to get rid of him.

'Hogwash,' said a retired diplomat who knew Dean in Berlin. The KGB and CIA conspiracy theories were hogwash. Dean's death was accepted as an accident until 'those people from Colorado got involved.'

Then there were the wild stabs: homosexual triangles; jealous women; jealous husbands; skinheads; louts who hated foreigners and roamed the fringes of East Berlin society. Most exotic was a rumour that Renate fingered Dean to the Party because he wanted to go home to America. There was no end to it.

Dixie, who said she spent $37,000 to send two private detectives to East Germany, wanted to go to a hypnotist to see if she could recall anything more from her subconscious.

Johnny Rosenburg was convinced that neo-Nazis killed Dean, as they had killed the deejay, Alan Berg. But how did they get to East Berlin?

In Los Angeles, Dean's daughter Ramona sued the East German government for mental injury she suffered over her father's death.

When Dixie was still busy trying to set Dean up in America, a bunch of kids came after her at her country property up near Grand Junction. Dixie said they were from the Aryan Nation and they were after her because of Dean. A journalist from Boulder named Jennifer Dunbar, who met Dean at the Denver Film Festival, said they were just rich punks.

On the other hand, Dunbar said — and I knew yet another wiggy scenario was in the works — how come when Dixie called the police, twenty-eight FBI agents turned up?

Without doubt, the craziest of all the scenarios was the one in which, according to the Scientologists, Russell Miller killed Dean Reed. Miller had written a book about L. Ron Hubbard; the church was suing to keep his book off the stands. They accused Miller of Dean's death, referring to the article he had written for the *Sunday Times*.

There were rumours that Dean's daughter, Ramona, belonged to the Church of Scientology.

Everyone was suspect; everyone was part of the conspiracy. Every scrap became evidence in their fevered brains, even the origins of *60 Minutes*. The truth about *60 Minutes* was simply that it had been suggested separately by Erik Durschmied and Anne de Boismilion, a staff producer working out of Paris.

The mystery grew not out of the facts, but out of the desperation to make it an important death. Like Moscow's intellectuals who, at the end of 1989, sat around the cafés promising themselves civil war and chaos, the more terrible the scenario, the more it lent itself to self aggrandisement. Who wanted to settle for the ordinary when you could have a revolution?

'He would never get old. He said he would take a gun and go to some revolution,' a friend of Dean's said. 'He would have loved a famous death.'

Johnny called Dixie and told her Dean had died. 'You're gonna get Dean shot,' she said.

What! Johnny said, and told me Dixie had come unglued.

Johnny called Will Roberts. 'Is Dean alive?' he said.

'Johnny, all I can say is I've got a lock of his hair,' Will replied mysteriously.

A West German reporter, who had no proof, said she saw Dean the day after he died. Someone saw him buying pencils in Schmockwitz.

There was plenty of evidence that Dean *was* alive, if you looked for it, except that none of it had any real substance. There were some who pointed to the fact that the man described in the autopsy report was taller than Dean. But when I finally got hold of his file from the State Department, I saw that in applying for his first passport in 1961, he listed his height as six foot one; by 1970, in a second passport application, he gave his height as six foot four, and it was, no doubt, from these records that the precise Germans took their data.

'The whole of Berlin was talking about the mock suicide,' said Vashek Nectar, who believed, among other things, that the arm-slashing was partly a publicity stunt, partly a tactic to psych up Renate for her performance in *Wounded Knee*. Others said Dean wanted to flee, but to spare Renate he faked his death and the body in the lake belonged to a singer who looked a lot like Dean. In that case, you had to wonder how Dean got hold of the spare body.

Dixie asked me to check Dean's account at the Berliner Bank. If money had been withdrawn since Dean died, it was to be proof he was alive. She was hearing those voices over the phone. The bank account was checked: nothing had been withdrawn.

Still, it spooked me for a while. It got so I expected to pick up the phone and hear Dean Reed's voice.

Instead, I got Dixie.

For a long time Dixie was in regular contact. She helped out with information, sent letters and tapes, and was generally cheerful. When she disappeared, I figured she was on one of her long-haul routes across country. Johnny Rosenburg called. There was a 'Wanted' poster in the post office with Dixie's face on it. She failed to respond to a summons by the police for some misdemeanour, and then she fled.

In April, 1989, my phone rang at eight in the morning.

'Hi,' said a voice muted by pain. 'D.J.'

Dixie.

'I'm in hiding,' she said. 'I can't tell you where. I just wanted to stay in touch, be friends. If Dean's alive, which I still believe, he won't be able to get in touch with me unless he gets in touch through friends in Minnesota.'

But the word on the street was suicide.

'Towards the end Dean could hear the doors shutting, one at a time,' said Victor Grossman.

Johnny could not accept it.

'I think the chance of his committing suicide is about as good as my putting on my shoes and walking to the moon. I just do not believe Dean did not want to push his shoeshine one more time across this earth,' he said.

I felt it was what Renate believed in her heart, though.

Drowning was a common enough form of suicide, the forensic pathologist at Manchester University said. It was common and quite easy – you sucked in a little water and gave yourself up.

And there were the cuts on Dean's arm.

It was a classic suicide attempt, those cuts – fifty was a classic number. The pathologist was an expert who could find nothing fishy in the autopsy reports. The report might come out of the GDR, he said, but it was German, nonetheless. In so far as death was concerned, the Germans were meticulous.

An unintentional suicide perhaps, a bumbled, messy panic attack that led to the lake behind the house in Schmockwitz. A man running out of time, his hair grey, his voice fading, his marriage come to pieces, Dean missed his America, but there was nothing in America for a fifty-year-old cowboy rocker who was losing his voice and, in any case, America did not want some commie who went on *60 Minutes* to defend the Berlin Wall. And when Dean looked the other way, he saw his diminished career, the record sales down, the Russians listening to their own music. He was yesterday's man. As passionate as he was for Glasnost, it gobbled up the ground from under him and left him with nowhere to stand. But as a scenario, suicide was unacceptable to Dean's family because it was a betrayal.

Maybe I was wrong. Maybe there had been some unspeakable crime. It was every journalist's nightmare and for months I lay awake every night, imagining that on the day this book was published, some crack reporter would discover that Dean Reed was murdered after all.

It was hard to untangle Dean, the man, from this mess. Leslie thought him the dupe of two cultures, too easily taken in by both myths, a rebel only by stance, and Leslie could not forgive Dean for his wilful disregard of political reality and thought him stupid for it. Like a flame, Dean sucked you in, but delivered no heat. There was a malign magic to it all, Leslie thought; it pulled the microbes out of the woodwork for everyone who shared it. Everyone was enlarged, changed, disarrayed by contact with Dean Reed, who serviced their needs in the way stars do. But for Leslie, Dean had no reality of his own.

By then I cared much more about what he did than about who killed him. If it was suicide, you could feel passionately for Dean. His anguish brought him down off of his soap box, this messy, handsome man. I liked him not because he was a martyr to his cause, but because, while most everyone else stayed home and watched TV, he *did* something.

But there was no way I could tell his mother that.


In Beverly Hills, on a balmy winter night, I met Sasha Gurman from Tblisi. He had thick wavy hair and impish eyes, and he was sexy, like a magician, which in a way he was. He was an interpreter, the sort who gets not just the words, but the magic.

The sky was a rich tuxedo blue that night and the art director had put in plenty of stars. Beverly Hills was tidy and lush as a starlet's shaved armpit. Drinking it all in, Sasha inspected the crowd on the patio at Roland Joffé's house where, a kind of vigorous human sputnik spun off by Glasnost, Sasha had put down for the evening.

Glasnost had come to Hollywood in the shape of Elem Klimov, the director, and Roland Joffé was giving him a dinner. Sasha had come to interpret.

'Tell me about Dean Reed', I began to say, as I did to every Soviet I met. Dean Reed, the man who brought rock and roll to Russia . . . but before I could get to him, Sasha smiled and shrugged and was spun away again because everyone wanted to hear of the extraordinary changes in the Soviet Union.

Later that night, we drank to peace and friendship and, I think, to Salvador Dali.

Ah, Glasnost! It was the fashion in the winter of 1989. Elem Klimov gave me a button with Gorbachev's face on it. Roland raised his glass.

'We may not share our politics, but we have to share our planet,' Roland said.

I cornered Sasha Gurman, the magician.

'Sasha!' I said urgently.

Detaching himself from the others, he spun in my direction, and presented himself.

'Have you ever heard of Dean Reed?'

'Ah, Dean Reed,' Sasha said, and told me a story.

When he was seven, Sasha's mother asked what he wanted for his birthday. I want to see Dean Reed, he said, and his mother took him to a concert in Tblisi.

He was very nervous because Dean Reed, the American singing star, was particularly big in Georgia where his picture was sold alongside that of Joseph Stalin. Anyhow, Sasha was taken up on the stage to meet Dean; the singer shook hands with the little boy and then he did one of his stunts: the big, handsome blue-eyed American flipped the child head over heels. He laughed. Then he kissed Sasha and gave him an autographed picture.

For years, Sasha kept the picture of Dean Reed in his school notebook next to a picture of Lenin. By the time Sasha was a teenager, the notebook had come to bits but he clung to it, nonetheless. In the late 1970s, his mother took him to East Berlin for a holiday. There they climbed the television tower at the Alexanderplatz.

Sasha looked out. He craned his neck so that he could see over the Wall into West Berlin, where he noted there was enough neon to fuel a small African nation, enough lights to fuel his dreams.

227

He imagined a world populated by tall, blond, blue-eyed American cowboys like Dean Reed who gave little kids a hug and sang them rock and roll.

'That's for me,' Sasha said.

# After the Wall, 1990

Between the summer night in 1988, when I said goodbye to Renate at the lake, and the beginning of 1990, everything changed. Mikhail Gorbachev freed the countries of the Soviet Bloc to pursue what his spokesman referred to as the 'Sinatra Doctrine'. Eastern Europe did it *their way*, and in November 1989, the Berlin Wall came down. The planet shifted on its political axis. Hungary declared itself a republic; in Poland, Solidarity became a government. In Prague, where a dissident playwright was made president, Alexander Dubček appeared on a balcony at Christmas and smiled. The streets were vibrant with music, noise, political gossip. In Wenceslas Square, after twenty years, the soundtrack was turned back on.

And in Romania, where Dean shot his movies because the countryside had hardly any television aerials, the television station became the headquarters for a revolution. After Ceausescu was executed, Romanians went into his office and rolled around on the priceless Persian carpets, grinning, their Kalashnikovs beside them.

'I would never have believed the Wall would come down in my lifetime,' Johnny Rosenburg wrote. 'I wonder what Dean would have thought. I sort of feel he would have adjusted real quick and went along with the flow . . . Why in God's name did he have to die at this point in time?' Johnny wrote. 'With things changing the way they are, he could have played such an important part in the whole affair . . . What a waste . . . '

What Johnny couldn't see was that, without the Berlin Wall, Dean Reed had no role. The Wall made him; crossing it gave him glamour. When Dean crossed to the East, what he did looked seditious, foreign, American, sexy, which was always ironic, of course, because he owed his existence to officialdom, to the Party.

To those who believed in the Party, in the system, the presence of Dean was also comforting as the Cold War raged, for here, after all, was an American who was not the devil incarnate.

He was an exquisite piece of propaganda. During the endless years of stagnation, for twenty years behind the Iron Curtain, from 1968, Dean Reed seemed to be a force for life. At least he gave the illusion of it.

As things changed, even in the short time I had been looking for him, Dean Reed seemed to recede towards some far horizon defined by the Cold War. When America was centre stage, so was Dean Reed. When, in the East, it was everything desirable and completely unattainable, Dean Reed *was* America. Without the Berlin Wall, he lost his platform. Glasnost sucked up his myth and he became a curious tale from the Cold War.

'There was no profit in a dead man,' Vashek said in Prague, where a million portraits of Vaclav Havel replaced a million pictures of Vladimir Lenin. In a record store up a cobbled street near Havel's castle, an old lady in carpet slippers searched the bins in vain.

'Dean Reed? I am so sorry, but it was a very long time ago,' she said.

The Dean Reed movie, which had been the pretext for all these trips, all these encounters from Hawaii to Moscow, was on hold. Leslie had gone to Nigeria to make a film. The producers were busy changing their minds, trying to decide what was in vogue, which was like trying to figure out if Albania would go capitalist before spring.

The little Dean Reed industry, which had arisen when Dean died, hummed along in the hinterlands – Dean's first wife, Patty was said to be writing a book, so were half a dozen others – and now and again, it broke out into the main stream: Martin Scorsese was interested in making a film, I heard; so was Stewart Copland of the Police. The ever elusive Will Roberts, whose answering machine continued to play Greensleeves, was said to have sold the rights to *American Rebel* to Blake Edwards. Indeed, Will seemed to have sold the rights to Dean Reed's life to half of Hollywood. When he was alive, Dean couldn't get an agent. Dead, he was a hot property.

On the day that Leslie and I first began the research for the film about Dean Reed, I read in the *Los Angeles Times* that Ed Pressman, the producer, had a picture ready to roll. He and Roberts were in business, it seemed. For us, it was not an auspicious beginning.

Nothing happened.

Finally, in the winter of 1989, from his room at the Château Marmont in Hollywood, Leslie got hold of Will on the telephone. For ten minutes, they swapped evasions.

'Don't you make anthropological films?' said Will to Leslie, who was a little unnerved by how much Will knew about him.

'Why have you guys been avoiding me?' Will whispered. 'I have 150,000 pages of Dean Reed transcripts. Five writers have been after my stuff. It's just ten years since I first saw Dean Reed in Red Square. I'm the only person who saw the whole body. Patty just saw the feet.' Will droned on.

They spoke of plots and counterplots. Leslie suggested a meeting.

'I'm not that easy to find,' said Will.

Will's deal with Ed Pressman was running out, it seemed. Nothing much had come of it.

'You're having wonderful meetings, Will, what else do you want?' Pressman said to him.

We were in Hollywood.

Months later I got an urgent message. *60 Minutes* had called. They wanted to get in touch because they were planning to do a follow up to the Dean Reed story. Nothing happened.

I went East again after the Berlin Wall came down. The film script I had written was out of date. Everything was out of date. In an astonishing poll, sixty-two per cent of Americans said that, with Gorbachev in power, they trusted the Soviet Union. Watching the East was like watching water flow. Not only had Darth Vadar pulled up his vizor, he'd taken off the whole damn costume. Journalists who covered the Soviet Union yearned for the old days, when they could take a night off for poker instead of working a twenty-hour shift because now everyone in the country had a story to tell.

By the time I got in to Moscow in early 1990, Sheremetyevo Airport was awash in electronic junk as the new-style Soviet traveller returned from New York, humping his toys – computers, videos, television sets – fresh from Uncle Steve's warehouse on

Canal Street. Uncle Steve's stocked answering machines geared specially to Soviet-style telephones.

Moscow itself was awash in Glasnost and Perestroika, free speech, anti-semitism, hamburgers, hookers, private enterprise and long lines that led to food stores which were completely empty. It was as if the city were trapped in some frenzied halfway house: it couldn't go backward; it couldn't go ahead. At the Sovincenter, half the lights were out.

The Sovincenter was Moscow's first mall. The huge complex, on the banks of the Moskva River, included a conference centre, a hotel with elevator pods that slid up and down its walls, and plastic trees. It had a credible imitation of an English pub which, with greasy plaid carpets, purveyed stale beer. Those who had the hard currency hurried in and out of the shops, buying fresh fruit, Tampax and air tickets.

In 1990, what had once been a glistening testimony to the glories of free enterprise a year earlier, was in disrepair; the lights were out; hoods loitered in the hall; it was the ugly face of Perestroika, this crappy steel and glass building whose whole purpose was to hold out its begging bowl to the West.

Outside, the chauffeurs smoked Marlboros and leaned against the Chaikas and Mercs, waiting for their clients. Ordinary Russians, who could not enter because they hadn't the hard currency, pressed their faces against the glass doors.

'At least when Stalin was in power, there was a real man and we had food on the table.'

That is what Vera heard in her meat queue. She heard it two or three times a week: 'If only we had Stalin . . . ' they said.

'I am the Jesus of Cool,' Art Troitsky said as we took the subway to Moscow University for a rock concert. The gig was half empty.

'People are scared to go out at night because of crime,' said Art. 'Rock is dead in Russia, anyhow,' he said.

As a political act, rock and roll let you declare your otherness, but when the state withdrew its opposition, rock and roll lost its heart. Fed up with Leningrad, even Boris Grebenshikov left and went to London, where he wore baggy brown cords and spent most of his time painting pictures and drinking malt whisky.

'I'm tired of being the ambassador of rock in the country that's got no rhythm,' he sang.

All the myths were banging around in some crazy, unpredictable fashion and Art was gloomy. He could hear the sound of breaking Glasnost, he said. Civil war was coming to the Soviet Union – Lithuania, Azerbaijan, the Ukraine. He could not quite explain how it was coming but it was inevitable.

'Why don't you leave?' I asked.

He shrugged.

'If what's coming is what you say and you stay, it's a prescription for your own death.'

'But if I'm wrong, I want to be part of it. Wouldn't you?'

So we toasted Glasnost and Gorbachev.

So much *stuff* was going on in Moscow that it was hard to get Dean Reed into focus again. Intellectuals found him loathsome or ridiculous, if they remembered him at all; the 'peasant young people' as Art called them, had other things on their minds.

They were cynical about everything, these Soviet kids, and when they grew up, they said, they wanted to be racketeers and hard-currency hookers. When the Australian embassy offered to process emigration forms, half a million Muscovites came to the gates. They had been promised better times for seventy years and better times had never come and they were fed up to the teeth. They wanted to have some fun before they died. Meanwhile, they preferred Michael Jackson.

'The best thing for this country is to sell it off a piece at a time to the highest bidders,' Art said as we strolled into Pushkin Square.

Oh, McDonald's!

In shimmering plastic and neon, in yellow and red arches, with rock music playing and a sea of stainless steel palm trees, the biggest McDonald's on earth glittered like a set from 'Miami Vice'. Even if you usually thought fast food was common or crummy, you couldn't help but thrill to the sight of all that food! At McDonald's, Pushkin Square, kids waited a couple of hours in line because they knew that, at the end of this line, unlike any other in Moscow, you got something.

Beeg Mek. Yum.

It was the new People's Palace, and if the fantastic yearnings of Imperial Russia were once re-created in the glories of the Metro, what the Underground was for Stalin, so was McDonald's for the 1990s.

His eyes shining, my friend Tolya, who dreamed of going to Malibu, stood beside me as we ordered our cheeseburgers and fries and apple pie. At last, I was an American. Me and McDonald's.

The more often I went to Moscow (I went again later in 1990), the more often I met Americans, like me, who could not get enough. As often as not we were the grandchildren of Russian immigrants, the children of the old American Left, urban coastal Jews who had grown up during the sixties and were cynical about America. Having seen the Soviet Union now, we were cynical about it, too, and very knowing (Russia was in vogue), yet we were drawn back to this mess of a country. What was it?

Over lunch in New York with a friend who, like me, was busy calculating how soon he could wangle another trip – for he, too, had his own friends, his Arts and Svetlanas and Tolyas – I realised what it was: they wanted us. They loved us, for our jeans, our dollars, our hamburgers, our good nature – it didn't matter. They loved us and, as Americans, we were crazy about them for it. That was just the point: if we had spent the sixties posturing about the evils of America, we were off the hook now. Their passion for us turned us back into Americans. Going to Russia gave us back America.

I took a picture of McDonald's.

'Not allowed!' shouted a uniformed boy.

Pictures were not permitted except by special arrangement, he said, casting a sharp eye on the squads of young Soviets who scrubbed at the clean floors relentlessly.

These were the rules and in this, I thought, McDonalds, the result of perfect regimentation, was ideally suited to the Soviet Union. This was the company that was built on the inviolable principles of the University of Hamburgerology. Outside Moscow, in specially equipped factories, any bun that did not meet its standards, was killed.

For a moment, I tried to tell Tolya that fast food was not always wonderful, but he only wanted to know how to eat a hot apple pie with cold ice cream. I showed him, and he smiled and ate his pie and thought about Malibu.

'When I saw Dean's death on television, I thought, am I next?'

It was Oleg Smirnoff. Oleg the Nerd had become Oleg, the

Yuppie. No longer did he wear a row of ballpoints, no longer did he talk like a socialist speak-your-weight machine. He wore a navy blue blazer from Next and he lectured me on the meaning of it. He talked about 'communist assholes' and about his advertising agency. Oleg had a fax machine. His biggest client was Pizza Hut and for its Moscow opening, he planned to commission a song about pizza. I suggested 'That's Amore'.

"When the moon hits your eye like a big pizza pie, that's . . . " I sang.

Oleg seemed non-plussed.

We moved back to Dean's death.

Oleg was no longer reluctant to talk to me. I was a Westerner with hard cash; there could always be a deal.

'The death was played down and made little of in the USSR, which made everyone suspicious. Dean talked about America a lot. Maybe somebody in East Berlin got pissed off.'

'I can go home again, Oleg. I met people in Colorado who told me they remembered me. I can have a career there. I can go home,' Dean said to Oleg in the spring of 1986. It was the last time they met.

'Dean, at the end, was a man who could not acknowledge he wasted his life. It was too late for him,' Oleg said. 'He was an idealist.'

Oleg had his fax machine and a gun in the glove compartment of his car – what good was Dean's idealism to him, after all?

Crime was rife in Moscow in 1990. Guard dogs went at a premium, guns were easy to buy and I heard of taxi drivers who murdered their passengers for twenty-five roubles. At the National Hotel, the bartender asked me to bring him a can of mace on my next trip.

'Tell him I can't get it in America. Tell him to ask a German,' I said.

Oleg and I drank our coffee in the Savoy, Moscow's newest hotel, where the chairs were covered in turquoise nylon brocade, and the dissident poet, Andrei Voznesensky ate steaks. All around us, men sat on the little chairs and signed deals that would never come to much. Upstairs in a casino, pimply boys, in tuxedos, worked as croupiers.

Svetlana and Boris were in London. In Prague, Vashek Nectar could order the *New Musical Express* and think about going to

London to meet Cliff Richard. Tolya dreamed of Malibu. I thought of the eight hundred thousand children dying from leukaemia from the spill at Chernobyl and of the mutant babies with six toes who were born there and the trees that grew upside down and the kids with AIDS. And of Vera, who was leaving for New York because her husband was afraid of the anti-semitism that was one of the ironies of Glasnost. With permission to speak freely came the ugly things once hidden behind the official pretence of a just society. The conventions of hypocrisy were withdrawn and people felt free to hate each other.

On days when pogroms were scheduled by the Pamyat – it was physically shocking to write the word pogrom in 1990 – Yelena's momma put a scarf over her head and stayed indoors. I asked Vera to show me her passport. In plain Russian it was marked: Jew. And in the main square in Vilnius, a sign appeared: *Lithuania for the Lithuanians. Poles to Poland. Yids to the crematorium.*

Asleep in my room at the Savoy, I dreamed that I heard the hotel management howling for all of the Jews to assemble in the courtyard. Then I dreamed of a horse that had fallen into a swimming pool. When it was hoisted up, it had no legs.

And I thought of the freedoms that meant, at least, that in the Moscow streets, people smiled fearlessly at you, just for the hell of it.

Oleg finished his coffee at long last and offered me his videotape. When I looked at it, it was mostly a memorial concert in honour of Dean Reed. I thought of how I had sweated that night in the Hard Rock Café in Gorky Park, sure that if anyone had the key, Oleg did.

Oleg got up and we shook hands. He gave me his fax number.

'I'll tell you this. Whatever else, Dean was very nervous his last trip here. It was just before his death. Wiebke was giving him a lot of trouble,' said Oleg.

'Wiebke?' I said. 'Wiebke?'

'Well, you knew she was Stasi,' he said.

I mumbled.

'Or at least an informer. She was put into Dean's bed in the first place to watch him. He told me that long ago, back around 1978, when he had to dump her. It made him very sad.'

*

236

Wiebke. Wiekbe who, when Dean dumped her, found herself a house with a swimming pool, just down the road from Dean. Wiebke, who made frequent trips to the West, because she had a father who was a pensioner and was allowed to live there. Who worked as an interpreter for foreign dance companies when they were on tour. And who knew the doctor who treated Dean when he slashed his arm that hot summer afternoon. Wiebke, who reported that we had offered her $50,000 for her story, a rumour Renate heard within twenty-four hours. Who did Wiebke report to? How did Renate hear?

I went back to Berlin. Some prophet I was! A couple of years earlier, I sat in Checkpoint Charlie, convinced nothing would ever change. At Christmas, Bloomingdale's sold 15,000 pieces of the Berlin Wall, at twelve and a half bucks a pop.

Clink. Clink. Clink.

The sound you heard as you approached the Wall from West Berlin, was the same sound I had once heard in Moscow when I passed a dog decked out with war medals like a little general.

Clink. Clink. Clink.

The sound of the hammer and chisel. The sound of the Wall coming down.

'The sound of freedom,' I said.

'The sound of money,' Leslie said.

For a few minutes, after the Berlin Wall was breached, a handful of idealistic East Germans imagined that there was a 'Third Way' – a kind of fantasy combination of socialism and capitalism. It lasted exactly as long as it took the East Germans to go shopping in the West. Any second, I thought, East Berlin would simply disappear up the ass of West Germany. And so, by the following Christmas, it did.

The Wall was coming apart. I bought a piece of it from a New Jersey boy who was in business with a hammer and chisel, and I chatted with a pair of burly ex-GIs from Texas.

'We come on over to get us a piece of that there Wall,' they said cheerfully, while a gang of drunken teenagers did a rock version of 'Winter Wonderland' for KOOL, America's oldest golden oldies station. KOOL was in town from Arizona, doing live remotes from the Berlin Wall.

'The rock and roll revolution is right here, babe!' the deejay screamed.

Checkpoint Charlie held no more terrors. It was, at worst, irritating, and I saw now that the daunting military uniforms the border guards wore were falling apart. Their epaulets were made of plastic; one hung by a thread from the shoddy shirt a young soldier wore and, in it, you could read the demise of the whole system. It was only a flimsy costume, from a period film, shot on lousy stock.

'Have a nice day,' said the border guard. He had no choice.

East Berlin was as dreary as ever. There were no posters, no banners, no slogans. As soon as the Wall came down, the revolution was over. Unlike Prague, there was no joy. Unlike Moscow, no craziness, no kitsch, no Gorby dolls. There were no taxis either. In those first few weeks of freedom, 300 East German taxi drivers went west in their plastic Trabants. Then, Volkswagen simply took over the Trabant factory.

There were still no Dean Reed records in the Melodie record store on the Leipzigerstrasse, where I had begun.

Renate was waiting with her bright red Peugeot. I gave her a piece of the Wall I had bought and she turned it over slowly in her hand. She was terribly thin. Sasha was in the army and she was living alone in the house in Schmockwitz. It was winter again. At the Karl Marx-allee, we collected Victor Grossman, who was much in demand, for East Berlin was full of journalists who wanted an interpreter.

'Have you been to the West?' I asked Victor.

'No, it has been indicated to me that I would be arrested. I still owe the US Army some time. My wife has been,' he said equably.

I gave Victor a bag of avocados.

Full of pep at the Moscow Restaurant where we had lunch, Victor ordered a pair of steaks with brandied peaches on them like two big yellow breasts.

Victor still believed. He worried that the gains made by East Germany would be wiped out by the big West German companies. As always, A. G. Farben popped out of his mouth between bits of steak.

What gains? Believe in what! I wanted to cry. What? In Erich Honecker's gains?

I ate steak with Victor just as the corruptions that had been East Germany were revealed in the press: the gold bars hoarded in Swiss banks; the country estates at Wandlitz; the rigged football games; the sale of museum pieces to the West for hard currency; the arms sales to South Africa. A quarter of a million pounds of state money had been spent for a watch that had once belonged to Lenin for Herr Honecker to wear.

Dean Reed had hard words for Imelda Marcos, for Ronald Reagan, for the grasping maw of the West, but what about Honecker, with whom he shook hands, from whom he took a medal? What about Honecker and his jacuzzi?

Gains?

A sea of mud slid away from the country and revealed a night-mare landscape: women forced to handle chemical wastes without gloves; a countryside poisoned by sulphur dioxide. In those weeks there were the flashes of violence when a mob in Leipzig, screaming 'communist swine' threatened to lynch the Stasi. Hoodlums, deliri-ous with freedom, accosted a Jewish girl and cut the Star of David into her naked flesh with a knife.

What gains? And how many other Victors were there, true believers, left behind in the East, stranded by their politics. What gains, I wanted to shout, but I knew there was no point. With the whole rotten enterprise revealed as a sham, Victor and the others, having made a lifetime enterprise of their beliefs, were impaled on the necessity of believing.

And what of Wiebke? In the week, at the end of 1989 when I saw Renate and Victor, they did not want to talk about the subject – and who could blame them. Many of the Stasi files were sealed, as the citizens of East Berlin tried to decide what to do about them, in a country where one third of the population of fifteen million had been involved. By August 1990, some of the facts about the Stasi were widely reported. It was then that I began to have doubts about the suicide scenario, began to think that Oleg's casual farewell words – 'You knew Wiebke was put in his bed' – were not just a paranoid supposition.

East Germany's Ministry for State Security – the *Staatssicherheit* or Stasi – had run the country. From forty-one buildings on the Normannenstrasse, in 10,000 rooms, the Stasi developed a network that extended to every citizen. It was reckoned that there were more than a hundred thousand full-time informants; that up to two million East Germans worked part-time for the Stasi, that, in effect, nothing happened in the whole country without the Stasi making it happen. Friends were made to spy on friends, children on parents, colleagues on work-mates, the *New York Times* reported. Sex, *The Times* noted, was a favourite Stasi tool in getting information. The males were known as 'Romeos'; the young women were called 'Swallows'. If Wiebke was put into Dean's bed, then Wiebke was Dean's 'Swallow'.

Millions of telephone calls were recorded by the Stasi and no breath Dean drew could have gone unnoticed. Perhaps that was why he crossed the Wall towards the end of his life to telephone Dixie, to tell her he was afraid.

In 1986, the *New York Times* also reported, 'As the Soviet Union began liberalising its society and the East German economy deteriorated, the Stasi, foreseeing unrest – but not the end of the Wall – put more than 2,000 members of an elite secret task force into the highest levels of East German government departments, business and universities.'

1986. The year of Dean's death. All the whispered theories which I had rejected began to resonate in my head in the middle of the night: Vashek Nectar's recollection of the wheel that nearly came off Dean's car as he drove to Prague; Oleg's convictions about Wiebke; even the Countess.

In 1986, after his glorious trip home to America, Dean was increasingly disaffected with the East. No doubt he talked about how he felt; he always did. Threatened, obsessed, certain that Dean was about to defect and to take with him what he knew – and he must have known plenty about the inner workings of East German society – maybe the secret police cornered him that night near the lake and killed him. They were good at murder.

If the Stasi went for Dean Reed on that lonely road at night near the lake, why had they left Leslie and me completely alone? Not once in East Berlin had anyone stopped us, except once, I suddenly remembered: one afternoon, emerging from the underground parking lot near the Grand Hotel, a man on the sidewalk took a picture of us.

'Just a tourist,' said Leslie.

'Taking a picture of you and me in a particularly boring Hertz rental car?'

'Maybe he had begun doing errands for the West,' said Leslie.

'Maybe he became a real problem for the East Gemans. If he telephoned Gerrit List to say he was on his way the night he disappeared, it would have been easy enough for Gerrit – who was certainly a Party official – to have let someone know that Dean was on his way, alone, at night. I'm not saying that Gerrit did, I'm just saying it would have been easy.'

It was all speculation, of course. Throughout 1990, as the nightmare world of the Stasi was exposed, a billion pages of files were uncovered. It became clear that, because so many East Germans were involved, one way or another, that the files would have to be permanently sealed, or burned. As they waited to disappear up the ass of West Germany, the East Germans felt that it might be wisest to burn the past.

And then, finally, late in 1990 – it was on Hallowe'en, in fact – as I was just about to send the last draft of the last page proofs of this book to the printers, I talked to Anne de Boismilion at CBS in Paris who said that she, or was it her researcher? had had a phone call from Will Roberts – wherever Will was – to say that someone, perhaps Renate, had seen Dean's Stasi file in Berlin. In it was a suicide letter. But, as always, news of Dean came in a phone call carrying a rumour of a possible sighting by someone I could not reach because it would have been the middle of the night in Berlin and anyhow, the lines were always busy.

After lunch, Renate drove me back to Checkpoint Charlie and she seemed reluctant to let me go.

I asked her how Dean would have felt.

She was correct, cheery and loyal to her dead husband. 'He would have been happy for a multi-party system, but worried about many problems, for he understood the need for the Wall. People in the East are very, very frightened. Everything is coming apart.'

'And you?'

'Hitler, Stalin, Honecker, we believed them all. Now we believe in nothing. We know all is bad. That we are bad people. We don't know what to believe.'

As I got out of the car and headed toward the border, Renate waved. Then we both turned to watch a middle-aged couple kiss. They kissed for a very long time until, with a doleful gesture, the woman turned back towards the East and the man went through to West Berlin and I remembered that Renate's first role was in a film called *Divided Heavens*. In it, a couple were separated by the Berlin Wall and because of the Wall, love died, she said.

I crossed Checkpoint Charlie. I looked at the phone booth where Dean made his last, desperate calls to Dixie and the sweep of his life got to me. It was never the politics that had me hooked; it was the scale of the life; this enormous life, loony, heroic, a remarkable stunt. With the awesome determination to be loved, to be a star, the longing for the stardom itself, Dean Reed had the aspirant energy of America in its prime. I longed for him to be alive. How he would have loved to strut his stuff on top of the remains of the Berlin Wall.

   Then I put my arm through it. It was a peculiar sensation because the Wall, what was left of it, was no thicker than a child's hand. A prop wall. The remnants of another world.

   I put my arm through the Berlin Wall one last time, then I went home.